Water Buffalo Theology

Water Buffalo Theology

Twenty-Fifth Anniversary Edition
Revised and Expanded

Kosuke Koyama

ORBIS BOOKS

Maryknoll, New York 10545

Copyright © 1999 by Kosuke Koyama
Published by Orbis Books, Maryknoll, New York, U.S.A.
Originally published in 1974 by Orbis Books and SCM Press, London.
All rights reserved. No part of this publication may be reproduced or transmitted in any form or by any means, electronic or mechanical, including photocopying, recording, or any information storage or retrieval system, without prior permission in writing from Orbis Books, P.O. Box 308, Maryknoll, NY 10545-0308, U.S.A. Manufactured in the United States of America.

"My Pilgrimage in Mission" first appeared in *International Bulletin of Missionary Research* 21 (April 1997): 55-59. It is reprinted here with the permission of the publisher, the Overseas Ministries Study Center, New Haven, Connecticut.

Library of Congress Cataloging in Publication Data

Koyama, Kosuke, 1929–
    Water buffalo theology / Kosuke Koyama. — 25th anniversary ed.
      p.   cm.
    "Revised and expanded."
    Includes bibliographical references and index.
    ISBN 1-57075-256-7 (pbk.)
    1. Theology, Doctrinal — Asia — History.   I. Koyama, Kosuke, 1929–
Waterbuffalo theology. II. Title.
    BT30. A8K68   1999
    230´.095—dc21   98-53749
                                                      CIP

Contents

Preface to the Twenty-Fifth Anniversary Edition
Water Buffalo Theology after Twenty-Five Years   vii

Preface to the First Edition
From Water Buffaloes to Theology in Thailand   xv

Part I
Interpreting History   1

1. Theological Situations in Asia and the Mission
   of the Church   3

2. Will the Monsoon Rain Make God Wet?
   An Ascending Spiral View of History   20

3. Gun and Ointment
   The Future of the Christian World Mission in Asia   32

4. The "Efficiency" of the Crucified One in the World
   of Technological Efficiency   44

Part II
Rooting the Gospel   51

5. Bangkok and Wittenberg   53

6. Aristotelian Pepper and Buddhist Salt   56

7. "Neighborology"   64

8. The Wrath of God in a Culture of Tranquility   68

9. Ten Key Theological Issues Facing Theologians in Asia   76

10. Theological Re-Rooting in the Theology of the Pain of God   82

Part III
Interpreting Thai Buddhist Life   **91**

11. Buddhist, not Buddhism   93

12. Cool *Arhat* and Hot God   96

13. Apostle James in Thailand   118

Part IV
Interpreting the Christian Life   **125**

14. In Search of a "Personality" of Theology in Asia   127

15. Tokyo and Jerusalem   137

16. Is Christ Divided?   140

17. Toward a Crucified Mind   150

18. Three Modes of Christian Presence   160

Epilogue
   My Pilgrimage in Mission   171

Acknowledgments   181

Index   183

Preface to the
Twenty-Fifth Anniversary Edition

Water Buffalo Theology after Twenty-Five Years

In the hot season, relishing the taste of the incomparable mango, and in the rainy season, listening to the fugue of the bullfrogs, I once wrote memos and short reflections. They had a common thread—the experience of a Japanese missionary in northern Thailand. When I had accumulated a number of them I pondered how to name the collection. At a meeting of the Association of Theological Schools in South East Asia I talked about the inspiration I received from the sight of farmers working with water buffaloes in the paddy fields. My *guru*, Shoki Hwang, gave his light-hearted approval to naming my gathered reflections *Water Buffalo Theology*. Since then, more than twenty-five years have passed.

Few copies of the book remain in print after twenty-five years. I am grateful that my friends urged Orbis Books to consider doing a silver anniversary edition and that Orbis agreed. The reader may wonder what is new in this book. First, convinced by my publisher that "water buffalo" is two words, not one, the anniversary edition bears the title, *Water Buffalo Theology*, not *Waterbuffalo Theology*. It doesn't feel quite right, but English is not my first language.

Second, I have reread every page, many of them several times, and have made numerous revisions and improvements, in some cases even inserting paragraphs that make the meaning of the original text clearer. In addition, I have tried to use non-sexist language throughout the anniversary edition.

Third, this preface is new. While not a *retractatio* in the way Saint Augustine reviewed and commented on his earlier work, the preface does, I hope, bring into relief what I consider the most important elements in *Water Buffalo Theology*. In similar vein, I have added an epilogue, entitled "My Pilgrimage in Mission." Written at the invitation of my friend and colleague Gerald H. Anderson, it first appeared in the April 1997 *International Bulletin of Missionary Research* and is reproduced here with the permission of the publisher. More than anything I have written, this autobiographical essay traces my inner and outer pilgrimage.

Finally, I felt it wise that two chapters of the first edition not appear in this one. They are Chapter 3 ("Particular Orbit Theology") and Chapter 18 ("The Man Wears the Coat").

In 1959, celebrating the centennial of the arrival of Protestant Christianity in Japan, the United Church of Christ in Japan expressed her deep gratitude for the work of love done by missionaries from many countries, and her hope to send her own missionaries to other countries of Asia. Thus I became a missionary teacher sent by the United Church of Christ in Japan to Thailand where I served on the faculty of the Thailand Theological Seminary in Chiengmai from 1960 to 1968. Ever since then, whenever I hear of or speak of Thailand, "my heart is strangely warmed."

The General Secretary of the Church of Christ in Thailand, Acharn Charoen Wichiaidist, and the principal of the seminary, Dr. John Hamlin, embraced me and my family warmly. The Thai people welcomed this Asian missionary family, a strange new species! For the next eight years, they walked with us on the hot dusty streets of Bangkok and Chiengmai, introduced us to the delicacy of sticky rice cooked with coconut milk, and spoke to us of their culture, religion, and life in quiet compounds of Buddhist temples in Chiengmai. Trying to understand the new culture, we were sometimes aware of "the bush that was burning but not consumed."

The context of *Water Buffalo Theology* is Thailand. This context was in fact a dialogical inter-context because I brought in, intentionally or unintentionally, my own previous contexts: Tokyo and New Jersey. Thailand was my third context. Tokyo began to speak in Chiengmai, and New Jersey could not stay silent. But Chiengmai was the immediate context. *Water Buffalo Theology* is the outcome of a three-cornered conversation. The converging nature of its origin makes it, I believe, able to engage in a wider ecumenical dialogue in the present as well as, hopefully, in the future. The Chiengmai dialogue between "cool religion" and "hot religion" continued in my own mind and expressed itself in *Mt. Fuji and Mt. Sinai* (1984). In my theological pilgrimage the theology of the *pathos* of God which I encountered in Abraham J. Heschel's *The Prophets* (1962) has been decisive. Years later I realized that through Rabbi Heschel *Water Buffalo Theology* was connected with the heart of the biblical proclamation. As long as it speaks about the *pathos* of God — "hot God" (*theologia crucis*) — it has its mission, I whisper to myself, even after twenty-five years!

It has been a turbulent quarter century! In it the superpowers have held hostage every living being with the threat of nuclear extinction. It was, however, also in this time of potential cosmic conflict that a self-conscious theology appeared in Asia. D. T. Niles, M. M. Thomas, U Kyaw Than, and Lesslie Newbigin spoke of the "Selfhood of the Church in Asia." In the broader ecumenical scene other theologies have appeared: Latin American liberation theology, black theology, feminist theology, interreligious dialogue theology, and, of late, ecological theology. Theology has begun to speak many languages.

The ground-breaking Bangkok conference on "The Christian Prospect in Eastern Asia" (1949) was fully aware of global tension. "The darkest shadow that hovers over our thresholds today is the possibility of another war with its atom bombs," says Rajah B. Manikam in his opening remark. Yet he could see the future in Christ and confidently spoke of the "ecumenical" nature of theology in Asia.

> This conference, though East Asian, is in an ecumenical setting and linked in the strong bonds of ecumenical fellowship. It is rightly *of* East Asia and *for* East Asia but it is at the same time *of* the ecumenical Church and *for* the ecumenical Church. . . . We of the East have also our own unique contribution to make in interpreting Jesus Christ, who was an Oriental, in our own oriental way, based on our experience of him as our Lord and Master, and Saviour of the West as well as of the East. We shall have to learn how to present the eternal gospel in terms intelligible to the cultural, historical and social heritage of our peoples.

Bangkok was again the scene of a "Conference on Theological Education in Southeast Asia" (1956) in which seventeen theological schools and colleges were represented. Theology responsible to the local situation of Southeast Asia was the focus of the conference. Yet, the conference decided that such *theologia in loco* can flourish only if it maintains its ecumenical linkage. Russell Chandran of the United Theological College, Bangalore, India, emphasized "the rediscovery of the Church's unity in the ecumenical movement" in the context of Southeast Asian theological education.

In 1957, as the superpowers were reaching the operational capability of their intercontinental ballistic missiles, the East Asia Christian Conference (later, Christian Conference of Asia) was formed. The historical background of the original *Water Buffalo Theology* (1974) was not tranquil. I was keenly aware of a nerve-wracking tension between the global conflicts (World War II, 1941-45; the Korean conflict, 1950-53; the Vietnam conflict, 1964-73); and the ecumenism of reconciliation.

The World Conference on Mission and Evangelism of the World Council of Churches was held in Bangkok in 1973 under the theme "Salvation Today." The theme suggested two major emphases: "culture and identity" and "social justice in a divided humanity." The conference focused on the meaning of the universality of the biblical faith which inevitably contained stumbling blocks. Interreligious understanding of "Salvation Today" was further explored in my adopted city, Chiengmai, in 1977 under the theme "Dialogue in Community." *Water Buffalo Theology* was "surrounded by a great cloud of witnesses." It was one small contribution to a great conversation.

At the time of writing *Water Buffalo Theology* I realized the danger of speaking of "Asian theology," and opted for the expression "theology in Asia," following the apostolic example of "Churches in Galatia" and "the saints in Rome." I took a second look (and a tenth look!) at the maps of Asia and of the world and became convinced that there is no such thing as a neatly packaged and unified reality called "Asia" historically, religiously, culturally, or philosophically. Asia is a geographically defined area divided by many cultural and linguistic differences. "Asia" moreover, has been in extensive communication with the cultures and languages of "outside Asia" since ancient times. The image not of an Asia separated-from, but of an Asia webbed-with the whole *oekumene*, is the reason I preferred "theology in Asia" over "Asian theology." *Water Buffalo Theology* is simply a theology engaged in the north of Thailand, a *theologia in loco*. It is, following the advice of Rajah Manikam, distinctively local and openly ecumenical. It rejoices in being a part of the global webbedness of many cultures within which the culture of northern Thailand finds itself.

Apart from this lively sense of intersection between the local and the ecumenical, *Water Buffalo Theology* shows little interest in formulating a methodology. It does not discuss how to approach such a *theologia in loco*. What are source materials for this theology? How should the Bible be used? In what way can "Asia" be theologically articulated? What is this theology's relationship with western theology? These questions are not taken up theoretically by *Water Buffalo Theology*, but they are demonstrated concretely in the narratives it tells. But how can any theology be written without conscious discussion of methodology? Should not responsible theology begin with a precise methodology accompanied by at least two or three conceptual definitions?

The primary reality of *Water Buffalo Theology's* methodology is that one day in 1960 I came to live in Thailand as a Japanese missionary. My theological experience in the community of faith in Thailand became an open-ended methodology. The decisive moment in this *lived methodology* came to me when I decided to learn the Thai language. When, after some months at school, I was not yet able to communicate the most basic concepts in Thai, I felt ruthlessly denuded and reduced to the zero point. This experience of humiliation is the foundation of the methodology of *Water Buffalo Theology*. For me, learning the language was a spiritual experience of repentance. And what is theological methodology if it is not repentance?

My "methodology" in Thailand and ever since has been "to see the face of God in the faces of people." Can this be called "methodology?" Should this not be called "focus" or "passion" or "commitment" instead of methodology? I have come across a number of inspiring books on theology in Asia written by Asians who begin their books with impressive discussions on methodology. The question rises in my mind: How do they know where they are going before they start walking? How can they describe the changing scenery before they see it? What space is there for such unexpected events as the disciples encountered on the way to Emmaus? When asked to appear at a certain time, the Buddha, so the tradition goes, only nodded silently. He retained the freedom to break the appointment if something urgent happened in the meantime. Do not methodology and definition erode such freedom? Do they kill the possibility of surprises? The Abrahamic faiths, Judaism, Christianity, and Islam, treasure the image of the one who went out "not know where he was going" (Heb. 11:8). With so much preoccupation on methodology, does not theology become a scheduled journey instead of a journey full of surprises? Is a scholarly analysis of "chop sticks" more revealing than the experience of eating with them?

Water Buffalo Theology is little concerned about its place in the academic world. In spite of all the pontifications of university theologians about the establishment of theology as an academic science, *Water Buffalo Theology* is quietly convinced that theology—God-talk—belongs to the realm of poetry. If poetic intuition and poetic expression are outside academically respectable discourse, then *Water Buffalo Theology* must accept its place outside the zone of academic prestige. In my view, this same verdict could be applied to Heschel's *Prophets* and Tillich's *Systematic Theology*, to the Bible and the Qur'an. "God-talk" is poetic, not scientific langue.

But there is a poem that responsibly expresses a keen sense of social justice in the name of God. The poetic mind can observe human society with unusal sharpness: "The voice of the Lord cries to the city. . . . Can I tolerate wicked scales and a bag of dishonest weights? Your wealthy are full of violence, your inhabitants speak lies, with tongues of deceit in their mouth" (Mic. 6:9,11,12). This kind of poem is theology. This keen observation of "a bag of dishonest weights" binds the poem to the academic disciplines of sociology, psychology, and economy because it certainly affects these subjects. As long as *Water Buffalo Theology* speaks passionately of *human* welfare, it is potentially related to all branches of human knowledge.

Interreligious dialogue came to *Water Buffalo Theology* naturally, without any coercion or definition. The Christian community in the heart of the Buddha land has for some time engaged in interaction and dialogue with the community of the Buddha. I found the two communities innocently animistic and friendly to one another. Buddhist respect for Christ was reciprocated by Christian respect for the Buddha. Thailand has experienced no violent religious conflict or uprising. Thai Buddhists or Christians are not militant. I did not find Thai Christians or their pastors discussing the two religions in terms of superiority or inferiority. They know that the two religions are *different*. Difference need not cause conflict.

Thai Christian language is extensively influenced by Hindu-Buddhist language. Respectful words and verbs used primarily for the Buddha or monks are used in relation to Jesus. This simple fact establishes an emotional connection between the two faiths. For the Thai translators of the Bible, there was no language other than the language of the Buddhist-animist culture. Inheriting Buddhist vocabularies, Bible translators appropriated the wealth of centuries of religious and philosophical experience as did the New Testament writers when they utilized Greek vocabulary. Words of Jesus that were once accommodated to Greek words were again accommodated to Thai expressions. With great effort Thai translators insured enrichment. It is not a distortion.

My encounter with Thai Buddhism helped me understand how Christianity itself was a continuous interreligious dialogue between synagogue and church. It appeared to me that the monastic, Theravada tradition of Thai Buddhism would dialogue more readily with the Old Testament's focus on ethical endeavor than with the savior figure of Jesus of the New Testament. I was deeply impressed by the sincerity of Thai Buddhist monasticism. *Water Buffalo Theology* tries to combine the biblical moral endeavor with the unconditional grace manifested in the form of *theologia crucis*. I hold that there cannot be true religion apart from self-discipline *and* an open acceptance of grace.

Thai Buddhism is monastic. But general Thai culture is a colorful mixture of life perceptions. In fact, if a certain group of people (*bhikkhu*) commit themselves to live according to the 228 Buddhist injunctions of monasticism, the society will not disintegrate, even though the lay world may be morally lax. Thai monasticism relaxes the community in this way. Thai culture assimilates important religio-philosophical concepts such as *nirvana* and *karman* to the common life of people in an equally relaxed fashion. *Water Buffalo Theology* moves from the monks' understanding to lay people's understanding of *nirvana* and *karman*. It is interested in popular Buddhism and popular Christianity.

In Thailand I was often asked whether the Hindu *Upanishads*, the Buddhist *Tripitaka*, or the Confucian *Analects* could replace the Old Testament. The argument was: if the Old Testament is a preparation for the New Testament, can the *Upanishads* be for Asians a preparation for the New Testament? My response was the *Upanishads* cannot replace the Old Testament, but the study of the *Upanishads* will profit our understanding of the Old and New Testaments. Why can it not replace the Old Testament? There is, as it were, a blood relationship between the Old Testament and the New Testament which is not there between the *Upanishads* and the New Testament. The discussion on replacement has never become serious enough to challenge the core of Christian theology. Rather, the question was an expression of the generally felt Asian frustration that the church has failed to accord proper recognition to Asia's own scriptures.

Into a mind busy with Christ and Culture in Thailand, the word "preparation" intruded with unexpected urgency. In the discussions of the East Asia Christian Conference I was confronted with the theological idea of *preparatio evangelica*. Somehow this Latin phrase impressed me. When someone suggested that religious instruction of any kind prepares people for the gospel of Christ, I rejoiced, but later I experienced some uneasiness; first, does just *any* kind suffice? and second, would not Buddhists, Hindus, and Muslims be irritated to hear this? They would certainly object to the idea that their religion is just a preparation for some other religion. I settled this question by meditating upon the great seventeenth-century Jesuits, Matteo Ricci of China and Robert De Nobili of South India, who studied the difficult languages of those cultures to "prepare" *themselves* to preach the gospel. I thought, if I "prepare myself" following the honored Jesuit examples, then, without conscious effort and strategy, or even missiology, I may prepare people for the gospel. No other enterprise can possibly pay more respect to a people than to learn their language. I became aware of the danger of *preparatio evangelica* becoming a veiled imperialism. *Preparatio evangelica* is not for "them," but for me.

Then I took a second look at the *Upanishads*. If I preach the gospel in a culture steeped in Upanishadic spirituality, the question as to whether the *Upanishads* can replace the Old Testament becomes immaterial since they will read both the Old and New Testaments from the Upanishadic outlook anyway. In all religious discourses, I concluded, replacement is an artificial concept. Instead of replacement we should speak of "mutual enrichment." *Water Buffalo Theology* is not happy with a missiology of replacement. Christianity will not replace Buddhism or Islam.

Water Buffalo Theology is, however, concerned about religious syncretism. Religious syncretism is ambiguous, being at times artificial and at other times natural. Religions artificially mixed will be deprived of genuine spiritual power. In fact, religious realities are resistant to such quick and superficial mixing, but at the same time religions influence each other in the longer time scale. This takes place in a natural fashion apart from human attempts to mix them. *Water Buffalo Theology* understands that all religious teachings are composites of many traditions. There is no pure or intact Buddhism or Christianity. It is not apart from but by means of the sometimes confusing voices of plurality *within* Christianity that the gospel displays power. And it is there we are to hear the gospel message.

Emotionally, *Water Buffalo Theology* anticipates ecological theology. It was written as I listened to the persistent, solemn croaking of bullfrogs. Often I wondered if J. S. Bach taught the *fugue* form to these frogs! They were there — with fish, snakes, mosquitoes, and millions of insects — engaged in the cycles of life. All comes and goes according to the seasonal circle. I have come to see affinity between the circle and ecology. The ecotheology of *Water Buffalo Theology* stops at the point where it suggests the friendly relationship between the image of circle and that of ecology.

Water Buffalo Theology sees certain specific challenges.

(1) Contextualization of theology implies two critical movements. First, to articulate Jesus Christ in culturally appropriate, communicatively apt words; and second, to criticize, reform, dethrone, or oppose culture if it is found to be against what the name of Jesus Christ stands for. That name leads us to reject what is "repugnant to reason or moral sense" (Gandhi). Theology's relationship with culture is relative (temporal), not absolute (permanent). This is the factor that distinguishes *theologia in loco* from tribal theology. Theology becomes tribal when it fails to engage in these movements. The globalization of theology cannot be built upon tribal theology. Such globalization of theology would be a cheap exercise in neoimperialism. I insist: *Theologia in loco*, not tribal theology, nurtures human history.

(2) Buddhism does not and cannot engage in dialogue with Christianity. Buddhists can. Christianity neither eats nor sleeps. Christians do. Buddhism does not sweat under the hot Bangkok sun. Buddhists do. Islam does not recite the Qur'an. Muslims do. I place priority in Buddhists, not in Buddhism; in Christians, not in Christianity; in Muslims, not in Islam. Obviously, there would be no Christians apart from Christianity. But Christianity without people called Christians would be inconceivable. I cannot imagine Buddhism without Buddhists, and Islam without Muslims. There would be no Christianity apart from the person called Jesus Christ. No Islam without Muhammad, and no Buddhism without Gautama Siddhartha. Even Hinduism, which does not have an identifiable founder, cannot exist without people who adhere to the Hindu spiritual traditions. I look at Buddhism through Buddhists, Christianity through Christians, Islam through Muslims, and so on. The *reality* of these traditions lies in living persons who so often fail to practice what they believe.

(3) The urgent commitment to the protection and maintenance of ecological health and justice required of the human community has brought Christian theology to an unexpected connection between *ecology* and *ecumenism*, both words that denote the taking care of house, *oikos*. Ecumenism which is not committed to the ecological health of our planet will be discredited and rejected by humanity as a movement of narrow tribal interest. The Christian faith must be expressed in terms of the webbed relationship between the life of the planet and the life of all living beings. The *ekklesia* can live and remain meaningful if the *kosmos* stays healthy. The Christ ecologically understood must illuminate the Christ ecclesiastically understood, though apart from the tradition of the church no one can envision the Christ ecologically understood.

What do these thoughts mean for the future of *Water Buffalo Theology?*

Preface to the First Edition

From Water Buffaloes to Theology in Thailand

I will read the Scriptures and theological works with your needs in mind. . . .

> To the weak I became weak, that I might win the weak. I have
> become all things to all men, that I might by all means save some.
> I do it all for the sake of the gospel, that I may share in its blessing
> (I Cor. 9:22f.).

On my way to the country church, I never fail to see a herd of water buffaloes grazing in the muddy paddy field. This sight is an inspiring moment
for me. Why? Because it reminds me that the people to whom I am to bring
the gospel of Christ spend most of their time with these water buffaloes in
the rice field. The animals tell me that I must preach to these farmers in
simple sentence structure and thought development. They remind me to
discard abstract ideas, and to use objects that are immediately tangible.
"Sticky-rice," "banana," "pepper," "dog," "cat," "bicycle," "rainy season,"
"leaking house," "fishing," "cock-fighting," "lottery," "stomachache" —
these are meaningful words for them. "This morning," I say to myself, "I
will try to bring the gospel of Christ through the medium of cock-fighting!"
   Proceeding to the country church on my Japanese motorcycle, I once
more recite mentally the scripture text that is to be used, and I try to formulate the approach to the intended message. Then I ask myself, "Is this
introduction understandable and realistic in terms of *their* daily experiences? Is this message digestible and nutritious to *their* ethical and theological needs?" When I reach the church, I concentrate on understanding
my audience. I count how many older people there are. How many
younger? Are there new faces, sick persons, pregnant women, physically
challenged? Then I say to myself, "I am sent to *this* congregation today." I
begin speaking from where they are (i.e., cock-fighting). From talking
about the human situation I go on to call God into this real human situation. It is not I, but my audience, who determines this approach of "theology from below." The truth of "self-emptying" ("Jesus Christ who . . . *emptied himself*," Phil. 2:5-7) in the God Incarnate means, to me, beginning my
sermon with "sticky-rice" and "cock-fighting" when preaching to my people, farmers of northern Thailand.

I decided to subordinate great theological thoughts, like those of Thomas Aquinas and Karl Barth, to the intellectual and spiritual needs of the farmers. I decided that the greatness of theological works is to be judged by the extent and quality of the service they can render to the farmers to whom I am sent. I also decided that I have not really understood *Summa Theologiae* and *Church Dogmatics* until I am able to use them for the benefit of the farmers. My theology in northern Thailand must begin with the need of the farmers and not with the great thoughts developed in *Summa Theologiae* and *Church Dogmatics*. But is not this approach uncouth and even sacrilegious? Do I mean to say that I dare to give priority to the farmers over Thomas Aquinas and Karl Barth in my theological thinking? Yes. The reason is simple: God has called me to work here in northern Thailand, not in Italy or Switzerland. And I am working with neither a Thomas Aquinas nor a Karl Barth. God commanded me to be a neighbor to these farmers. I make this decision because of my involvement with the farmers. Is not such involvement the only soil from which theology germinates? This decision — "I will read theological works with *your* (the farmers') needs in mind and I will give your needs priority over even the greatest theological works, because I am sent to you" (Lk. 10:33-35) — means that the theology for northern Thailand begins and grows in northern Thailand, and nowhere else. Northern Thailand theology, the theology that serves Jesus Christ in northern Thailand, will surely come into being when we dare to make this decision. In this decision is the beginning of a theology for Thailand and for Asia.

PART I

Interpreting History

Theological Situations in Asia and the Mission of the Church

- In Singapore, Thailand, China, Hong Kong, the Philippines, Indonesia, Burma, Vietnam, Japan, and Taiwan.
- "Contextualization" applied to the Asian situations.
- "History-gravity" means "suffering-gravity."
- The missiology of the "crucified mind."
- Challenges we face together in Asia and the West.

This chapter has two sections: in the first I wish to highlight, as concisely as possible, how I see, at this moment, theological issues in the different Southeast Asian countries. I would like to raise interrelated questions without attempting to give the answers. "Third World Theology" begins by raising issues, not by digesting Augustine, Barth, and Rahner. This is, in short, an attempt to call your attention to some of the Asian theological "raw situations" that have been on my mind for some time. This exercise may give you a feeling of a "scatter-brain" theological travelogue, but I trust that we can together make such a trip as we confess that "in him all things hold together" (Col. 1:17).

On the basis of the first section I invite you to think with me, in the second section, on the mission of the church.

FROM COUNTRY TO COUNTRY

Singapore: Toward a slower and more human "*erets*-ology"

Let me begin with the youngest nation in the region. Singapore has 150 years of history since the time of Stamford Raffles, and it has been a republic only since 1965. It is an island of 244 square miles with an energetic Chinese majority who refuse to live according to the "rhythm of the tropics." There is a disturbing sense of psychological incongruity which any visitor would notice, between 85° Fahrenheit, 85 percent humidity, and 16 hours hard work a day. The skyline is changing every week. Between 1960 and 1969 a total of 106,418 living units were constructed by the government housing project. The streets have been widened for the ever-increasing number of vehicles (156,000 in 1974). The whole island is covered with disciplined "worker ants." It is a showcase of nation building. It is an island of efficiency in an ocean of Southeast Asian inefficiency. Singapore (Lion City) is not a "lion" that eats and sleeps. Rather, she is represented by the 747B, telephone-telegram, S$500 fine for littering, court without jury, non-stop reclamation of land to gain one more square foot, air-conditioned attractive shopping complexes, with an infinite number of cosmetic counters each displaying 36 kinds of lipsticks, and a strongly teleologically-minded political leadership. The kingdom of God, Singapore style, is just around the corner! "Convert to Prime Minister Lee Kuan Yew, for the kingdom of God is at hand." In the constant 85° climate, this is an amazing achievement.

The theological issue here is the relationship between "being efficient" ("fast") and "being human" ("slow"). May I ask the following questions?

(a) Is not the biblical God an "inefficient" and "slow" God because he is the God of the covenant relationship motivated by love? He walks forty years (!) in the wilderness with his people, speaks through the "ox-cart history" of three generations of the united monarchy, twenty kings of Judah and nineteen kings of Israel, exile and restoration, diaspora, and so on. Isn't this simply too "inefficient" and "slow" for Prime Minister Lee Kuan Yew (efficiency incarnate)? The image of the crucified Christ ("nailed down" — the ultimate symbol of immobility, the "maximum slowness") is an intensification of the forty years wandering in the wilderness. Can this "immobile" inefficient Christ speak to "mobile-efficient" Singaporeans? How are we to retain "being slow" in Singapore, which is constantly getting to be "fast?"

(b) To realize that the biblical God is "slow and inefficient" in the midst of Singapore life — is this "salvation today?"

(c) What kind of lifestyle would communicate salvation in the "slow God" in Singapore?

(d) The whole of Singapore is after money (as is the case in Japan). Shall we just say, "You cannot serve God and mammon" (Matt. 6:24) and sit down? What is the missiologically meaningful interpretation of this passage?

(e) Thousands of people are living in concrete square boxes (government housing project). Some of them live on the fifth floor or the nineteenth floor. Their lives have been "uprooted" from the ground. "Distance from the ground" is causing psychological problems. "To be human" is "to be on the ground," particularly for the Singapore Malays. Theological "*erets*-ology" is needed (*erets* = earth in Hebrew, see Gen. 1:1).

Thailand: Let's discuss *meedtaa-karunaa* while eating banana and pizza

I would like to highlight two interrelated areas of theological issues: 1) Thailand One and Thailand Two; and 2) "Showing mercy" in the theology of the ideal person, the king, and Jesus Christ.

Mother nature, the monarchy, and Theravada Buddhism are the three basic continuities in the life of the Thai people. The people live in the land of fertile paddy fields (fertile in producing not only rice but also mosquitoes). There are three regular circling seasons: hot, rainy, and cool. When you have been through this eighty times you are eighty years old! Thailand's nature is hospitable to the people. There are no typhoons, earthquakes, floods, droughts, and bitter cold.

There, people have been blessed by the stable and benevolent monarchy of the Chakri Dynasty since 1782. The tradition of this dynasty is for the monarchs to adhere to the Ten Virtues according to the ethics of Buddhism. The Ten Virtues are: 1) charity, 2) moral living according to the known code — *sila*, 3) support for religion, 4) honesty, 5) compassion, 6) freedom from wrongful ambition, 7) freedom from thoughts of revenge, 8) love for the people as their father, 9) moderation in punishment, 10) constant care for the people's welfare and happiness.

In 1932 the absolute monarchy was changed into a constitutional monarchy. The people show deep-felt affection for the king. They see the walking symbol of the *nirvana* ideal in the persons of 240,000 monks throughout the kingdom. They visit Buddhist temples, the centers of their rural communities, regularly according to the waning of the moon. This Thailand of continuities which lives according to the messages of mother nature, the monarchy, and Buddhism is the Thailand I wish to call Thailand One. It is the Thailand in which banana and mango taste so delicious.

Alongside this Thailand One there is another Thailand, which I call Thailand Two. This is, in short, the Thailand of modernization. It centers upon the fast-increasing number of modernization agencies and institutions: the modernized concept of political system, education, employment, hospitalization, communication, transportation, agricultural production, distribution, housing, and so on. This Thailand Two is sometimes called "Americanized Thailand" or "busy-business-Thailand." It is the Thailand going through "modernization and cultural revolution." The center of Thailand Two is Bangkok. This Thailand is symbolized by such mixtures as FNCBs in Bangkok, well-equipped modern hospitals, the Central Post Office, 9,000 taxis (Datsun Bluebird) within the city limits of Bangkok, and finally American B52s stationed there. For the last twenty-five years this Thailand Two has achieved tremendous advancement in growth in both positive and negative directions. It is the Thailand in which coffee and pizza taste delicious. And one can even speak English!

The traditional Thailand One and modernized Thailand Two exist side by side. Every Thai person, it seems to me, is living at the intersection of Thailand One and Thailand Two. Isn't this a historically pregnant moment? Co-existence of "banana-mango" and "coffee-pizza!" This is the dynamic *historical context* in which many other changes are taking place in the life of the people of Thailand. This observation itself is a challenging subject that demands far more than the present treatment. Theological questions:

(*a*) "Who is Jesus Christ?" at the intersection of Thailand One and Thailand Two?

(*b*) Is Jesus Christ a part of "Americanized Thailand?"

(*c*) Are there two gospels? One for Thailand One, another for Thailand Two?

Now to the second theological issue. "To show mercy" is the enduring tradition in the land of Theravada Buddhism. The concept of mercy (*meedtaa karunaa*—to be merciful, to be kind) is constantly nourished by two distinguished personages: Gautama Siddhartha, the Buddha, and Bhumibol Adulyadej, His Majesty the King. The Buddha taught the people of Thailand "to be merciful" without concluding that sentence with "as your heavenly Father is merciful." The king is the Buddhist who practices mercy. In his practice of mercy the royal glory emanates from him. His word is salvific. His presence is blessing. His acts are compassionate. He is actually the *ideal* man. He is religious. He holds supreme authority. He is healthy. He is rich. He has the most beautiful wife. He is the Head of all Thai people in whom "all things hold together!"

(*a*) How is the mercy shown in the name of the Buddha related to the mercy shown in the name of Jesus Christ? If mercy which is pleasing to the biblical God is found "outside" the name of Jesus Christ, what is the meaning of "no other name" (Acts 4:12)?

(*b*) How is the Christian understanding of mission related to the Thai teaching on '*meedtaa-karunaa?*'

(*c*) Is Jesus Christ an ideal man? In what way? How do we speak of Jesus Christ among people who experience the presence of the ideal one, the King, in whom "all things hold together?"

China: Invitation to a dialogue on two *credos*

That China is "the middle kingdom" in the world is the historic cornerstone of Chinese self-identity as a nation. In her long course of history many neighboring nations came to the Imperial Court of the Middle Kingdom to pay tribute. The peoples outside the reign of the Emperor to whom heaven gave mandate to rule are thought to be "barbarians." This political and cultural "middle-kingdom complex" is not unique to the Chinese race. It happened to many other countries, such as the Greeks, Romans, and Japanese until their defeat in 1945. (And it is swiftly coming back to the Japanese again!) When the United States, with 250 million people, consumes 40 per cent of the non-renewable energy resources of the world, there must be a strong middle-kingdom complex with her too!

In 1921 the Chinese Communist Party came into being with eight members. In 1949 it assumed the ruling power under the chairmanship of Mao Tse-tung over 800 million people. Mao Tse-tung was born in 1893. He came to know the ideology of Marxist-Leninism. After accomplishing the Long March (1935) in 1941, he wrote his *credo*, comparable to the ancient *credo* which appears in the Book of Deuteronomy, 26:5-10:

For a hundred years, the finest sons and daughters of the disaster-ridden Chinese nation fought and sacrificed their lives, one stepping into the breach as another fell, in quest of the truth that would save the country and the people. This moves us to song and tears. But it was only after World War I and the October Revolution in Russia that we found Marxist-Leninism, the best truths, the best of weapons for liberating our nation. And the Communist Party of China has been the initiator, propagandist and organizer in the wielding of this weapon. As soon as it was linked with the concrete practice of the Chinese revolution, the universal truth of Marxist-Leninism gave an entirely new complexion to the Chinese revolution.

Here is the biblical *credo*:

A wandering Aramean was my father; and he went down into Egypt and sojourned there, few in number; and there he became a nation great, mighty, and populous. And the Egyptians treated us harshly, and afflicted us, and laid upon us hard bondage. Then we cried to the LORD the God of our fathers, and the LORD heard our voice, and saw our affliction, our toil, and our oppression; and the LORD brought us out of Egypt with a mighty hand and an outstretched arm with great terror, with signs and wonders; and he brought us into this place and gave us this land, a land flowing with milk and honey. And behold, now I bring the first of the fruit of the ground which thou, O LORD, has given me.

Here one great liturgy (one history) encounters another great liturgy (another history).

(*a*) What is the *theological* assessment of the "middle-kingdom complex" (and parochialism) in our day? Why is it that the world, so full of fantastic technological means of communication, can remain so parochial? Why does the kangaroo image haunt us: great hind legs (mobility-communication) with small head (parochial mentality — middle-kingdom complex)? What is the spiritual power that emancipates us from the grip of parochialism?

(*b*) How do we compare the two *credos*, of Mao Tse-tung and of the Pentateuch? Is the former part of the latter? Is the former an expression of the latter? Is the former a Christian confession or a pagan confession? How should the former be "evangelized" by the latter? Or *vice versa*? Are there really two histories, two liturgies encountering each other here?

Hong Kong: Between the times — Hong Kong style

Hong Kong consists of two large areas: Hong Kong Island, Kowloon (which has belonged to the British since the Treaty of Nanking in 1842), and the New Territories. The New Territories, 356 square miles, was leased to the

British Crown colony by China for 99 years. In 1997 this lease expired. As a matter of fact it could have expired at any moment, since Beijing did not recognize the existence of such a humiliating agreement. The New Territories cover 92 per cent of the area known as Hong Kong. It was obvious that without the New Territories Hong Kong could not survive. There was naturally a sense of uncertainty among the people, particularly those who were in business and who were trying to make as much as possible beyond their initial investment. The precarious situation was expressed by a journalist: "If at any time China's leaders choose to reclaim what they consider Chinese soil, they can do so with a single telephone call."[1] Any time can be "eschatological." 1 July 1997 was a specially "eschatological" moment. 4.2 million people of Hong Kong were overshadowed by the reality of precariousness. There had been a massive inflow of refugees since the Communist takeover in China. It is said, for instance, that in 1962 17,500 refugees fled to Hong Kong each month. In the tiny island adjacent to the giant nation life went on. There was a strong dedication among people to make the best of life and gain whatever one can gain in this context of uncertainty.

(a) Does not Hong Kong suggest an image of the "wandering Aramean," not in the sense of nomadic camel caravans crossing the steppes, but in the sense that their life is precarious and that time may run out for them at any moment? How can life be made meaningful and Christian ("made to be slow") in the context of time running out? How can they be invited to come to the thanksgiving service (a Hong Kong style one!)? ". . . he brought us into this place and gave us this land, a land flowing with milk and honey. And behold, now I bring the first of the fruit of the ground . . ." Hong Kong must not be, according to the biblical "*erets*-ology," a parking lot or heliport from which one takes off as soon as one gains what one wanted to gain. That would be raping *erets*. Hong Kong must celebrate a "slow" thanksgiving liturgy. Not in a parking lot or a heliport, but where?

(b) How does Jeremiah's message to the exiles speak to Hong Kong in 1973?

> Build houses and live in them; plant gardens and eat their produce. Take wives and have sons and daughters; take wives for your sons, and give your daughters in marriage, that they may bear sons and daughters; multiply there, and do not decrease. But seek the welfare of the city where I have sent you into exile, and pray to the LORD on its behalf, for in its welfare you will find your welfare (Jer. 29:5-7).

The Philippines: "Four Philippines" in one Filipino

Filipinos are Asians. But they have Spanish names (Jose Rizal, Ferdinand Marcos). This is unique in the Asian world. Some in Ceylon (today,

---

1. John B. Koffend, *The Asia Magazine*, 7 October 1973.

Sri Lanka) have Portuguese names. (Think of a nation like the occidental United Kingdom with its population having oriental Chinese names!) Every time Filipinos are called by their names, the perceptive mind does not fail to see the history this great people suffered for 400 years under Spanish colonialism. The name, the Philippines, itself derives from King Philip II of Spain. The Spanish expedition led by Ferdinand Magellan arrived in the southern island of Cebu in 1521. Fifty years later in 1571 Miguel Lopez de Legaspi made Manila the Spanish colonial capital. Spanish rule continued until the Spanish-American War in 1898. Then the Philippines came under the rule of the United States. William Howard Taft was the first American governor of the Philippines. He was appointed in 1901. The Philippines remained under American rule until the Japanese attacked in 1941. After the defeat of Japan, they achieved independence on 4 July 1946. The pre-1521 Philippines are Philippines One, the Philippines under the Spanish rule Philippines Two, the Philippines under the American rule Philippines Three, and the Philippines since independence Philippines Four. Colonial experiences of the Southeast Asian countries are unique in each nation. Yet, it seems to me, colonialism meant generally the destruction of indigenous (rooted in *erets*), integral self-identity.

As long as people live in a concrete historical world of interactions, it is obvious that there is no such thing as a "pure, intact self-identity." Self-identity is a concept of historical interaction. It is always "shared identity." We must ask the questions relating to "shared self-identity" with all nations in the world. Mission is to relate God's history of shared self-identity with people's history of shared self-identity. The Filipinos are a dramatic example. Every Filipino has at least "four Philippines" within, seen from the aspect of political history alone. They may have more "Philippines" when they are seen religiously, anthropologically, ethnically, and so on. Perhaps one Filipino has "fifteen Philippines" within. This observation is, of course, surrounded by many ambiguities. Yet it can serve as an indicator to certain serious theological and missiological issues. What we are thinking about now is not a self-identity in terms of an IC (Identity Card) or a travel passport, but the historically produced crisis of individual, communal, national, and global shared self-identity and shared self-understanding.

(*a*) Why must Christian understanding of mission take the historically constructed, shared self-identity crisis seriously? Who is Jesus Christ against the background of "four Philippines" Filipinos?

(*b*) What is the relationship between diversified self-identity and Christian understanding of Jesus Christ?

Indonesia: Many spirits, several spirits, One Spirit

Indonesians are "spiritual" people. They live with spirits. For them the presence and work of spirits are real. The fascinating study on this subject is found in *The Religion of Java*, by Clifford Geertz.[2] People live with many spirits, some benevolent and some malevolent. One cannot understand Islam, Christianity, or Hinduism in Indonesia without having a proper understanding of "many spirits." The people and the spirits share one integral community life. Life in such a community is not lonely. The traditional spiritual world of the Indonesians is that of many spirits. Into this world of many spirits came the impact of modernization.

When Japanese military power was swiftly declining in April 1945, the "Body for Investigating Efforts in Preparation for Independence" chaired by Sukarno was set up in Indonesia. This body discussed "the basic principles upon which the future state should be founded."[3] On 1 June 1945 Sukarno delivered an address *Lahirnja Sila* (The Birth of *Pantja Sila*). The *Pantja Sila* (Five Principles) were incorporated in the draft constitution (1945) and thus became the "basis for further development for the Indonesian nation's progressive national ideology" (Preface by Sukarno). The *Pantja Sila* are as follows: 1) Belief in the One God, *Ke-Tuhanan Jang Maha Esa*; 2) The Principle of Humanity, *Perikemanusiaan*, 3) Nationalism, *Kebangsaan*; 4) Sovereignty of the People, *Kedaulatan Rakjat*; 5) Social Justice, *Keadilan Sosial*. In 1964, commemorating the occasion of *Pantja Sila*, Sukarno wrote:

> Finally, may we at all times hold fast to the three basic meanings of the *Pantja Sila*, namely: 1. *Pantja Sila* as the sublimation of Indonesia's unity of soul. 2. *Pantja Sila* as the manifestation of the unity of the Indonesian nation and territory. 3. *Pantja Sila* as the *Weltanschauung* in the Indonesian nation's way of life, nationally and internationally (Preface by Sukarno).

These *Pantja Sila* must not be seen as five separate principles. They are all vitally interrelated. In his exegesis of *Pantja Sila* Sukarno summarizes the whole *Pantja Sila* into *Ekasila* (one principle), *gotong-royong* (mutual cooperation).

> We are establishing an Indonesian state which all of us must support. All for all. Not the Christians for Indonesia, not the Islamic group for Indonesia, not Hadikusumo for Indonesia, not Van Eck for Indonesia, not rich Nitisemito for Indonesia, but the Indonesians for Indonesia — all for all! If I compress what was five into three, what was three into one, then I have a genuine Indonesian term, *gotong-royong*, mutual co-operation. The State of Indonesia which we are to establish must be a *gotong-royong* state. How wonderful that is; a *Gotong-Royong* state (p. 35)!

---

2. Clifford Geertz, *The Religion of Java*, Free Press of Glencoe, 1965.
3. *Pantja Sila. The Basis of the State of the Republic of Indonesia*, p. 10.

Here is a spark of genius of "Bung Karno." *Pantja Sila* is a *modern* "progressive national ideology." It is a strong expression of modernity! But he lets the spiritual message speak through the indigenous concept of *gotong-royong* (meaning "to carry heavy burdens together"). He was able to build a bridge, at the crucial juncture of ideological struggle for the new nation, between the value of modernization and traditional values. As long as the Indonesian people see the relationship between the *Pantja Sila* and *gotong-royong* there will be "Indonesia's unity of soul." In this fundamental sense the state ideology of *Pantja Sila* is not an invasion of iconoclastic modernity, but a moment of inspired accommodation.

Yet at the same time one notices that there is spiritual uneasiness among the people who find themselves between "many spirits" (the animistic spiritual world) and "several spirits" ("Five-*pantja*-Spirits," the spiritual world of modernization). "Many spirits" fascinate people. Many spirits keep community life colorful and prevent it from falling into destructive loneliness. They can occasion many social gatherings. The world of several spirits (several strong modernized ones!) is attractive in a different way, too. It points to the future. It sheds light and helps clarify the direction and quality of national life which many spirits have failed to do. The several spirits are supported by national economic advisers and a national development board. The situation is this: people are oscillating between the "traditional world of many spirits" and the "modernized world of several spirits."

(*a*) What is the Christian assessment of the historic example of Sukarno's accommodation? Does *Pantja Sila* point to the saving truth of the biblical God?

(*b*) People are sandwiched, as it were, between "many spirits" and "several spirits." How is the Holy Spirit of God whom God sent to the world "in my name" (John 14:26) related to many spirits and several spirits? Indonesia demands the doctrine of the Holy Spirit between many spirits and several spirits.

Myanmar (formerly Burma): An interdependent world, not simply an interrelated world

There is a special attractiveness in Yangon today. No traffic jams, no pollution, no din of building construction; it is a quiet place. Since 1962 General Ne Win's BWSP (Burmese Way to Socialism Program) has taken the policy of closing Burma to other countries. The contrast between Bangkok and Yangon is incredible, although which is better can become a great debate. In nearly every aspect they represent opposites. The quiet of Yangon must not be understood, however, to be a pastoral, peaceful quietness. The people of Burma are going through the hard experience of isolation and destitution. People are experiencing loneliness. In our interrelated world this is an unusual situation. Today what happens in one corner of the world finds its repercussions at the other end of the world with electric speed. Tucked between the Indochinese Peninsula and India (two power-ful symbols of the interrelated world), Burma lies in isolation, as it were, in its "Burmese Way to Loneliness."

The world is indeed interrelated. But it is not interdependent. There is a critical difference between an interrelated world and an interdependent world. An interrelated world can cure national as well as human loneliness to a certain extent, but an interdependent world can heal loneliness in a much more satisfactory way. Such a thought may be simply too romantic. Thailand depends militarily and economically on the United States in the face of the Communist threat to her northeast province. The United States, however, does not depend on Thailand. Since nations are interrelated but not interdependent, peoples suffer. In such a world situation, isolation may not be so demonic an alternative.

(a) Will the national isolation bring people to Jesus Christ?

(b) What is the missionary participation in the effort to bring forth the reality of an interdependent world from an interrelated world? What is the role of the church in this? What kind of interdependent world is our Christian vision?

Vietnam: Can man blow the coat off God?

I am not going to discuss the tragic history of Vietnam. At present I wish to call your attention to only one observation. Vietnam stands, in my mind, for the poignant truth, which came through the apocalyptic quantity and quality of suffering, that somehow the world's mightiest nation, with all her B52s and 400 billion dollars, could not achieve the objective she desired to achieve. It reminds me of the famous fable of Aesop when he told of the contest between the Sun and the Wind: ". . . it blew, it blew, it blew." Can we with all our power blow the coat off God? ". . . Thus says the LORD God: 'Behold, I am against you, Pharaoh king of Egypt, the great dragon that lies in the midst of his streams, that says, "My Nile is my own; I made it"'" (Ezek. 29:3). All Asians have seen it. The world has seen it. Both Mr. Brezhnev and Mr. Nixon have seen it. It is the planetary fact of this century. Let me stop here.

How should Christians interpret military power?

Japan: Between Article Nine and the question "What is this industrialization for?"

Since the turn of this century Japan has unwittingly played the role of a catalyst within the Asian international situation. Her victory over "white" Russia in 1905 caused a tremendous psychological boost among Asians. The history of the rise and fall of the Japanese military conquest stirred up a strong sense of nationalism in the Asian countries. Japanese evil, in the strange way of history, promoted and prepared many nations for independence. In August 1945, Japan became the first country in the history of the human race to suffer the attack of nuclear bombs over two of her heavily populated cities. Out of the ashes of these nuclear bombs came the Peace Constitution in 1946. The famous Article Nine has this to say:

Aspiring sincerely to an international peace based on justice and order, the Japanese people forever renounce war as a sovereign right of the nation and the threat or use of force as means of settling international disputes.

In order to accomplish the aim of the preceding paragraph, land, sea, and air forces, as well as other war potential, will never be maintained. The right of belligerency of the state will not be recognized.

Any Japanese above forty years of age today has consciously experienced "discontinuity" between pre-war and post-war Japan. It was an experience of the end of the old life and the beginning of a new. Such experience has made the Japanese mind perceptive to the biblical proclamation: "Behold, I make all things new" (Rev. 21:5). Since the war she has achieved tremendous advancement in her economic recovery. She has outstripped all other countries in Asia and finds herself in the position of taking part in "foreign aid," which is unfamiliar to the Japanese mind. Japan is a highly industrialized and modernized Asian country. People were spending so much money in 1973 in order to enjoy the pollution-free, quiet, pastoral Japan of 1923. It takes exhausting travel, both domestic and international, to find such a peaceful place.

(*a*) What is the theological defense of Article Nine? This must become a joint theological discussion between Japan and the United States, whose citizen General MacArthur was.

(*b*) How can the experience of radical discontinuity ("national death and resurrection") of 1945 be Christianized?

(*c*) What theological support for "foreign aid" will speak to the Japanese people?

(*d*) What is modernization for? What is industrialization for?

Taiwan: "The Emperor's Clothes" situation between Mount Sinai and many mountains

In 1949 the Communist Mao Tse-tung drove the Nationalist Chiang Kai-shek to Taiwan. The latter came with two million mainlanders and took control of fifteen million defenseless Taiwanese. Chiang Kai-shek in Taiwan was, to the nationalists and in their vociferous propaganda, the ruler of the whole of China. He was "the saving star of the whole Chinese race," as the omnipresent billboards throughout the island of Taiwan proclaimed. The fundamental policy of the Chiang Kai-shek government since 1949 has been liberation of the mainland. This is more than a national policy and ideology, it is a *creed* which every person in the island is required to recite liturgically at all occasions. This strange unrealistic creed is the official political "religion" of the Chiang Kai-shek island. The United States supported this "confession of faith." In short, the people in Taiwan have lived for many years in an "Emperor's New Clothes" situation. Everyone, including perhaps Chiang Kai-shek himself, knew well of the impossibility of such an enterprise. To use the classic expression, "the passing of the Heavenly Mandate," the ruling of

China, moved from Chiang Kai-shek to Mao Tse-tung. Yet the nation must propagate the illusion and on the basis of that illusion survive, justify, and unify its existence. No one really believed in the liberation of the mainland, and yet all are required to live as though they are dedicated to this "noble ideal." (Sometimes said to be the "noble *Christian* ideal!")

The situation is that of idolatry, since such an illusion is the center of national policy and "integrity." Is it not precisely the same situation as that of the children of Israel worshipping the golden calf in the process of Exodus? ". . . And they said, 'These are your gods, O Israel, who brought you up out of the land of Egypt!'" (Ex. 32:4). In this case idolatry becomes directly manifest because people ascribed the historical experience of salvation from Egypt to the golden calf they made of earrings and amulets. It takes the history of salvation to produce idolatry. That is why only in the tradition of biblical faith in the history-involved God is idolatry a possibility. Only those who are married can have the possibility of divorce. It is idle for a bachelor to speak about divorce. In the spiritual tradition of Mount Sinai, idolatry becomes possible. Outside that tradition, then, there is no idolatry. Is that so? Is it wrong, then, to call the Taiwan situation idolatrous? Perhaps we should say that it is only a situation of dangerous illusion.

Obviously the whole *oikoumene* does not stand in the Sinai tradition. There are many different mountains in the world. On their slopes people and gods can have a nice picnic with 7-Ups. Some contain sacred stones and trees which people must approach carefully. Some have gentle spring rain and no thunder and lightning. The message of Mount Sinai — the presence of the history-concerned *impassioned* God and people's ability to destroy themselves by distorting their relationship with this God — is, in diversified ways, reaching the peoples living in the lands of different mountains. One way in which this message has reached Taiwan is through the "Emperor's New Clothes" political situation. This painful situation forces people to think about the issues suggested by Mount Sinai. Liberation of the mainland is not immediately the "golden calf" situation for the Nationalists in Taiwan. Educational, religious, cultural, and military situations are forcing the peoples of the lands of the different mountains to see the serious issues involved in the "golden calf." Mount Sinai is silently and steadily becoming the prominent mountain among many other mountains.

(*a*) How can Taiwan's "idolatrous situation" be placed in the theological context of Mount Sinai? At what point should the church say, "Your Majesty, you are naked?"

(*b*) In search for a new way of theologizing the subject of idolatry, what does the experience of Taiwan suggest?

(*c*) The church, the people conscious of Mount Sinai and Mount Calvary, lives not outside but inside the world of idolatrous situations. The church, however, can itself become an idolatrous situation. How does that tragedy influence her mission to the peoples of different mountains?

PROPHETIC ACCOMMODATION

I appreciated your company as we traveled around Asia. I have pointed out to you in my own way how I see theological issues. Someone else may do the same and give a different report on the theological situation.

I began this paper by saying rather flatly that third world theology (every time I hear this expression "third world" it makes me think of the "Atlantic middle-kingdom complex") *begins* by raising issues, and not by digesting Augustine, Barth, and Rahner. I must say, though, that they do help in raising theological issues. You may know that the overarching theological principle of the Third Mandate of the Theological Education Fund (TEF) is expressed by "contextualization." (My native English-speaking friends tell me that this is an ugly English word. But being a non-native English speaker it does not bother me.) What is meant by contextualization of theology has been the debate on many occasions. I would like to quote two key passages from one of the important recent publications of TEF entitled *Ministry in Context. The Third Mandate Program of the Theological Education Fund (1970-1977)*:

> It means all that is implied in the familiar term "indigenization" and yet seeks to press beyond. Contextualization has to do with how we assess the peculiarity of third-world contexts. Indigenization tends to be used in the sense of responding to the gospel in terms of a traditional culture. Contextualization, while not ignoring this, takes into account the process of secularity, technology, and the struggle for human justice, which characterize the historical moment of nations in the Third World.
>
> Yet a careful distinction must be made between authentic and false forms of contextualization. False contextualization yields to uncritical accommodation, a form of culture faith. Authentic contextualization is always prophetic, arising always out of a genuine encounter between God's Word and his world, and moves toward the purpose of challenging and changing the situation through rootedness in and commitment to a given historical moment (p. 20).

The message I hear from these paragraphs is this: contextualization of theology is something more than taking the historical and cultural context seriously; it is letting theology speak in and through that context. This much is already a tall order indeed. The TEF concept of contextualization "seeks to press beyond" this. Theology must consist of critical accommodational-prophetism and prophetic accommodation. This is authentic contextualization. TEF theological reflection locates the ultimate moment of such authentic contextualization in the incarnation of Jesus Christ. I quote one more paragraph from the same document.

If, then, contextualization becomes a chief characteristic of authentic theological reflection, a request for support submitted to the TEF will be judged to have potential for renewal when:
1. There is evidence of contextualization in *mission*.
2. There is evidence of contextualization in *theological approach*.
3. There is evidence of contextualization in *educational method*.
4. There is evidence of contextualization in *structure* (pp. 20f.).

A tremendous challenge is expressed here. In all of these four areas, are we engaged in critical accommodational-prophetism and critical prophetic accommodation and moving "toward the purpose of challenging and changing the situation through rootedness in and commitment to a given historical moment?" Are we doing this in Singapore, Jakarta, Hong Kong, London, Geneva, and Virginia? I believe that this TEF challenge is on the right track. But I feel that "evidence" may not often be self-evident. Critical accommodational-prophetism and prophetic accommodation are most likely done in a *hidden* manner. This is, in short, because such an intensified theological involvement suggested by authentic contextualization cannot be done outside "if any man would come after me, let him deny himself and take up his cross and follow me" (Matt. 16:24). This "terrible" passage packs the substance of authentic contextualization. It is such a *life* that engages in authentic contextualization. When theology tells us that the Christian faith takes history seriously, it means far more than the understanding that history is not *maya* (actually to say that history is *maya* betrays a strong interest in history!). That means history is not a real history unless one participates in one way or another ("take up his cross and follow me") in the life of the Crucified Lord.

Ordinarily it is said that Buddhism does not take history seriously. Such a remark has become a favorite saying among Christian theologians. My eight years in Thailand, the land of Theravada Buddhism, radically changed my view. Often Buddhists take history more seriously than Christians! Whatever one sees in the 240,000 monks throughout the kingdom of Thailand, one cannot fail to see the religious ideal of poverty. "Spiritual" poverty is — allow me to make an ironical remark — easier to achieve than "economic" poverty. One can have two Mercedes Benz and be spiritually poor! But for the same person to lose even one of those "aircraft-carrier-sized cars" would be too painful to endure. Living among people who are mad about making money, the life of these 240,000 monks demonstrates, in spite of all human frailties and short-comings, the virtue of a simple life. They renounce material possessions. This is the right way to live in this evil historical time, free from all the snares of history. Don't they take history seriously? They are committed to overcome history. If history is not taken seriously, what is the use of practicing renunciation to overcome history and to reach the salvific tranquility of *nirvana*? Anyone who has traveled inside India has experienced the reality of the catastrophic proportion of economic poverty. They come back shocked. I frequently go to India, but I cannot get used to its staggering poverty. Some say that India's religion is Hinduism. Hinduism does not take history seriously. For them history is *maya*. The Christian message to Hindu India is that Christianity takes history seriously. It is the religion of incarnation (into history, into culture, into language, into the religious situation, and so on) of the Son of the history-minded God. But what escapes their notice is the primary fact that people there experience history — its hope and despair — with tremendous realism through their famished stomachs. The visitors probably experience it through their (Bachelor of Divinity) brains. I do not want to pit "stomach" against "brain" in the discussion on "taking history seriously." But the global truth (the evidence of which may not be self-evident) is that those who can afford to eat much experience history more superficially than those who are not so affluent. A bank account and an abundant diet somehow (I cannot explain it quite satisfactorily) insulate a person from coming to feel the primary truth of history.

The primary truth of history? Yes. For me it is Matthew 16:24. History is not there as a coffee cup is there. We live in history. "We live" means "we experience history." But there are "varieties of historical experiences." The way authentic contextualization suggests we should experience history is, in my mind, through Matthew 16:24. Such a *life* must be the life of critical accommodational-prophetism and prophetic accommodation. In this context the famous saying of Luther comes to us with full force: "Not reading books or speculating but living, dying and being damned make a theologian." Critical prophetic accommodation and accommodational-prophetism cannot come out of a suffering-free source. In Christian language "history-gravity" means "suffering gravity." At the moment of inspiration in Israel's history of theology, theological contextualization came out in the moving language of one suffering for another.

> Surely he has borne our griefs and carried our sorrows; yet we esteemed him stricken, smitten by God and afflicted. But he was wounded for our transgressions, he was bruised for our iniquities; upon him was the chastisement that made us whole, and with his stripes we are healed (Isa. 53:4,5).

He indigenized the message of God through his life of suffering. Suffering was the point of indigenization. This indigenezation took a mysterious course. He "pressed beyond" and challenged the present context of wholeness. By enduring the chastisement and stripes, he opened up a new possibility for the community. He accommodated salvation through his suffering. In this act he became prophetic. Doesn't this point to Jesus Christ of the New Testament? Why "with his stripes we are healed?" I don't know why. I don't quite understand why. But I feel that something very crucial to human history is there. And this must be vitally related to the style of life declared by Matthew 16:24.

I would call the mind portrayed by Matthew 16:24 a "crucified mind." It is the crucified mind that can meaningfully participate in authentic contextualization. It is the mind of Christ. It is not a neurotic mind. It is not a morbid mind. It does not have a persecution complex. It is a positive mind. It is a healthy mind. It is the mind which is ready to deny the self (". . . deny himself," "he emptied himself . . .") for the sake of building up a community. This mind is a theological mind. It is a free mind. And it is the missionary mind in contrast to the "crusading mind." This mind does not live by itself. It lives by constantly creating the life that practices such a mind. It lives with constant frustration and a sense of failure. Yet, it is joyous. It is resourceful. It is accommodational and prophetic. It knows that only by the grace of God can it be, and remain, accommodational and prophetic at all. "I believe, help my unbelief!" (Mk. 9:24). Chinese theology cannot come out instantly when theology is recast in the Confucian category from a neo-Platonic category. If that were all that it took to contextualize theology, it would not be such a difficult arrangement. It has in reality to do with the emergence of theological work engaged in by a Chinese crucified mind.

In the first section I hope I was able to communicate to you that there are diversified historical and cultural events and changes taking place which are full of human, spiritual, and theological implications. They are, as it were, theological "raw situations." The mission of the church begins with the nurture of the crucified mind, the mind of Christ in the context of theological raw situations.

In the light of the first section and the insight of contextualization — accommodational prophetism and prophetic accommodation engaged in by the church's crucified mind — what have we to say about the following seven topics?

(1) How do we understand accommodation in the mission of the church, in the church structure, in liturgy, in theology? What is accommodation in its relationship to proclamation, syncretism, and iconoclasticism?

(2) Worship — how does centrality of divine worship give life to the mission of the church?

(3) Evangelism — to name him at all times when he names himself.

(4) The mission *of* the third world — Jakarta is as central as Jerusalem and London in the mission of the Risen Lord. When I hear God's intention "Behold, I make all things new" (Rev. 21:5), I hear the call of God to the mission *of* the third world. It is already *very much* under way, I believe, although we may not see it clearly. It has not worked in the way we are accustomed to. The Lord's hands are on us. ". . . Do you see anything? . . . I see men; but they look like trees, walking" (Mk. 8:23,24).

(5) Salvation in the personal and social sense — the image of *horizontal* and *vertical* salvation — has done harm. It is a strange discussion in the

world which historically has lived with the "anthropology of totality" to which Jesus Christ himself belongs (. . . if you are offended by my saying "Your sins are forgiven," may I say *the same thing* in a different way, "Take up your pallet and walk"). I can interchange these two sayings as I "name myself" (Mk. 2:1-12). In both the personal and revolutionary situations Jesus names himself.

(6) Asian spirituality and religiosity — Asia has a great historic tradition of a sense of value, human relationship, philosophies, and religions. Their spiritual life has been fertile and rich. The modernization drive and economic development are overshadowing the great reality of the Asian spirituality and religiosity at this moment. The church's mission is enriched by knowing the Asian heritage of spirituality and religiosity. They are the spiritual and mental background, and only against this background can "the shape of Christ" (Gal. 4:19) be formed. Dialogue with people of other living faiths and ideologies becomes, then, the area of critical importance for the mission of the church.

(7) Global ecumenical partnership in mission — how can we increase *interdependence* between the churches in the West and the churches in Asia? Practical suggestions involve such advice as "missionary go home," "moratorium," "we need as many missionaries as possible," "send Asian missionaries to U.S.," "funds not personnel," "Australia needs Indonesian pastors," "support our Methodist work in Malaysia," and so on. Interdependence is, theologically speaking, the "form of Christ."

CHAPTER 2

Will the Monsoon Rain Make God Wet?

An Ascending Spiral View of History

- The biblical view of history is linear and emphasizes the quality of "once-for-all" in history. Under the influence of nature, however, history appears to be dominated by a quality of "many-times-ness." Frogs do not have a view of history. But the seasonal croaking of frogs influences the human mind to look at history as a circular movement.
- The proper location of the circular view fostered by nature is *within* the biblical linear view of history. The circular nature must be illumined by the linear history. Theological thinking must hold both history and nature to be equally important. *Within* here does not suggest the disappearance of the circular view. It means for nature to become a universal sign for the time. God is the Lord of history-and-nature.
- When the two images, linear and circular, are put together in the land of the monsoon orientation, one can, and perhaps should, use the image of an ascending spiral in speaking of history-and-nature.

THE MONSOON ORIENTATION

Frogs Croaking and Mosquitoes Humming

About five minutes walk from the back gate of our theological seminary there is a rustic open-air cremation site. Often I watch funeral processions passing by my office window. Long before they appear I hear them. Sorrowful tunes emanating from bamboo flutes and coarse gongs of several pitches draw me to put down my pen and join them mentally in their walk toward the cremation site.

20

Everybody has been registered by Phaja-Madcura-d, the chief of death, and we are now waiting for our turn to be called by Phaja-Madcura-d. Who is this Phaja-Madcura-d? Somewhere in an old sermon it is written that Phaja-Madcura-d is a big giant with two eyes — one is a ball of fire, and the other is a diamond. He has seven hands and thirty teeth. He catches his victims with his hands and eats them. He will kill everybody without exception, even the Lord Buddha or a king. The meaning of this Phaja-Madcura-d is as follows: the giant represents death; the two eyes are the sun and the moon; the seven hands are the seven days of the week; and the thirty teeth are the days of the month. Death comes to a person on any day of the week or the month, at any time, whether it be day or night![1]

As the procession draws abreast of my window, I see first two or three flag-bearers hoisting flags of shredded white cloth on which appear strange black symbols. The flag is called *thong samhang* and is said to be of Tibetan origin. The coffin decorated with colorful tropical flowers is placed upon a wagon. Between the flag-carriers and the relatives and close friends of the deceased who pull the wagon walks tranquility itself in the form of a chapter of saffron-robed monks. I can hear in my mind the monks, seemingly passive and untouched, preaching to the people as they walk.

> The Lord Buddha said death is the change of the name and the body of a spirit from one form to another. Nothing in the world, even life or matter, can vanish; it only changes.[2]

The cremation site lies at the end of the narrow road. Suddenly the mourners invade it. They squat on the grass while the monks chant sacred Pali sentences in a melody harmonious with the surrounding stillness of nature. The face of the dead is washed with coconut-water, the fruit taken from atop a tall tree. The coconut-water, it is said, will beautify his appearance when he is reborn into the world. An old man sets fire to the pyre. People immediately gather around the cremation platform to throw their flowers onto the coffin. They turn and walk away. The monks, too, have vanished. As soon as they are gone, the quietude of nature resumes her reign in and around this small cremation site, as though the whole event were an episode in an ecstatic dream. The man is dead. He is gone. From whence to whither? From the bosom of nature to the mysterious depth of mother nature!

---

1. Konrad Kingshill, *Ku Daeng — The Red Tomb*, Bangkok Christian College, 1965, p. 169.
2. Ibid.

His soul left his body;
Like a candle burning at night
It shone brightly.
But when it blew out
The light disappeared.
And it became dark.
. . . Life is born and dies;
It is not excellent
It may be extinct;
Nothing is more comfortable.[3]

When the people have deserted the site, I hear birds singing, frogs croaking, and mosquitoes humming. After the people have vanished, water buffaloes wallow languidly in the warm black mud as though nothing had happened during the last hours. As the black smoke trails and fades away in the groves of bamboos and among the tops of coconut palms, the dead man has gone home to nature. From benevolent nature to benevolent nature — he returned. The silence of the universe is not terrifying. It is, rather, a benign expression of the tranquility to which humans, after some years of precarious existence, are destined to return.

I still hear birds singing, frogs croaking, and mosquitoes humming. I say to myself, nature in Thailand is fertile, benevolent, and rarely moved to wrath! "In the paddy field is rice, in the water, fish" is a common saying among her people. The annual mean temperature is about 80° Fahrenheit. Rainfall varies from 760 to 3050 millimeters a year. Plenty of rainfall and sunshine (and rice and fish) fill the bosom of the warm-hearted nature in which thirty million people live. Thailand is not located in the Pacific typhoon route on which the Philippines, Taiwan, Hong Kong, and Japan lie, periodically to be visited by the fierce wrath of nature. Nature in Thailand pursues her undisturbed course of seasons with a cosmic regularity. Hot season, rainy season, cold season, hot season . . . nature circles. In that black smoke fading away among the tops of coconut trees I see the reign of nature's cyclicism which controls and numbs the claws of Phaja-Madcura-d. Nature circles. Frogs croak and mosquitoes hum.

Not "Once-for-All" but "Many-Times"

In Thailand nature circles emphatically. One season is succeeded by another with distinctive accent. The rainy season (monsoon) begins in May and continues to October. Cool air and abundant rain revive all nature into green youthfulness. Hope and salvation come with the monsoon rain! Farmers begin to plough the paddy fields now inundated. The water buffalo plodding before the plow again becomes the most familiar and essen-

---

3. Ibid., p. 122.

tial part of the rural scene. The dried well is replenished. *Every year* at about the same time the faithful monsoon arrives, impressing the people that mother nature does not forget them and that she is, in all that she does, dependable and benevolent.

Nature is cyclically oriented. Human life itself is a small circular movement within mother nature's broader circular movement. When life is viewed and experienced in terms of a circular movement, it becomes relatively free from the sense of despair and crisis. Once-for-all-ness breeds psychological tension and turmoil. Circular movement is, without really intending to be so, a negation of once-for-all-ness. There are always second, third, fourth, fifth . . . chances for people and nature to accomplish what they intend to do. Peace and tranquility — what great virtues they are! — will come when we view and experience our lives in terms of the many-times-ness which is the genuine child of nature's cyclicism. Remember, no case is a terminal case!

The once-for-all life is a life in tension. It is life against the spirit of mother nature. The many-times-ness of nature confronts the doctrine of once-for-all-ness. The once-for-all style of life is an *unfamiliar* style of life in the land of benevolent nature. On the contrary, life lived in accordance with the instructions of nature is a harmonious and familiar style of life. It accepts nature's cyclical hope and salvation. Hope is not conceived as a perpendicular promise. It is a familiar occurrence. Hope is an intimate member of the family of life which visits people regularly for reunion in the circle of nature. The Thai people intuit that the view, be it philosophical or religious, which sees human life in the light of once-for-all-ness is incongruous to the real experience of their life. Cyclical time is the image of many chances, hence tranquility. It is *apatheia* translated into the language of time.

When the monsoon rain dampens the fire of the once-for-all interpretation of our life, we find a workable basis for an optimistic view of our life. We have many chances to improve our lot. Our destiny is something we ourselves realize in a process which has no time limit. This interpretation is assured every year between May and October. When that giant with the eyes of fire and diamond calls us, it does not mean the once-for-all end of life. There are still many more chances beyond it. We must not be irritated and become impatient. Learn from nature! She "walks confidently" and "goes to sleep confidently" like the *arhat!*[4] Cosmic regularity "walks confidently" over the power of Phaja-Madcura-d! The face of the dead is washed with the coconut water. Why? To prepare the dead for the next appearance!

Nature has appointed her spokesman to announce her objection to the confidence-stealing once-for-all view of life. The monsoon frogs, *uung-aang*

---

4. "Worthy One," the person who has reached the highest stage of spiritual discipline.

(the big frogs so named because of the sound of their croaking), are the ones appointed. The door of heaven opens. The dark cloud hangs low. The water comes down. Everywhere it is wet. The grass is freshly green. The country roads once more become impenetrable. Mud, pools, and floods begin to surround us. The *uung-aang* know that their time has come. After dusk one of them begins to croak, "uung-aang, uung-aang . . ." From every corner others join to produce an impressive monsoon frog fugue. The music is comforting to the tired farmers. Perhaps there is only one group of people who do not listen to this monsoon *uung-aang* orchestra. They are the Asian theologians! *Uung-aang* do not comfort us once-for-all, but many times in every monsoon season.

THEOLOGICAL RESPONSE

The Lord Who "Sits Enthroned over the Flood"

Is nature, even in Thailand, truly so benevolent and dependable? Is not the peace of the monsoon-orientation view of nature too naïve and too optimistic? True, there are no avalanches in the land which extends from latitude 5°40′ to 20°30′. True, too, that the monsoon rains dependably visit the land every year. Yet, is Thailand's nature all so harmless and affectionate? Do not malaria-mosquitoes and poisonous snakes find Thailand's nature agreeable to them? Doesn't nature prepare a congenial environment for such dreadful diseases as cholera, typhoid, and dysentery? Isn't there obviously some evil in nature of Thailand? Are there not sudden mutations and crises in nature?

Yes. I must insist that there is indeed evil in nature. It seems to me, however, that in Thailand nature is accepted *non-argumentatively* as the benevolent mother. We may look at the presence of evil in nature argumentatively or non-argumentatively. Thailand's non-argumentative approach to the problem of evil in nature must come, to a significant degree, from the ever-present influence of the inevitable cycle (non-argumentative cycle) of tropical seasons represented by the regular coming of the life-giving monsoon rain. An argumentative approach to non-argumentative nature is an "unnatural" mental posture which results in psychological difficulty. Here again, the monsoon rain, accompanied by the *uung-aang* music, dampens the arguments about the evil in nature. The monsoon rain grants fertility to the soil. Fertility based on cosmic regularity is not a problem. We live in it. We live by the familiar and non-argumentative hope of nature's blessing. We cannot become suddenly serious about the problem of evil in nature. We must be led to the insight of unfamiliar hope and an argumentative interpretation of history in order to become serious. It takes something more than the sense of nature's regularity to engage us in the appreciation of nature that surrounds us.

The idea of the biblical God is an "argumentative" idea. The word "argumentative" is used here not with its negative sense but in the positive sense of creating something new out of involved discussion and an involved way of life. The God in the Bible is not controlled by the monsoon. God is not cyclical. God is linear. God is not many-times, but is once-for-all. When the black smoke fades away in the groves of bamboos and among the tops of coconut trees non-argumentatively, faith in God makes us look up to that same smoke argumentatively. We will meditate on the life just ended in the light of the reign of God who does not circle but moves purposefully toward a goal. Our meditation is argumentative. It is not a familiar meditation among the people of Thailand. We listen to the *uung-aang*'s magnificent fugue in its counterpoint, inspired and comforted, saying,

> I listen to the marvellous music of the monsoon frogs. From whence does my help come? My help comes from the Lord, who made the monsoon frogs.

What a strange argumentative idea! Why should the monsoon frogs and "my help" be joined together in one thread of thought?

Cyclical cosmic regularity and its saving dependability without hurry and without argument constitute the spirit of the monsoon orientation. The cosmic cyclical regularity is, however, intended by the Creator God according to the biblical faith.

> While the earth remains, seedtime and harvest, cold and heat, summer and winter, day and night, shall not cease (Gen. 8:22).

Regularity is there not by itself, but *by the promise of God.* The promise was given when "Noah built an altar to the Lord" representing the new community after the Flood. The cosmic regularity is pronounced not as "cyclical words" but as the word of decision of the Creator who intends "*never again* to curse the ground because of *man.*" The concept of regularity is severed from the tranquility of that black smoke and natural appreciation of the *uung-aang* music. Not god or gods, but God, the God of Israel stepped in, and all thought on nature's regularity has been given new dimensions. When Israel's God, the Creator, confronts the monsoon orientation, our old relationship with nature is deepened and we are given a new appreciation of nature.

Creator? Isn't this a disturbing thought? Why should there be Someone who disturbs nature's natural arrangement? *Pen* (to be) *eng* (of itself)! Nature is there of itself! There is no unnatural agent, be it intellect or spirit, behind and above nature. Any possibility of the existence of a "beyond-nature" agent would make nature — and, of course, our life — "unnaturally" complicated. Nature must be a zone cleared of the invasion of "beyond-nature" (or "unnatural") mind! Genesis 8:22 is quite acceptable if it is a description of the *pen eng* nature. But it is not! God rules nature. God is the "beyond-nature" mind over nature. God is not a part of nature.

> The voice of the LORD is upon the waters;
>   the God of glory thunders,
>   the LORD, upon many waters.
>
> The voice of the LORD is powerful,
>   the voice of the LORD is full of majesty.
>
> The voice of the LORD breaks the cedars,
>   the LORD breaks the cedars of Lebanon.
> He makes Lebanon to skip like a calf,
>   and Si'rion like a young wild ox.
>
> The voice of the LORD flashes forth flames of fire.
> The voice of the LORD shakes the wilderness,
>   the LORD shakes the wilderness of Kadesh.
>
> The voice of the LORD makes the oaks to whirl,
>   and strips the forests bare;
>   and in his temple all cry, "Glory!"
>
> The LORD sits enthroned over the flood;
>   the LORD sits enthroned as king for ever.
> May the LORD give strength to his people!
> May the LORD bless his people with peace!
>   Psalm 29:3-11

The God of Israel who is not a part of nature, but who "shakes the wilderness of Kadesh" and "sits enthroned over the flood," is bound to be an unfamiliar God to the understanding of people of monsoon orientation.

Let us briefly look at a critical portion of the history of Israel. The years leading up to 587 B.C.E. were a time of great upheavals. The land promised to the covenant people was not a "lotus-land." It was a strip of corridor land, ever threatened by the neighboring imperial powers of the Fertile Crescent and Egypt. Their predatory military devastation extended from one end to the other of this small patch of land. The Northern Kingdom of Israel fell to the Assyrian Sargon II in 721. Ahaz, the king of Judah, found his Southern Kingdom immediately exposed to the insatiable Assyria. From 627 to the Fall of Jerusalem, Jeremiah spoke to his people. He witnessed the fall of Assyria's Nineveh to the Medes and the Babylonians in 612. Babylonians stepped onto the scene of history as the new masters of the world. Their lordship was soon confirmed by the victory of Nebuchadnezzar over Pharaoh Necho in the battle of Carchemish in 605.

As soon as Babylon reached her zenith of power under Nebuchadnezzar she began to decline. Nabonidus (555-539), a successor to Nebuchadnezzar, was defeated by Cyrus and yielded his empire to the sovereignty of Cyrus. In the seventh and sixth centuries, the world of the Fertile Crescent experienced political and military shaking of the foundations. Deutero-Isaiah begins his ministry among the exiles in Babylon. He sees the coming of Cyrus whom God "stirred up" (Isa. 41:2,25) on the horizon of the chaotic power struggles. He senses that God is "mobilizing history"[5] for divine purposes. Jerusalem has fallen, as Jeremiah had prophesied. But God, "who is the controller of world-history," has not fallen,[6] but is now restoring God's people in a *new* way:

> Remember not the former things, nor consider the things of old. Behold, I am doing a new thing; now it springs forth, do you not perceive it? (Isa. 43:18,19).

The one who "shakes the wilderness of Kadesh" and who "sits enthroned over the flood" is the one who is in firm control of history between the destruction of Jerusalem (the City of God!) by the Babylonian Nebuchadnezzar in 587 B.C. and the overthrow of the Babylonian empire in 539 by the Persian Cyrus! God controls history, and does not allow nature to be confined in a compartment of nature, or history in a compartment of history. God, the "controller of world-history," is the inner meaning of the rule of God over nature (waters, thunders, cedars, calf, wild ox, wilderness, oaks, forests, flood). Hosea, the prophet from the Northern Kingdom who spoke in the years preceding the capture of Samaria by the Assyrians in 721, puts the issue with devastating clarity:

> And she did not know that it was I who gave her the grain, the wine, and the oil, and who lavished upon her silver and gold which they used for Baal. Therefore I will take back my grain in its time, and my wine in its season; and I will take away my wool and my flax, which were to cover her nakedness (Hos. 2:8,9).[7]

Israel's sin is that she gave God's glory to others by failing to see the relationship between the giver (the Lord of history) and the gifts (nature and its produce). The Lord of history is the Lord of nature, says Hosea!

---

5. Gerhard von Rad, *Old Testament Theology*, Vol.II, Oliver and Boyd, 1965, p. 244.
6. Ibid., p. 242.
7. "These amazing words represent Jahweh as the bestower of all the precious gifts of the soil. Israel, however, misunderstood both the giver and the gifts; she failed to see that she had been brought into a *status confessionis* before Jahweh because of these gifts; rather, she fell victim to a mythic divinization of husbandry and of its numinous, chthonic origins" (ibid., p. 142).

This is Israel's Creator-Ruler-God, who is a beyond-natural someone over nature if judged by the monsoon orientation. This God created all and sustains all. This much is already quite a puzzling idea, but what follows is intensely *unfamiliar*. It describes the intimate relationship between this Creator God and Israel, a tiny nation in the ancient Near East. God called Israel. God works through the instrument of Israel "to open the eyes that are blind, to bring out the prisoners from the dungeon." Bringing "prisoners from the dungeon" (Isa. 42:7) is the work of God who set "seedtime and harvest, cold and heat, summer and winter, day and night." This God refuses to sit and listen passively to *uung-aang* music staged by the cosmic regularity as though nothing else existed. On the contrary, this God pays attention to those who listen to *uung-aang* orchestras in prison or in hospitals, the *Pen Eng* at work, not only in the nature of cosmic regularity, but in an area which cannot be confined in the idea of nature, the area which theology calls "history."[8] God who sets the "seedtime and harvest" (nature) is the same God who "stirs up Cyrus" and is concerned with the "prisoner in his dungeon" (history).

The cosmic regularity itself is not of the devil. This is clear. It expresses, as we have seen, the mind of God who gives "help" to the prisoners and the blind. The God who emancipates from dungeon and darkness is the same God who desires the regular coming of the monsoon. The "emancipation from dungeon" (history-event) and the "coming of the monsoon" (nature-occurrence) are one in expressing God's intention to "help" humankind. The former does not work according to the rhythm of cosmic regularity. The Chiengmai prison does not let one hundred prisoners go free regularly every year. The Chiengmai prison takes an unpredictable course of development in sharp contrast to the regularity of the monsoon. History reminds us of the "road from Jerusalem to Jericho" (Lk. 10:29-37), where unexpected events of encounters with robbers *can* happen. The "road from Jerusalem to Jericho" (history) is different from the "road from cold season to hot season" (nature) where only that which is familiar and known

---

8. In the Thai language '*Prawàd*' (account, story, history), *pradwàdkàan* (history chronicle of event). *Prawàdsàad*', *prawàdtisaad*' (history) refer to events in the past. We say, "He has a bad *prawàdtisaad*'." This means that the person has a bad life story, a bad record. At this point the biblical concept of *prawàdtisaad*' has something very important to add to the Thai concept of *prawàdtisaad*'. History, in the biblical sense, refers to both past and present. Past, present, and future are one continuous story of God's involvement with humankind. God visited the prisoner, is visiting the prisoner, and will visit the prisoner. God visited the man of bad *prawàdtisaad*', is visiting the man of bad *prawàdtisaad*', and will visit the man of bad *prawàdtisaad*'. God's work is continuous. So history is a continuous story into the future. Since God visited, is visiting, and will visit the man of bad *prawàdtisaad*', the man of bad *prawàdtisaad*' may become a man of good *prawàdtisaad*'. God's visitation brings salvation. God will visit the prisoner and emancipate him. History will see that visitation and emancipation. In this saving and creative way history is not just a story of the past, but the future is included and the possibility of change from a son of bad *prawàdtisaad*' to the man of good *prawàdtisaad*' is included.

can happen. One may travel from "Jerusalem to Jericho" "non-argumenta-tively," as though walking on the nature-road from "season to season," understanding life in terms of nature's cyclical movement, history over-shadowed by nature. It may be called the monsoon interpretation of his-tory which says: "One must not take history so seriously and impatiently since history is a journey between two points, 'Jerusalem and Jericho,' *within* the grand circle of 'season to season.'"

This *within* poses a problem. Is history ("road from Jerusalem to Jeri-cho") *within* nature ("road from cold season to hot season") or is nature ("road from cold season to hot season") *within* history ("road from Jerusalem to Jericho")? Should we understand our unpredictable life (his-tory-event) in the light of the predictable movements of nature (nature-occurrence)? Or should it be the other way around? That would make a great difference. If the message of cosmic regularity is taken as the *final* word, then the travel between "Jerusalem and Jericho" will be "regular-ized," "tranquilized," and made familiar. But if the message of the history-event controls the meaning of the nature-occurrence, then what happens between "cold season and hot season" will be "historicized," "disturbed," and made to be thought "anew every day" (Lam. 3:23; Matt. 6:11).

The Bible affirms the latter over against the former. It announces that we should see nature in the light of the Creator God. Nature must not be understood only naturally. It must be theologically appropriated, since "in the beginning God created the heavens and the earth" (Gen.1:1) and *not* "in the beginning the heavens and the earth created God." "*He* sends his rain" (Matt. 5:45)! The rain is theologized, historicized, and becomes more than just drops of water from heaven. It is God's rain. It is God's monsoon. Scientifically speaking, of course, a certain combination of meteorological arrangements will produce monsoons every year. This is a scientific truth. Not in conflict with this scientific truth, Jesus gives another *kind* of truth.

> But he replied, "When the evening comes you say, 'Ah, fine weather — the sky is red.' In the morning you say, 'There will be a storm today, the sky is red and threatening.' Yes, you know how to interpret the look of the sky, but you have no idea how to interpret the signs of the times" (Matt. 16:2f.).

The Pharisees and the Sadducees were competent in judging the meteo-rological situation (nature). But, even with their sharpened religious per-ceptivity, they failed to grasp "the signs of the times" (history). The One who sends "his storm" sends "his Son," who is himself the sign of the times! The One who promises the cycle of seasons can behave in an "un-meteorological" way. Rain must be theologized as "his rain," and "his rain" that he sends must be seen in the perspective of "his Son" whom he sends. The cosmic regularity of nature must be placed *within* (or under) the pur-pose of God who is the Lord over meteorological and cosmic realities.

> It is he who sits above the circle of the earth, and its inhabitants are like grasshoppers; who stretches out the heavens like a curtain, and spreads them like a tent to dwell in; who brings princes to naught, and makes the rulers of the earth as nothing (Isa. 40:22f.).

But this *within* never means that nature ceases to be nature and begins to take some "divine" character. Nature is placed under the rule of God, but nature continues to be nature. ". . . If salt has lost its taste, how shall its saltness be restored? It is no longer good for anything except to be thrown out and trodden under foot by men" (Matt. 5:13). This is why we can eat fish. Fish (nature) is fish (nature). It is fish while it is swimming in the river. It is fish while we are cooking it, it is fish while we are eating it, and it is fish while we are digesting it. Its character of being fish does not change. Fish is fish. It is predictable. If fish became banana or bamboo-shoots while we were cooking it, we would never know how to season it. It would be too unpredictable. But this unpredictable situation does not occur in the normal experience of our life. Atoms, the scientist say, make unpredictable movements. But that does not mean that atoms become something other than atoms. Nature remains nature. It is in that sense predictable. It is like monsoon orientation. In June the monsoon will *surely* come to Thailand. Suppose nature changed itself to un-nature, something demonic, terrible, or divine, we would then fear that "unnatural nature," "demonic-nature," "terrible-nature," and "divine-nature," and we would not dare to "eat" it. How could we dare to eat the fish if half of it were "god" — a bad-tempered god?

> And he became hungry and desired something to eat; but while they were preparing it, he fell into a trance and saw the heaven opened, and something descending, like a great sheet, let down by four corners upon the earth. In it were all kinds of animals and reptiles and birds of the air. And there came a voice to him, "Rise, Peter; kill and eat." But Peter said, "No, Lord; for I have never eaten anything that is common or unclean." And the voice came to him again a second time, "What God has cleansed, you must not call common" (Acts 10:10-15).

"All kinds of animals and reptiles and birds of the air" are placed *within* the context of the purpose of God. God cleansed them. Peter can kill them, cook them, and eat them. While he is doing so, cow will remain cow, pig will remain pig, and chicken will remain chicken. God, the Creator, will not allow chicken to be changed into something else. He has cleansed chicken as it is for our use. We do not need to fear chicken. "Without fear" we can eat chicken because we understand chicken "theologically." Theological understanding of chicken is that chicken remains chicken since it is "his" chicken in the same way the rain is "his" rain. It is strange that we always try to change nature into something more than nature. We should feel thankful for nature which God has given us, but this gratitude must not be corrupted so as to make nature "some kind of god." Nature expresses the mind of the Creator.

> You have heard that it was said, "You shall love your neighbor and hate your enemy." But I say to you, Love your enemies and pray for those who persecute you, so that you may be sons of your Father who is in heaven; for he makes his sun rise on the evil and on the good, and sends rain on the just and on the unjust (Matt. 5:43-45).

The monsoon orientation (cyclical movement) is placed *within* the purpose of God (linear movement).

> The heavens are telling the glory of God; and the firmament proclaims his handiwork (Ps. 19:1).

The monsoon rain cannot make God wet! God is the Lord of the monsoon rain. God sends "his" monsoon. The biblical view of history is not circular. It is linear. But life in Thailand is strongly influenced by the circular movement of nature. This circular nature is not of demons. It is, as we understand, from God. We see the glory of God both in history and in nature. Circular nature shows God's glory as much as linear history. Both are purposeful. Yet, as we have seen, circular nature finds its proper place *within* linear history. In this proper location, circular nature finds its purpose. When two images, circular and linear, are put together, why can we not have the image of an ascending spiral view of one unified history-nature? Is not this image helpful and even necessary in the land of the monsoon orientation? Is not this at least one way to see the sign of the times in Thailand? Will this not bring the presence of God closer to the people of Thailand?

CHAPTER 3

Gun and Ointment

The Future of the Christian World Mission in Asia

- The West is both *gun* (wounding) and *ointment* (healing) for the East.
- Asia's theological thinking must be engaged in against the background of this peculiar history of *gun* and *ointment*.
- Theology must be pursued with the crucified mind, not with the crusading mind.
- A theological examination of Asia's experience of the impact of modernization is a priority for Asian theologians. This examination must be done in the context of a particular cultural orbit.
- The Christian proclamation is that the lamb slain is the victor forever. The methodology and content of *missionary ointment* derive from this amazing quality of the person and work of the Lord Jesus Christ.
- The crucified mind, the mind of *missionary ointment*, sees and appreciates the overwhelming complexity of history in which Asia lives today.

. . . and the house was filled with the fragrance of the ointment (Jn. 12:3).

The paper will have two sections: first, I must attempt to outline the historical perspective in which I may be able to place Asia, keeping missiological concern in mind. There may be varieties of methods by which to formulate this perspective, and consequently varieties of perspectives. I propose to locate Asia, the region of fascinating histories and diversities, in the historical perspective of the West's "gun" (wounding) and "ointment" (healing).[1]

---

1. How to determine the historical and theological position of Asia involves great debate. How is Asia's own history to be assessed *vis à vis* the message of Israel and the church? Before the coming of the proclamation of Christ, was the history experienced by Asia not full history? Was it only marginal to "real" history? What is the theological

The West has meant and is *both* threat and salvation for Asia. Asia's experience of the "gun and ointment" has aroused an active sense of participation in history among its peoples and its nations' leaders. In the second section, I must examine the missiological implications of the participation in history developed from the background of the West's "gun and ointment" perspective.

THE "GUN AND OINTMENT" PERSPECTIVE

It was in 1511. The Portuguese fleet, propelled by greed for the monopoly of the Asiatic trade (spice!) and hatred of the infidel Muslim, approached the fortress of Malacca. The captain of the fleet, Alfonso de Albuquerque, spoke to his men to inspire them on the eve of the successful assault on the city. The speech contains a highly interesting theological interpretation of the event.

> It is, too, well worthy of belief that as the King of Malacca, who has already once been discomfited and had proof of our strength, with no hope of obtaining any succour from any other quarters — sixteen days having already elapsed since this took place — makes no endeavour to negotiate with us for the security of his estate, Our Lord is blinding his judgment and hardening his heart, and desires the completion of this affair of Malacca.[2]

Contary to Albuquerque's imperialistic theologizing, I am afraid that God had hardened the captain's heart and blinded the judgment of king D. Manuel. The heart of the Portuguese captain was hardened, first, by his drive after wealth and his antipathy to the Muslims, and perhaps secondly, by a very direct application of a biblical doctrine — a doctrine which happens to be a controversial and abstruse one which must not be used without soul-searching! — to his historical situation, for his own advantage. The guns he carried on his fleet symbolize the first hardening, the cross he hoisted high on his fleet symbolizes the second. Albuquerque was convinced that God Almighty was on his side. He was hardened to an intensive

---

meaning of the word "before" here? What is the theological understanding of the enduring value of the great Asia civilizations? General Simatupang of Indonesia finds Bishop Newbigin's phrase, "'people who have no history' before the experience of the modern Western invasion," quite difficult to accept. Cf. Alan C. Thompson, "Faith and Politics: The Indonesian Contribution," *The South East Asia Journal of Theology*, Spring 1970; Lesslie Newbigin, "The Gathering Up of History into Christ," in C. C. West and D. M. Paton (eds.), *The Missionary Church in East and West*, SCM Press, 1959.

2. H. J. Benda and J. A. Larkin, *The World of South East Asia*, Harper & Row, 1968, p. 78.

degree unknown to the Asians who had not the "theological maturity" to utilize biblical doctrine to their own advantage![3]

Malacca in 1511 stands as an incident burdened with a symbolic historical value. In the person of Albuquerque one can discern the structure and character of the relationship between the West and Asia. In her dealing with Asia, the West has often been hardened by commercial avariciousness and by theological self-righteousness. These two "hardening" elements constitute the main ingredients of the gunpowder of the West against Asia. Professor K. M. Panikkar's *Asia and Western Dominance* is an extensive historical investigation of the acts of the West's "gun" since 27 May 1498, the day of the arrival of *San Gabriel* at Calicut. Whether we begin in 1498, or in 1511, or in 1564 (the first Spanish settlement in Cebu by Miguel Lopez de Legaspi), or in 1602 (the formation of the Dutch United East India Company — *Vereenigde Oostindische Compagnie* — to which "was granted the monopoly of trade in the regions between the Cape of Good Hope and the Magellan Straits for an initial period of twenty-one years, together with power to make treaties, build forts, maintain armed forces and install officers of justice"), we can discern the same psychological structure of the West's aggression on Southeast Asia.[4] The study of the history of the "new power"(K. M. Panikkar) since the sixteenth century involves complicated historical processes and accidents which differ significantly from one locality to another. Economic, political, anthropological, and cultural assessment of Asia's experience of the West's expansion, conquest, and empire-building from 1498 to 1914 poses a formidable assignment. The point I wish to make here is that the twenty cannons mounted on the deck of *San Gabriel*, the flagship of the Vasco Da Gama expedition, meant far more than some 20 mechanical arrangements in which gunpowder could be ignited. They symbolized the coming of a time of radical crisis and upheaval for Asian life, the shaking up of her economic, political, and cultural life. This process is a process of "wounding," particularly as it came at the hands of the countless "hardened and blinded" Albuquerques!

Concomitant with the process of "gun" came "ointment," also from the West, to Asia. "Gun" was accompanied by "ointment!" "From the same mouth come blessing and cursing. My brethren, this ought not to be so. Does a spring pour forth from the same opening fresh water and brackish?" (Jas. 3:10f.). In the West's relationship with Asia, however, history has produced both "fresh water and brackish" in a remarkable fashion. Sixteenth-

---

3. Historical and theological investigation into the origin and development of the European background of the "aggressive theology" up to the appearance of Albuquerque in the East would be a worthwhile study. The church's negative attitude toward the Jews and Moslems and the church's powerful position that enabled her to suppress other religious persuasions certainly must have to do with the future appearance of Albuquerque.

4. D. G. E. Hall, *A History of South East Asia*, Macmillan, 1968, p. 271.

century Europe has the unique distinction of being the century from which both "wounding" and "healing" began to reach the East. It was a stormy century for the European nations in their political, religious, and scientific life, accelerating the process of the momentous transition from the medieval to the modern which took place between the twelfth century and the eighteenth century.

What is that "healing" which the West brought into Asia, perhaps as an "unintended gift" of the age of an extended Albuquerque?[5] It is *modernization*. The impact of modernization upon Asia has been a gradual process of historical development which began its acutely ascending phase at the end of the Second World War. Modernization does not simply mean a spread of modern technological information and practices. It is a new orientation which has been effecting radical transformations in all areas of human life. It affects political systems, international life, community life, education, health service, employment, labor conditions, public works, and business enterprises. Professor C. E. Black attempts a definition of modernization "as the process by which historically evolved institutions are adapted to the rapidly changing functions that reflect the unprecedented increase in man's knowledge, permitting control over his environment, that accompanied the scientific revolution."[6]

Asia's traditional way of life in all these areas of human existence was "gunned" by the Albuquerquean invasion. But one discerns at once that the "dynamic and interventionist" valuation of modernization has gunned the "static" traditional values, too.[7] Here lies the great "ointment" aspect of modernization.

How far, however, has the Albuquerquean "wounding" prepared the ground for the modernization "healing?" Has the colonial "gun" accelerated or hindered the process of the modernization "ointment" in Asia? These questions require careful historical investigation. It is true that the simultaneous advent of "gun" and "ointment" has produced an unusually compact and fertile history for Asia.[8] Experiencing this accelerated historical process, Asians began to have a new feeling about history. From this feeling came two convictions: first, a growing conviction that Asians can become the main force in the universal history of humankind today and tomorrow, that through their active participation in history they can *change* history; second, an increasing confidence that history has some definite goal. In the "goal of modernization," they have found a practical goal toward which they can purposefully move. An "Asian Drama" has begun.

---

5. Henrik Kraemer, *World Cultures and World Religions*, Lutterworth Press, 1960, p. 67.

6. C. E. Black, *The Dynamics of Modernization*, p. 7.

7. Gunnar Myrdal, *Asian Drama*, vol.1, Penguin Books, 1969, p.73.

8. According to Dr. Masao Takonaka, six revolutions in the West which spread over the four hundred years since the Reformation came to Asia all at once, telescoped into five decades. Cf. Hans Ruedi Weber, *Asia and the Ecumenical Movement*, SCM Press, 1966, p. 21.

The modernization ointment consists outwardly in the transformation of everyday life, in increasing physical and environmental comfort, and inwardly in the sense of active participation in history. Modernization is, in this sense, an "ointment" for a stagnant and traditional Asia.

Thus the West's "gun and ointment" means the "colonial exploitation-disruption gun," and "modernization ointment." The results of the former are still quite visible today in South Asia, particularly when viewed from the perspective of the development issue. The modernization ointment must work to foster and restore health to the wounded process of development.

Modernization, however, is not all ointment! This becomes clear when one studies one of the main arteries through which the blood of modernization circulates in the world today, technological advancement. Technology, from the printing machine of Johannes G. Gutenberg in 1448 to the American NASA men who overcame both terrestrial and lunar gravitational pulls in 1969, has emancipated humankind, to a significant extent, from toil and suffering. It has succeeded in putting an unheard-of amount of educational material into the hands of millions. It has achieved miracles in hospitals. Technological advancement stands in a positive relationship with the "life abundant" for which Christ came (Jn. 10:10; Matt. 11:4-6). *But,* isn't it also technology that changed the twenty guns mounted on the deck of *San Gabriel* to the nuclear missiles deliverable by submarines or earth-orbiting bombing systems? The *San Gabriel* cannons, through the apocalyptic touch of technology, have become literally "cosmic guns!" Technological efficiency, however fantastic — computers, heart transplants, nuclear energy — none of these can solve the problem of history. There seems to be a demonic alliance between technocracy-psychology and the modern age. "The modern age, more than any other, has been an age of civil, religious and international wars, of mass slaughter in many forms, and of concentration camps."[9] Between 1820 and 1949 the world lost 46.8 million lives in wars.[10] Isn't this "the agony of modernization?"[11] Modernization itself, then, must be realistically understood as simultaneously "gun and ointment." "Colonial gun and modernization ointment" and "modernization ointment and modernization gun" are continuous, co-existing, and mingled.

PARTICIPATION IN HISTORY AND CHRISTIAN MISSION

Great empires and civilizations existed in Asia prior to the invasion of the West's "gun and ointment." Perhaps because of the abrupt onslaught of the West's "gun and ointment," the modern world has not fully under-

9. C. E. Black, op.cit., p. 27.
10. Ibid., p. 33.
11. Ibid., p. 20.

stood or acknowledged the vast and profound contribution of the Asian civilizations to the life of humankind. Asian sons, Gautama Siddhartha, the writers of the *Upanishads,* Confucius, Lao-tse, participated in the "axial period" of humankind with Elijah, Isaiah, Jeremiah, Deutero-Isaiah, Zarathustra, Homer, Parmenides, and Plato.[12] Asian histories have had their own "gun and ointment." If I may hazard a characterization of Asia's experience of history, I would say it has been *patient,* compared to the West's *impatient* history. This characterization is guided by a theological understanding of history. The strongly linear view of history in the biblical tradition, based on the faith that God is the governor of history, is not indigenous to the life and thought of the peoples of Asia. A linear sense of history, when appropriated by human *hybris,* can produce dangerous *impatience* with history.

The biblical God "experiences" history.[13] God has a purpose for human history. God does "strange things" in history (Isa. 28:21), hardening the human heart according to God's purpose. But for the mortal Albuquerque to say that God was on his side and blinding the judgment of his enemy was an egoistic monopoly of the biblical linear view of history! The relationship between the mystery of "hardening of heart" and the mystery of the "linear view of history" produces an extremely dangerous zone for us to walk in. Albuquerque became *theologically impatient* with the city of Malacca, since he was convinced that God was on his side. His impatience and aggressiveness are thus of a special kind, since they have a theological foundation.[14]

The Albuquerquean theistic impatience was given powerful expression in July 1937, in the land of "axial" Confucius, in the person of the Chinese atheist Mao Tse-tung (what a development!):

> In the present epoch of the development of society, the responsibility of correctly knowing and changing the world has been placed by history upon the shoulders of the proletariat and its party. This process, the practice of changing the world, which is determined in accordance with scientific knowledge, has already reached a historic moment in the world and in China, a great moment unprecedented in human history, that is, the moment for completely banishing dark-

---

12. Karl Jaspers, *The Origin and Goal of History,* Routledge, 1953, pp. 1-21.

13. "What concerns the prophet is the human event as a divine experience. History to us is the record of human experience; to the prophet it is a record of God's experience" (Abraham J. Heschel, *The Prophets,* Harper & Row, 1963, p. 172).

14. For example, in 1454 Henry the Navigator received Pope Nicholas V's bull: "We, after careful deliberation, and having considered that we have by our apostolic letters conceded to king Afonso the right, total and absolute, to invade, conquer and subject all the countries which are under rule of the enemies of Christ, Saracen or pagan," quoted in K. M. Panikkar, *Asia and Western Dominance,* Allen and Unwin, 1959, p. 27.

ness from the world and from China and for changing the world into
a world of light such as never previously existed.[15]

Mao Tse-tung, "the helmsman" of the world's most populous nation, here
speaks "theological" language. The *kairos*, decisive hour, has come to the
world and to China through his "proletariat ointment!" He speaks of the
once-for-all event of "banishing darkness from the world." His interpretation of a participation in history is based on the impatient criticism made
by Marx and Lenin of the economic substructure of the West's "gun and
ointment." Mao's passion and conviction betray their "Christian origin."
His proletariat ointment is a great historical agent bringing change into
Asian life today.

Mahatma Gandhi's life (1869-1948) was a continuous story of active participation in history. He organized campaigns of civil disobedience; he was
imprisoned because of his conviction of the direction of history; he
founded the *ashram;* he advocated *swaraj* (home rule); he improved the status of the untouchables. He experienced, through his own life and the life
of his people, the whole range of implications of the West's "gun and ointment" upon India. He appreciated the effects of the Christian missionary
ointment. But for his part, he presented to the millions of his fellow Indi-
ans "*ahimsa* ointment" (non-killing, non-violence), the first principle in the
satyagraha (holding to the truth) movement.[16] The *ahimsa* ointment used
by the Hindu Indian has been repeatedly referred to by the Burmese Theravada Buddhist U Thant, when Secretary-General of the United Nations:

> It was in an effort to assert the dignity and worth of the human per-
> son that Gandhiji started the first passive resistance movement called
> Satyagraha in South Africa at the beginning of this century. As its con-
> notation so clearly shows, Gandhiji believed that the weapon of truth,
> if firmly grasped and purposefully used, could head to peaceful
> change without resort to violence. This was indeed one of the great
> ideas of our century. Gandhiji has rightly been regarded as the apos-
> tle of Ahimsa or non-violence, a concept enshrined in the teaching

---

15. From Mao's philosophical essay "On Practice," *Essential Works of Chinese Communism*, ed. W. Chai, Bantam Books, 1962, p. 95. What he said in 1937 was reiterated
with an equal vigor in 1966: "Communism is at once a complete system of proletarian
ideology and a new social system. It is different from any other ideological and social
system, and is the most complete, progressive, revolutionary and rational system in
human history. . . . However much the reactionaries try to hold back the wheel of history, sooner or later revolution will take place and will inevitably triumph" (*Quotations
from Chairman Mao Tse-Tung*).

16. "The Satyagraha movement is an attempt to carry this ancient Indo-Aryan idea
into play against what would seem to the eye to be the vastly superior powers of the
highly mechanized, industrially supported, military and political equipment of the
Anglo-Saxon's victorious machine of universal empire" (Heinrich Zimmer, *Philosophies
of India*, Routledge, 1951, p. 169).

of practically all the great religions. It is really one of the basic tenets of my own religion, Buddhism. Intolerance, violence and the spirit of persecution are foreign to Buddhism. . . . A familiar phrase one often hears is that "the end justifies the means." Gandhiji categorically rejected this idea; he did not believe that a noble end could be achieved by ignoble means.[17]

The Secretary-General of the United Nations endorsed the *ahimsa* ointment as "in line with the principles and purposes of the Charter of the United Nations" and enshrined in "all the great religions."[18] *Ahimsa* ointment is rooted in the human conscience, which echoes back to the messages of the axial epoch. At the same time, it has cogently relevant applications for today's violently torn world. This great ointment activated itself in recent history through the Hindu man, who himself met a violent death. Martin Luther King, Jr. also stood for the *ahimsa* ointment and came to a violent end.

I have chosen two Asian ointments centered in the two great countries of the ancient civilization, China and India, whose spiritual and cultural influence upon the whole of Asia have been immense. In speaking of the present proletariat ointment and the ancient *ahimsa* ointment, I am not intending to be comprehensive. There may be other important Asian ointments. My aim is to clarify, if at all possible, some of the critical challenges the Christian mission is facing in Asia while speaking on the encounters between representative great "ointments" in the perspective of Asia's historic encounter with the West's "gun and ointment."

Both proletariat ointment and *ahimsa* ointment have histories. They are two outstanding examples of Asian participation in history. They are not just ideas. They have influenced millions of people in more than a superficial way. They are meant to heal the wounds of human history. Here are concrete ointments working in the concrete history of Asia. Both ointments have come out of frictions and irritations with the West. They are not ignorant of the history of the West's colonial-expansionist and modernization guns. Both realize the presence of a strange ointment called the missionary ointment which is trying to heal the wounds of history by the name of a man crucified two thousand years ago. Whether they realize it or not, it is true that the missionary ointment has influenced, to a great measure, their commitment toward the establishment of social justice in the human community. The name of Jesus Christ does not, however, occupy centrality in these two Asian ointments. The very necessity for these two Asian ointments (Mao Tse-tung, Gandhi, and U Thant) connotes to Asians a criticism of the "almighty" West's ointments, both modernization and missionary.

---

17. U Thant, "Non-Violence and World Peace," *Gandhi Centenary Celebrations*, Singapore, 1969, p. 15.
18. Ibid.

They see, rightly or wrongly, that both missionary ointment and modernization ointment have not really healed the wounds of history. Modernization is valuable, says the *ahimsa* ointment, as long as it increases the *ahimsa* value. It is valuable, says the proletariat ointment, as long as it contributes to the creation of the classless society. The same points must be made with the missionary ointment. The proletariat ointment positively accepts the proposition that "the end justifies the means" because it is intensely "impatient" with history. Its rejection of religious value is also rooted in the same impatience with history. Religious interpretation of and participation in history is too lenient and patient! The Chinese proletariat eschatological movement engages in a radical surgery of history. It cuts history open, puts its hand inside, and extracts the cancer of all evils from the body of history once and for all! The *ahimsa* ointment, reflecting the ancient Indo-Aryan wisdom, does not work or develop according to historical scientific dialecticism. It is not impatient with history. It desires to speak to evident human history through a simple *satyagraha*. It proposes to "hold all things" (Col. 1:17) by the invisible power of the eternal truth.

Against the background of the proletariat ointment ("impatient" in the tradition of Albuquerque) and the *ahimsa* ointment ("patient" in the tradition of the ancient Indo-Aryan spirituality), a critical event took place in 1964. "Impatient" China successfully detonated a device containing thermonuclear material in the Sinkiang test ground. Sinkiang 1964 stands out as the point of the Chinese transition from the message of the proletariat ointment to the dreadful modernization gun which was, until then, the monopoly of the West. There could be no Sinkiang 1964 without New Mexico 1945. China's apocalyptic gun began to overshadow her message of "completely banishing darkness from the world." Her cosmic gun has become a threat to humankind because of her ideologically impatient position that "the end justifies the means." India, the land of the *ahimsa* ointment, bordering on China, watched apprehensively the appearance of the super modernization gun in China. India was threatened by it and has explored the development of nuclear arms herself, in spite of the obviously devastating cost that the project entails! This move is a tragic Indian departure from the *ahimsa* ointment to the *himsa* gun. The *ahimsa* ointment had been the torch of hope in the world of the *himsa* gun. Sinkiang 1964 thus shook the foundation of both Asian ointments. The demonic fumes of the modernization gun are now beginning to paralyze the nervesystem of the two centers of the great civilizations in Asia, China, and India. The courtship with the modernization gun will immediately exhaust the resources for the projects of the modernization ointment. The modernization ointment has been recognized among Asians for its high value. But the astronomically expensive armament drive will destroy the modernization ointment. Slavery to armaments! The West's positive contribution of the modernization ointment is still there, but under the constant threat of the super-gun. How long can the modernization gun and modernization ointment stay together in this crowded history of humankind?

THE PARTICIPATION OF THE ANOINTED ONE IN HISTORY

From the sole of the foot even to the head, there is no soundness in it, but bruises and sores and bleeding wounds; they are not pressed out, or bound up, or softened with oil (Isa. 1:6).

In the house of Simon, the leper, at Bethany in an insignificant corner of the Roman Empire two thousand years ago, a nameless woman broke a jar of costly ointment and poured it over the head of Jesus. Her act was a symbol of the impending death of the Anointed One. "And truly, I say to you, wherever the gospel is preached in the whole world, what she had done will be told in memory of her" (Mk. 14:9). Wherever the gospel is preached — in China, India, Hong Kong, Vietnam, Cambodia, Laos, Thailand, Malaysia, Singapore, Indonesia, the Philippines, Burma — what she has done will be told in memory of her because she staged a symbolic act demonstrating the substance and manner of God's participation in history. The Crucified One (I Cor. 2:2) is the agent of God's participation in history! The fragrance of God's creation, participation, government, and fulfilment of history in Christ must fill the whole *oikoumene*. The substance of the missionary ointment is the entire story of God's work in history culminating in the death and resurrection of Jesus Christ. Can this event of Christ mean anything for Asians today? Theological discernment will reveal the missionary ointment's unique historical reality (II Kings 6:17; Mk. 8:24f.). When Albuquerque was storming Malacca, the Basque Francis Xavier was five years old. Between 1581 and 1712, of 376 Jesuits sent to China, 127 were lost on the voyage through sickness or shipwreck.[19] The history of the missionary ointment takes place *incognito* and patiently in the same history in which guns are being used.

Isn't it the mission of the missionary ointment to purify and strengthen the other ointments with the oil of God's judgment and salvation and let them participate in the movement of the missionary ointment? If God's participation in history is portrayed in the form of the Crucified One, the *morphe* (form or shape, Gal. 4:19) of absolute self-denial, in order to issue a mighty invitation to all "on earth or in heaven" (Col. 1:20), if the Lamb of God (Jn. 1:29; Rev. 5:12) is the victorious head of the *ekklesia* (church) and *cosmos* (world) (Col. 1:15-20), then should not the missionary ointment work toward the realization of a *koinonia*, community, of the ointments participating in history? Can we find any ointment at work in history which is totally healing and completely free from any possible taints of wounding, be it modernization ointment, *ahimsa* ointment, or proletariat ointment?

---

19. Stephen Neill, *A History of Christian Missions*, Penguin Books, 1969, p. 208.

Even missionary ointment? Isn't it true that there have been unfortunate incidents indicating the entanglements between missionary ointment and the conquest-expansion gun?[20]

The missionary ointment itself, then, can be fragrant only insofar as the fragrance of Christ is in it and the same fragrance is appreciated by the ones who *repent*. This repentant missionary ointment sees other ointments as having elements of Christ's ointment and unconsciously participating in the fragrance of Christ in history. Is it possible to say that the West's "gun and ointment" has provided stimulation to give vitality to the dormant Asian ointments and thus has made them historical forces in the life of the Asian? If so, cannot the "gun and ointment" of the West since 1511 be viewed in the light of Ephesians 1:10?

> He purposes in his sovereign will that all human history shall be consummated in Christ, that everything that exists in heaven or earth shall find its perfection and fulfilment in him (Phillips translation).

If so — if we look up to the Crucified One under Pontius Pilate as the One who will fulfill the history of all the "guns and ointments" — I wish to ask three *related* questions with regard to the future of the Christian mission in Asia:

(a) What are the specific ways by which the Christian mission can become even more an agitator of history in order to facilitate a healthy increase of modernization ointment?

(b) Are the people of the missionary ointment sure that they are not *Asian* Albuquerques who are eager (impatient!) to storm Hong Kong, Djakarta, Manila, Rangoon (and Buddhism, Hinduism, Islam, and animism) as though all these were "infidel Malaccas" (Hos. 9:7; Jer. 25:29)? Should we be more impatient with history than God is?

(c) Is it possible, particularly in these post-Sinkiang dangerous days, for the Christian mission to be "the salt of the earth" (Matt. 5:13) unless it lives *in* the confusion of history of "guns and ointments?" Christian mission will command the attention of the millions of Asians, by standing against the

---

20. In 1857 the execution of the Spanish Bishop of Tonking, Msgr. Diaz, by the Vietnamese ruler Tu-Duc (1848-83), gave France a long-awaited pretext for seizing territory in Annam. At Hue, de Montign presented three demands to Tu-Duc, one of which was "a guarantee of religious liberty for Christians." A war ensued. In June 1862, a treaty was signed at Saigon "by which Tu-Duc ceded to France three eastern provinces of Cochin China and agreed to pay a heavy indemnity in instalments over ten years. He promised the free exercise of the Catholic religion in his dominions and to open the ports of Tourane, Balat and Kuang-An to French trade" (Hall, op.cit., p. 613). Speaking of "the fortunes of Christianity" in the Moluccas, Hall writes that they "depended almost entirely upon the military strength of the Portuguese" (ibid., p. 233). The missionary ointment dependent "upon the military strength of the Portuguese" was a disastrous corruption. The peoples of Ternate and Amboina (Ambon) rejected Christianity. For the China scene, see K. M. Panikkar, *Asia and Western Dominance*, pp. 136f.

"guns" and giving passionate encouragement to all the "ointments." How can the Christian mission do this unless it begins itself to live under the "sentence of death?"

> For I think that God has exhibited us apostles as last of all, like men sentenced to death; because we have become a spectacle to the world, to angels and to men. We are fools for Christ's sake, but you are wise in Christ. We are weak, but you are strong. You are held in honor, but we in disrepute. . . . We have become, and are now, as the refuse of the world, the offscouring of all things (I Cor. 4:9-13).

CHAPTER 4

The "Efficiency" of the Crucified One in the World of Technological Efficiency

- One of the outstanding characteristics of our era is *orientation* on *technology*. Electric potato peelers (home attachment: Singapore $44)!
- How do we express the biblical message of "God is love" in the language of the technological efficiency?
- Amazing "inefficiency" of God? God wandered "these forty years" with his people to know what was in their hearts and to teach them that one "does not live by bread alone. . . ."
- The variety of human efficiencies must be viewed in the perspective of the "efficiency of the Crucified One." When we do this, we display our Christian *freedom* in the world of technological efficiency.

According to the social scientist, humankind today is living in the third great transformation period of its history. The first great revolution was the emergence of the human being itself about a million years ago, in our solar system of about four and a half billion years. The second revolutionary transformation was that "from primitive to civilized societies, culminating seven thousand years ago in three locations, the valleys of the Tigris and Euphrates (Mesopotamia), the valley of the Nile and the valley of the Indus."[1] The third revolution is going on now in our lifetime! "What is distinctive about the modern era is the phenomenal growth of knowledge since the scientific revolution and the unprecedented effort at adaptation to this knowledge that has come to be demanded of the whole of humankind."[2] This *change* taking place today is called modernization. Modernization is then a serious and comprehensive concept. It touches all human activity — intellectual, political, economic, social, and psychological. When education is universalized by a well-planned scheme, when giant

---

1. C. E. Black, *The Dynamics of Modernization*, p. 2.
2. Ibid., p. 4.

business enterprises operate systematically and efficiently for the public, when people begin to participate in the political life of their own nation as the dominant factor in deciding their own destiny — all these are the manifestations of the *change*, the modernization, taking place in the world today.

There is scientific revolution behind the historic thrust of modernization. Science discovers the principle of refrigeration, technology applies the principle and produces a refrigerator, then the product exercises far-reaching modernization influence upon human life. One of the outstanding characteristics of our era is its *orientation* on *technology*. A discovered scientific principle will be immediately applied and adapted for the benefit of human existence. The principle of combustion produced the jet engine, which has diminished our globe in size.

There is a powerful trend in our world today to turn away from the "ox-cart" (traditional, old) toward the "supersonic aircraft" (revolutionary, new). The old is vociferously rejected and the new indiscriminately accepted. Yet the "ox-cart" will not so easily be banished from the dynamics of history. It still wishes to make a relevant contribution to humankind, which in truth it can. Caught as we are in the great upheaval, we need to make a careful theological examination of the situation. A recent study conducted by the Theological Education Fund of the World Council of Churches has this to say:

> . . . local cultural situations are today characterized by the interaction between the traditional cultural and religious heritage and the universal technological civilization which penetrates into all parts of the world. The result is generally not the disappearance of the ancient culture and religion, but rather its renaissance and transformation.

The Prospectus of a study on *The Future of Man and Society in a World of Science-based Technology* by the World Council of Churches states: "The whole world is vitally affected by the constantly enlarging scope of science-based technology." Have we given thought to the coming of a universal technological civilization and its impact upon us who live in a certain locality, in certain cultural and religious traditions? But we may say that the universal technological civilization is not really our *immediate* problem. Or is it too enormous a problem to be taken up in Bangkok, Hong Kong, or Djakarta? Indeed, it is a challenge of immense proportions straight from the third revolutionary transformation of human affairs since the emergence of humankind! The coming of the universal technological civilization compels me to grasp again the essence of the good news of God in Christ. If we can do this, then the universal technological civilization becomes an occasion to point out the glory of Christ at this crucial period in the history of humankind.

According to the spiritual climate of this civilization, the "ox-cart" stage of technological achievement must be constantly improved to realize the technological miracle symbolized by the supersonic aircraft. Technology is able to change a desert into a green, habitable land. It can transport millions of tons of materials from one place to another with amazing rapidity. Its efficiency has implications for "salvation." Many believe that not the "spiritual" Jesus of Nazareth but today's dazzling technology should be our Messiah. It is sophisticated and mighty machines that can help us, and not a sermon on the love of God, they say. Even sharper criticism is directed against the love of God. The message "God is love" is empty. It is intangible, while technology's salvation is tangible!

Efficiency is the spirit of the technological civilization. Motorcycles, automobiles, aeroplanes, telegrams, communication satellites. . . . A technology that breeds inefficiency is not worthy of its name. A technological breakthrough by Johannes G. Gutenberg in 1448 eliminated the inefficiency of hand-copying by inventing the *techne* (art, artifice) of printing. In 1969 American NASA scientists efficiently overcame both terrestrial and lunar gravitations and placed men on the moon. Efficiency has been recognized as valuable since humans first began to use simple tools. Our ability to use tools indicates directly our ability to appreciate efficiency. But with the phenomenal advancement in scientific knowledge, efficiency has become acutely the arch-value in our lives. In fact, it may not be altogether an exaggeration to speak of the imminent coming of technological humans living in a technological city "efficiently" ever after. To "live in technological efficiency" may become for many the experience of "salvation."

We are, perhaps, more efficiency-minded than we realize. Today's generation is being educated and brought up on the creative surrounding of efficiency. I believe that efficiency is a positive value which goes back to Genesis 1:28: "And God blessed them, and God said to them, 'Be fruitful and multiply, and fill the earth and subdue it: and have dominion over the fish of the sea and over the birds of the air and over every living thing that moves upon the earth.'" But it is here, at the point of positive value of efficiency and our efficiency-mindedness, that we fail to hear the Word of God. Why? It is because to the efficiency-minded person the Word of God comes in the form of "inefficiency." In fact, it may be said that the contrast between the "inefficient God" and "efficient human" is becoming more and more pronounced. Everything is currently being streamlined (look at automobiles, computers, and even kitchen utensils, including electric potato peelers, to meet the demand of the efficiency-minded humans). In this world of salvation of streamlined efficiency, the Word of God sounds archaic to many.

The Word of God communicates the love of God. The love of God means God's resolution to love people, though it may call for supreme sacrifice, even when such sacrifice is implemented by "inconvenient" and "inefficient" processes. Being love, God is prepared to operate in history "inefficiently." God's love which is genuine proves its genuineness by working its way in history without any "magic formula," "easy quick ways," or "technologically efficient ways." Here is one classic example:

And you shall remember all the way which the LORD your God has led you these forty years in the wilderness, that he might humble you, testing you to know what was in your heart, whether you would keep his commandments or not. And he humbled you and let you hunger and fed you with manna, which you did not know, nor did your father know, that he might make you know that man does not live by bread alone, but that man lives by everything that proceeds out of the mouth of the LORD. Your clothing did not wear out upon you, and your feet did not swell, these forty years (Deut. 8:2-4).

God wandered "these forty years" with his people to know what was in their hearts and to teach them that one "does not live by bread alone. . . ." What an inefficient investment in order to teach this much of the truth of God! No matter how important the truth is, wasn't there a more efficient way? God is the almighty Lord of history. Why didn't and couldn't God act far more majestically and with amazing efficiency? Would it not enhance God's glory before all the people? Why didn't God short-circuit history and liberate Godself from all the troubles, inconveniences, and inefficiencies of "walking history" with the people? "The people stood and stared while their rulers continued to scoff, saying, 'He saved other people, let's see him save himself, if he is really God's Christ — his chosen!'" (Lk. 23:35). Jesus did not come down from the cross. He refused to free himself from the cross, and by doing so he refused to disengage himself from sinful human history. In this way, he forcefully demonstrated that he was "God's chosen!" God does not cut Godself off from human history. Because God is love, God became a nomad "for these forty years." God demonstrates faithfulness by protecting even "your cloth" and "your foot." (What a nuisance! What a chore!) God's care extends to all people who are journeying in the desert. God refuses to give up, no matter how "inefficient" the divine work becomes.

The Lordship of God has a *historical* substance. It is the love of God realizing itself in history through the violent storm of human (not technology's) disobedience and stubbornness. It is the crucified Jesus Christ in Golgotha under Pontius Pilate. "Yet the proof of God's amazing love is this: that it was while we were sinners that Christ died for us" (Rom. 5:8). God spoke, is speaking, and will speak to us through this miserable crucified prisoner! Does the crucified prisoner have a saving and relevant message for us of universal technological civilization? Does he really? There is no objective guarantee that he does. We believe that he does. We believe that the crucified prisoner holds the secret of living meaningfully through humankind's third great transformation in the last million years. This "fantastic" dimension is contained today when we say that we believe in Jesus Christ.

God speaks to both the "ox-cart" and the "supersonic" people, because he spoke to the innermost need of people.

Today we have the jet engine. But no one would attach a high-powered Rolls-Royce engine to the Four Noble Truths of the Buddha. An *immediate* connection between spiritual truth and technological devices is an absurdity. It is the person who *values* the Four Noble Truths *and* the jet engine. The traditional and the revolutionary do not meet directly; they meet only in people who shape them and value them. Local cultural and religious traditions are not in tension directly with the coming of a universal technological civilization.

The people in whom two great historic forces meet each other are "inefficient people" in the sense that value-judgment cannot be done with technological efficiency. The present situation of the clash between the two historic forces, the force of universal technological civilization and the force of local cultural and religious traditions, produces a sense of value-crisis in the minds of people.

The Prospectus says, "The steadily increasing development of science and technology poses a great paradox for mankind: it is the condition of man's survival and at the same time it threatens his destruction." This truth has been demonstrated to every one of us today by the frightful figure of $200 billion the world spends on arms annually. In order to vanquish the enemy "efficiently," the world engages in this astronomically "inefficient" enterprise. $200 billion wasted in the face of a poverty-stricken world will not eliminate our enemies: hunger, disease, illiteracy, and war. We must become "spiritually inefficient" (Blessed are the poor in spirit!) in order to see what kind of apocalyptic "inefficiency" we are in! "At the height of our power and technological might, we have our deepest moments of insecurity."[3]

We spend all our savings, and cannot achieve our objective. Against this background of immense frustration God stands as an efficient God. Going through a most inefficient process, God proved Godself to be the most efficient One. God's efficiency is not, however, an ordinary efficiency. It is the efficiency in a great paradox, the efficiency of the Crucified One! "Crucified efficiency" is the message which must be given to both the "ox-cart" and the "supersonic" people. In this "crucified efficiency" is hidden new life for the great issues we face within the framework of technological civilization, the problems of development, social justice, crisis of faith, and the search for the meaning of life. "Crucified efficiency" teaches us, whether we are lumbering along the inhospitable country road on an ox-cart, or penetrating into the depth of awesome space, that technological efficiency needs to be enlightened by the sense of the "efficiency" of the Crucified One. Technological *shalom* (peace, salvation) must sit in the *shalom* feast of the Messiah. "In him appeared life, and this life was the light of humankind" (Jn. 1:4). Who invites the technological *shalom* to come to the light of the messianic *shalom*? God who "was in Christ personally reconcil-

---

3. S. Radhakrishnan, *Religion in a Changing World*, Allen and Unwin, 1967, Preface.

ing the world to himself" (II Cor. 5:19) issues the invitation! We are invited
to see this grand process of history.

> Things which eye saw not, ear heard not,
> And which entered not into the heart of man,
> Whatsoever things God prepared for them that love
>   him.
>
> (I Cor. 2:9)

God has a purpose for universal technological civilization. "He purposes in
his sovereign will that human history shall be consummated in Christ, that
everything that exists in heaven and earth shall find its perfection and fulfilment in him" (Eph. 1:10).

We do not have in our hands God's "letter of invitation" sent to God's
servant, universal technological civilization. But we know that without
God's invitation to technological civilization, that is to say, apart from the
understanding of the "efficiency" of the Crucified One, universal technological civilization may be eventually occupied by demonic efficiency. And
here we have a promise that "all human history shall be consummated in
the efficiency of the Crucified One!" "The light still shines in the darkness
and the darkness has never put it out!" (Jn. 1:5).

The issue is not whether one is to use an "electric potato peeler" or an
ordinary hand knife to peel a potato. It is a deeply theological issue in
which we are inescapably involved.

If God is thus involved, isn't this involvement a challenge *to all Christians?*
How should we make the theological insight of the efficiency of the Crucified One the powerful leaven in the universal technologically efficient
civilization?

PART II

Rooting the Gospel

CHAPTER 5

Bangkok and Wittenberg

- *Because of* her love of her own daughter, the mother came to Jesus. *In spite* of Jesus' rejection, the mother hoped against hope — like Abraham!
- Human love ("my daughter!") is not depreciated but appreciated in the presence of the Son of David.

Some time ago, I studied the story of the woman in the region of Tyre and Sidon with a group of Thai Christians.

> And Jesus went away from there and withdrew to the district of Tyre and Sidon. And behold, a Canaanite woman from that region came out and cried, "Have mercy on me, O Lord, Son of David; my daughter is severely possessed by a demon." But he did not answer her a word. And his disciples came and begged him, saying, "Send her away, for she is crying after us." He answered, "I was sent only to the lost sheep of the house of Israel." But she came and knelt before him, saying, "Lord, help me." And he answered, "It is not fair to take the children's bread and throw it to the dogs." She said, "Yes, Lord, yet even the dogs eat the crumbs that fall from their master's table." Then Jesus answered her, "O woman, great is your faith! Be it done for you as you desire." And her daughter was healed instantly (Matt. 15:21-28).

Here is a Gentile woman who clung to Jesus in faith in spite of the chilling silence and rejection of the Savior. It is an astonishing story of faith! No wonder Luther, the great restorer of the depth of the biblical faith, loved to dwell on the story of this nameless Gentile woman. He saw here a "strong faith" in the midst of, and in spite of, severe *Anfechtung*.[1]

---

1. This notoriously untranslatable German word *Anfechtung* is interpreted by Dr. Bainton as follows: "It may be a trial sent by God to test man, or an assault by the Devil to destroy man. It is all the doubt, turmoil, pangs, tremor, panic, despair, desolation and desperation which invade the weight of man" (R. H. Bainton, *Here I Stand*, New English Library, n.d., p. 42). With this understanding, the English word "assault" will be used in what follows.

According to Luther, this Canaanite woman was chosen to taste the fore-shadowing of the *assault* which Christ himself later experienced on the cross when he cried, "My God, my God, why has thou forsaken me?" In the Crucified Christ we are given the incomparable image of *strong faith*!

> A strong faith! which can speak unto an angry God, call unto him when being persecuted, flee unto him when being driven back, praise him as your helper, your glory, and lifter up of your head, when you feel him deserting, confounding and oppressing you.[2]

The message of the story of the Gentile woman revolves around the amazing power and capacity of faith itself. "Luther! you are profound and powerful," I said to myself. "Your *assault* interpretation of the woman's situation must be *the* interpretation. I was deeply moved when I first heard it in New Jersey, as I am in northern Thailand today! I don't want to know any other interpretation than this! Those who have no understanding of doubt, turmoil, pangs, tremor, panic, despair, desolation and desperation are bound to fall short of the crucial message of this story. The basic fact about faith is that faith is faith when it believes in spite of *assault*!"

So I introduced Luther's theology of *assault* to my Thai Christians and I talked about "doubt, turmoil, pangs, tremor, panic, despair, desolation and desperation." Coupled with my language limitation, the result was disastrous. My audience went home with the impression that some kind of neurosis constitutes the vital part of the Christian faith.

Confused and despondent, I went home. I took a second look at the story and, after considerable hesitation, decided to "de-*assault*-ize" it. I felt as though I was committing a hideous crime against Luther and against heaven. Enjoying, however, light-hearted freedom from the overwhelming giant, Luther, which came to me suddenly when I decided to do it, I began to see something new in the story. I kept the needs of my neighbors in mind and studied the story. Then my "heart was strangely warmed," as my attention shifted from the nervous theme of *assault* to the words of the mother, "my daughter" — a natural and common concept — as the key to the whole story. I noticed immediately that the need of her daughter who was "tormented by a devil" sparked her theology, the depth of which was able to astonish even the Savior himself.

The woman's motherly love for her own daughter, her human concern for outright need, gave her a profound wisdom which burst out in one of the most imaginative and impressive forms of a confession of faith: "Yes, Lord, yet even the dogs eat the crumbs that fall from their master's table."

I concentrated my attention on finding the *beginning* of this woman's amazing faith. The beginning of faith must contain some universally valid and relevant factor which can erase religious, cultural, and political demar-

---

2. Weimar edition V, 96.13. Translated by Henry Cole.

cations. Otherwise, how can a Gentile woman sincerely come to Jesus Christ, an Israelite? Otherwise, how can the peoples of Hong Kong, Tokyo, Bangkok, and Djakarta come to Jesus Christ, a Palestinian Jew? My interest in this *beginning* of faith did not come from myself but was forced on me by my Thai neighbors.

There was a woman's faith in the "Son of David." And there was also "her daughter." The former was her confession of faith, and the latter was the total expression of her life's problem. In her these two were inseparably merged into one. The latter, however, propelled her to the former. The mother's love for her daughter — a universally valid and relevant factor (shall we call it *eros*, natural human love?) — was transformed and sanctified to the even profounder confession of faith in the presence of the "Son of David," just as the water was changed into wine at Cana in the presence of the same Lord. Human natural love met with the Lord of divine self-giving love (*agape*) and brought forth a "strong faith."

The *assault* interpretation points out the dimension of "in spite of," while the "natural love" interpretation emphasizes "because of." These are two emphases in one story, the first pointed out by Luther and the second by my friends in Thailand. Both direct our attention to the great event of believing. The two different emphases do not indicate the spiritual and the moral sense of the Scripture respectively, as some church fathers would prefer to say. Both point to the same presence of the Son of David. "My daughter!" — a straightforward human attachment has a legitimate place in our faith in God. Yet, the important point is that unchallenged and crisis-free human love cannot be the total situation between God and humans. In the relationship between God and humans, that is, in the believing situation, our "because of" must be *assaulted* by God's new situation in which we are confronted by "in spite of." This being said, I wish to call attention to the historical, cultural, and religious distances between Bangkok and Wittenberg. Wittenberg was perhaps ready to receive Christ enveloped in the bitterness of *assault*, and this presentation of Christ must have had tremendous historical significance at the crucial time of the Reformation. For Bangkok the theology of *assault* is both too overwhelming and strange, and only causes nervous discomfort. Strong faith must be viewed through another emphasis, the human factor — "my daughter who is tormented by a devil." In short, these two interrelated possibilities of interpretation are derived from particular historical, cultural, and religious backgrounds, those of the Wittenberg of the sixteenth century and of the Bangkok of the twentieth century. Both are equally significant and fundamental, either jointly or separately, to the believers in each historical situation.

CHAPTER 6

Aristotelian Pepper and Buddhist Salt

- In the process of appropriation of the gospel by the Christian people of Thailand one discerns that Aristotelian philosophy (West) and Buddhism (East) season the gospel and make it palatable for the Thai.
- The Buddhist psychology of "dependent origination" has prepared the Thai mind for the Aristotelian world-view of scientific causality. Aristotle is a fascination for those brought up in the Buddhist culture. The Aristotle-inspired cosmological proof of the existence of God is a favorite subject in their "theological" discussions.
- The Buddhist philosophy and the lifestyle of detachment season the religion of God's attachment to humankind. Thus, sometimes one is confronted by an "Asokanized Christ."
- Yet, Christ will become a genuinely "tasty" Christ not in the outright rejection of both Aristotelian pepper and Buddhist salt, but rather in using them. The question is, *what kind of use?* By what theological principles do we engage in this dangerous (and unavoidable) task? How can one use Aristotle and the Buddha (the two great sages!) to articulate Jesus Christ biblically in Thailand?

A letter to Dr. Daniel McGilvary (1828-1911), a pioneer missionary who served Christ for over half a century in northern Thailand

Dear Dr. McGilvary,

This is my sixth year in northern Thailand. About one-tenth the length of your ministry here! Your old teakwood mission house still stands by the Ping River, overlooking your town, Chiengmai. The residence of one of the Chiengmai princes, a house which you frequented, is now occupied by the American Consulate.

My letter to you is in the nature of an inquiry. I want to know the nature and place of my ministry in the context of the history of the church in northern Thailand. To what kind of spiritual and theological heritage am I heir? This question is of immediate concern for me, for how can I make my witness meaningful to my neighbors if I fail to understand where they are and where I am in the continuing story of the Christian church here? How can I engage in meaningful theological thinking if I do not understand the story of the development of theology in northern Thailand? Whenever I undertake the study of the church's past in northern Thailand, you are there, the dedicated pioneer missionary, whose immense spiritual and intellectual influence upon the Thai is still visible in those churches spread over the countryside, stamped with your own Christian piety. So I have studied your message.

I have read your book, *A Half Century among the Siamese and the Lao*,[1] with intense interest and eagerness. At certain points in your book you give some clues to the contents of your message:

Why do we worship Jehovah-Jesus? Because he is our sovereign Lord. The Buddha groaned under his own load of guilt, and was oppressed by the sad and universal consequences of sin among men. The Christ challenged his enemies to convince him of sin, and his enemies to this day have confessed that they find no sin in him. Buddhists believe that Buddha reached Nirvana after having himself passed through every form of being in the universe — having been in turn every animal in the seas, on the earth, and in the air. He did this by an inexorable law that he and every other being is subject to, and cannot evade. Our Jehovah-Jesus, as our Scriptures teach, is the only self-existent being in the universe, and himself the cause of all other beings. An infinite Spirit and invisible, he manifested himself to the world by descending from heaven, becoming man, taking on our nature in unison with his holy nature, but with no taint of sin. He did this out of infinite love and pity for our race after it had sinned. He saw there was no other able to save, and he became our Saviour. . . .[2]

The sacred books of the Princes teach that there is no creator. Everything, as the Siamese say, "*pen eng*," comes to be of itself. All this complicated universe became what it is by a fortuitous concurrence of atoms, which atoms themselves had no creator. We come as honest seekers for truth. We look around, above, beneath. Everything seems to imply the contrivance of mind. . . .[3]

We pressed home the thought, new to them, that there must be a maker of the world and of all creatures in it. We told them the old, old story of the infinite love of God, our Father, and of Christ, his

1. Daniel McGilvary, *A Half Century among the Siamese and the Lao*, Fleming H. Revell, New York, 1912.
2. Ibid., pp. 181f.
3. Ibid., p. 182.

Son, who suffered and died to save us, and of pardon freely promised to all who believe in him. This is the final argument that wins these people. . . .[4]

And then, before that motley crowd, drinking with them their native tea from an earthen teapot, the men seated close around, or reclining as they smoke their pipes, the women and children walking about or sitting on the ground — we tell of God, the great Spirit, the creator and Father of all — the Bible, his message to men — the incarnation, life, and death of Christ, and redemption through his blood. . . .[5]

Then our religion was explained in its two leading ideas — rejection of the spirit-cult and acceptance of Jesus for the pardon of sin and the life eternal. Questions were asked, and answered.[6]

These accounts, although brief and written for the English-speaking reader, allow me to sense the content of the message you preached and the theological approach you employed when you proclaimed Christ to the Thai. You spoke simply, forcefully, and straightforwardly to the listening Thai. When Paul proclaimed Jesus Christ in Athens, some Epicurean and Stoic philosophers remarked: "What is this cock-sparrow trying to say?" And Athenians asked: "May we know what this new teaching of yours really is? You talk of matters which sound strange to our ears and we should like to know what they mean" (Acts 17:18ff.). While you were preaching, "some Buddhist monks" or "Chiengmaians" might have been thinking, "What is this cock-sparrow trying to say?" But it may be that the oriental Chiengmaians are more courteous than Mediterranean Athenians, and they did not say it out loud. There is, however, something more significant involved than the issue of cultural modesty. I think that both in Athens and in Chiengmai, the story of Jesus Christ is a story that "sounds strange to our ears." But the basic character of "strangeness," the cultural historical context in which the "strangeness" manifests itself, and the degree of intensity with which the "strangeness" disturbs "our ears" are definitely quite different. My rough guess is that Paul in Athens had an easier assignment than McGilvary in Chiengmai. The nineteenth-century American McGilvary, speaking in the northern Thai dialect to Thai peasants, encountered more difficulties than the Mediterranean Paul speaking in Greek to the Mediterranean audience.

In the light of this brief observation, I have become very curious to know whether your audience understood your preaching or not, if you will pardon me for asking. In my ministry here today I am forced to see how thoroughly strange and unrealistic — how "Western" — is the Christian vocab-

4. Ibid., p. 328.
5. Ibid., p. 342.
6. Ibid., p. 344.

ulary to the ears of my Thai neighbors. How did you explain thoughts such as "Buddha groaned under his load of *guilt*," "Our Jehovah-Jesus is the *only self-existent being* in the universe," "He did this out of *infinite love* and pity for our race after it had *sinned*," "Everything seems to imply the *contrivance of mind*," "*suffered and died to save us*," "the *incarnation*, life, and death of Christ and *redemption through his blood*," and "*eternal life?*" Don't you think, Dr. McGilvary, that you spoke *too* directly or inflexibly to your audience? Each one of these terms invites cultural resistance, psychological antipathy, and emotional reaction! (But, again, your audience might not have been listening to your words, but watching your magnificent long white beard!) I am interested in you beyond my unlimited admiration of your beard. I am interested in your own mission theology.

My observation is that upon accepting the gospel, the Thai season the Christian ingredients — whether they be "infinite love," "sin," "incarnation," "redemption through his blood," or "eternal life" — with their own Buddhist salt. Why *Buddhist* salt? Very briefly, it is because the Thai culture is permeated with the strong influence of Theravada Buddhism, as Phra Anuman Rajadhon observes in his careful study of Thai life.[7] If you had said that "Buddha groaned under his own load of *dukkha*," "Our Jehovah-Jesus is the only *arhat* in the universe," "He did this out of *infinite mercy* for our race after it is caught by '*craving*,'" "Everything seems to imply the highest value of the *Nirvanic Mind*," "suffered and died to *instruct* the way out from *saṃsāra*," "salvation through the *dharma* to *Nirvana*," suppose you had said this, then your audience might have accepted your message without much distaste, and consequently they might not have added their own seasoning to the ingredients. It is pretty well seasoned already!

Suppose you wanted to say that "Jesus is an *arhat*," then you would have to do it with conditional sentences and explanatory paragraphs. That would require too much labor and only invite misunderstanding. There are, of course, certain key words which can be "baptized" and used more effectively in our communication of the gospel. According to Visser 't Hooft, Paul dared to use such loaded words as *logos* (word), *soter* (savior), *mysterion* (mystery), *metamorphosis* (transformation) for his own evangelistic purpose. He was confident that these "heathen" words could be employed as faithful servants when they are placed in the strong proclamation (*kerygma*) context.

Our dilemma is this: if we say "salvation through the blood of Jesus," our Thai audience is completely lost. If we say "salvation through the *dharma*," they would see no difference between the Christian faith and Buddhism. Perhaps the best possible way to avoid the difficulty and reach our goal is to explain that the *content* of the *dharma* is the sacrificial death of Christ. Of course, once again this raises the question, "Why such a sanguine *dharma?*" How can the *dharma* be *dharma* when it has "warm blood?" The concept of the *dharma* and "blood" are mutually incompatible!

---

7. Phra Anuman Rajadhon, *Essays on Thai Folklore*, Bangkok, 1968.

While we are baffled by these difficulties, Thai "Christian theological thinking" is at work. The dish prepared with the flavor of Buddhist salt has, inevitably, a strange, "ambiguous" taste to me. But for them I think the taste has been well "adjusted" to their liking.

Then, too, I have discovered that the seasoning takes place in the Thai theological kitchen, not in the broad living room into which missionaries have access. Their theological activity goes on while they squat on the dirt ground, and not while sipping tea with missionary friends in the teak-floored shiny living room. When I peep into the kitchen of their theology, the theological situation I see there is unique. No books have been written about this situation and no references are available in the best stocked theological libraries! I must confess my incompetence in grasping the details of the daring activities of this "kitchen theology". My experience in peeping into the kitchen is sometimes like watching a great Chinese chef throwing six different ingredients into a heated, oiled kwali. I can smell a most delicious aroma and I can see smoke, but I cannot identify the ingredients! Free theologizing is going on. No authorized "theological commission" is watching over the activity. Terribly fragmentary use of the Bible, not acceptable in any "accredited theological school," suddenly explodes with enormous energy and answers their theological needs. This process, I realize, is going on unconsciously, unintentionally, and almost semi-automatically so far as those in the kitchen are concerned. It is wrong to say that we must produce an indigenous theology. It is not necessary to produce one. It is there! Perhaps what we must do is to improve this indigenous theology by injecting more biblical information and helpful insights from the current ecumenical theological discussion.

Let me illustrate what I mean by kitchen-produced theology. The Christian message is based on the "infinite love" of God, as you say. According to ingrained Thai emotion and psychology, the word "love" (*khwamrak*) denotes people's attachment to things, persons, or supernatural beings. Attachment *inevitably* produces sorrow and trouble. Detachment *inevitably* creates tranquility, honesty, and genuine happiness.

Christianity teaches attachment. "So God *attached* himself to the world. . . ." What a doctrine! This doctrine makes our Thai friends think the whole thing in a completely different perspective and with a different feeling! This is great! This Christianity has something new to say to us! The kitchen becomes an exciting theological forum. The difference between attachment and detachment has been grasped, but not without much difficulty. But the hard-won difference between attachment and detachment is under the blight of *inevitability*. The old equation of inevitability: attachment produces sorrow and detachment happiness *inevitably* cripples the Christian concept of love. The basic distinction is won, but it does not show its creative newness since it is blighted. The Christian doctrine of "love" and the idea of "inevitability" are antithetical. "Love" is the least "inevitable" thing one can think of!

One of my students told me that the idea of *good* in Thai culture can be portrayed as clothing washed, neatly ironed and placed in a closed, undisturbed drawer. Don't wear it! It will get dirty! The clothing must stay "detached" from the dirty world. Several times, both on the university campus and at rural meetings, I have encountered violent objection to Jesus' censure of the servant who carefully wrapped his one talent and gave it back to the master when he returned. What is wrong about this "honest" servant who kept what was entrusted to him in a "tranquil drawer?" Jesus' blame is unreasonable and outrageous! The sense of commitment to a "tranquil drawer" (non-involvement) is in the very roots of Thai psychology.

By these two illustrations I am trying to point out how difficult it is for our Thai friends to break through the philosophy of detachment. In the philosophy of detachment, I sense their desire to pay respect to the great principle of "inevitability" taught by the Wise, the Buddha.

In the Buddhist doctrine of the dependent origination (*paticca samuppada*), if you wear clothing it will inevitably get dirty. If you give one talent to someone you will inevitably get one talent back. This is the inevitable rule of life. That attachment can be creative is a great message for Thai people. But if "love" is bound up with the general concept of "inevitability," then the Christian concept of love is sadly blurred. It is like a two-hundred-volt electric bulb operating on a hundred-volt current. I call this dimness a state of "chronic Asokanization of the gospel."[8] An Asokanized Christ is a "dim" Christ.

Here I must refer again to the question: "Why such a sanguine *dharma*?" The idea of a "warm-blooded" *dharma* constitutes a terrible stumbling-block in the Thai culture. If it is "warm-blooded," it cannot be a dependable *dharma*. Jesus Christ becomes a stumbling block in this way.

My letter to you is getting to be a long one. I did not intend it to be so. So far I have tried to outline the "kitchenized Christ" who is seasoned by the Buddhist salt. Relying on your patience, let me make one more point. I am interested in your statement: "We come as honest seekers for truth. We look around, above, beneath. Everything seems to imply the contrivance of mind." You seem to be pursuing, if I am not mistaken, the traditional "cosmological proof" of the existence of the intelligent God. The remarkable design one discerns in the universe compels one to acknowledge that this universe is not self-explanatory but must be explained in reference to Someone beyond it. This Someone is the cause of all other causes. The crucial point, which the users of this argument often overlook, is the question of what kind of mind it is that exists behind the universe. Is it a good mind or a bad mind? A redemptive mind or a destructive mind? A *Nirvanic* mind or a mind concerned with history? Isn't it true that if one

---

8. Asoka was a great Buddhist king in India. He died in 232 B.C.E. after having been instrumental in strengthening and spreading Buddhism wisely, contributing eventually to its strong pervasiveness in Thailand today.

speaks of orderliness in the universe, another can speak of disorderliness (accident, confusion) in the universe with the same vigor?

It has been made clear to me in my rural ministry here that this important question of the cosmological argument — *what kind of mind?* — is intensified if in my congregation there is one person who is born crippled or made blind by accident. People say to me that there may certainly be a mind behind the universe, but if that mind can produce such cruel limitations as disabled bodies and blindness, it must be capricious and erratic! (It may be that the mind is "warm blooded"; that would explain these troubles!) Where then, I ask myself, is the distinction between the God understood through recognition of design in the universe and the varieties of spirits my neighbors worship?

My Thai friends and I may come to an agreement, although not without much difficulty, that "in the beginning was the Word" (Jn. 1:1). But it is not self-evident what kind of word this is, even when "we come as honest seekers for truth." Honest seekers may find some objective religious truth, but the God of revelation is a hidden God, even to the most honest of seekers (Jn. 1:13; Matt. 16:17). May I quote from Kierkegaard: "Now Spirit is the denial of direct immediacy. If Christ be very God, he must be unknown, for to be known directly is the characteristic mark of an idol." Gradually I have come to see that the medicine of the cosmological argument, which has been widely prescribed in Thailand to be used at the levels of pre-evangelization, evangelism, and even the mature Christians, has proved to be a paralyzing tranquilizer. And it has, in reality, hampered my parishioners' way to the presence of the "undomesticated God" of the Bible, as Luther called him. This Aristotelian argument may be useful at the level of pre-evangelization (although I am not really sure!), but it produces unwanted and even destructive effects when it is incorporated into the substance of the Christian message.

I notice that on the dinner table of Thai theology, Buddhist salt and Aristotelian pepper go nicely together, since Aristotelian pepper has a flavor of *dharma*, tracing one cause to another cause. Thus Aristotelian pepper plays a role of wife to the husband Buddhist salt, to *dharma*-ize the *kerygma* of Jesus Christ. Why am I so concerned about Aristotelian pepper? I must confess to you that one uneasy look cast on me by a leprosty patient while I was happily discoursing on this "proof" for the existence of God in a hospital outside Chiengmai shook me. The patient, through his very existence, challenged and rebelled against Aristotelian pepper — so I understood. The God theorized under the influence of the overanxious rationality of the West is, I must conclude, as dim as the "Asokanized Christ."

Sometimes an interesting situation occurs in the Thai theological scene. The Aristotelian Christ is put in dialogue, or even in heated argument, with the Asokanized Christ. This is a theological traffic between the two "dim" Christs. By a remarkable development of discussion and insights, the Asokanized Christ sometimes comes out on top of the Aristotelian Christ, and at other times the reverse occurs. Of course, all this hot theological debate takes place in the "kitchen."

Let me come to my concluding remark. I admit that what I have written here is oversimplified. And the problems I raise would involve many thorny theological, historical, and cultural questions which would defy any easy schematic handling. Yet a persistent question comes to me every day: "Where is the sharp edge of the love (*khwamrak*) of Christ in our churches in northern Thailand? From what source did the blurring of Christ come?" I wonder if the "doubly blurred" situation, caused by the two distinctive blurring agents of East and West, have contributed to a very significant degree to the emergence of the Thai "dim" Christ.

As soon as I say this, however, a chain of questions comes into my mind. I ask myself, "Why have we been so incompetent in understanding the development of 'kitchen theology'?" Why have we kept the "living-room theology" more or less at a distance from the hot "kitchen theology"? Why have we been so unprepared to present a Christ who can be "bright" in the kitchen? Or is the "dim" Christ more salvific than the "bright" Christ to the Thai? Is Christ *supposed to be* seasoned by those elements in order to become a palatable Christ to the Thai? In order to become the neighbor of the Thai? Is it possible to have an unseasoned and raw Christ? Isn't it true that the incarnation of the Son of God means his "in-culture-ation"? Wasn't he a Palestinian Jew? Doesn't this mean that imagining an unseasoned and raw Christ is as absurd and impossible as a de-Hebraized Yahweh? Does this then mean that one must not simply reject the "pepper and salt" of any culture, but attempt to see *what kind of* pepper and salt is seasoning Christ, and try to present a well-seasoned Christ in *co-operation* with the local pepper and salt? What are the theological rules by which we should launch this *co-operation*?

Many questions indeed! I am asking all of them. I honestly do not know how I can manage them. And . . . the weather is too hot here and mosquitoes bother me. But, dear Dr. McGilvary, what should I do with the Aristotelian pepper and Buddhist salt?

Sincerely yours,
Kosuke Koyama

Chiengmai
Thailand

CHAPTER 7

"Neighborology"

- Often we look at our neighbors as though they were inanimate objects. Then we are treating them as *maya* (illusion). By making them *maya*, we make ourselves and the gospel of Christ *maya*.
- Our neighbors have an *important* message for us Christians!
- A distinction between "philosophy and neighbor" and "theology and Christ" is useful for understanding our Christian life in Thailand.
- Legalism takes the reality of personality away from our neighbors.
- Jesus Christ is neighbor to all of us in Asia today.

He who does not love his brother whom he has seen, cannot love God whom he has not seen (I Jn. 4:20).

As thou didst send me into the world, so I have sent them into the world (Jn. 17:18).

A conversation between a missionary and a woman suffering from cancer:

M. How are you today? I have come to visit you, hoping that I may talk with you a few minutes about the Christian religion.

W. I feel neither well nor bad. If you want to tell me your *dharma* — you are a teacher of religion, aren't you? — go ahead.

M. Yes, I am a teacher of the Christian religion. This book I have in my hands is the Scripture. Just as the *Tripitake* is very important for Buddhism, this book is very important for us. There is a prayer, quite short and concise, in the Scripture. The name of it is the Lord's Prayer. . . .

W. Just a minute! I am a northern Thai woman. Speak to me in the northern Thai dialect. You said that you are a teacher of religion, didn't you? How can anyone be a teacher of religion unless he is at home with the language of the people? Speak to me in the dialect, I am tired of hearing your poor Thai. . . .

64

M.   I am sorry. I can speak only the Bangkok Thai. . . .
W.   I thought so. You cannot! I don't like people like you. You mission-
     aries are always trying to teach people while you really do not under-
     stand the people. The Buddhist monks are much better than you mis-
     sionaries. I will call in a monk right now. I will listen to him. He will
     understand me. He can comfort me with his *dharma*. He can speak
     my own language. You are wasting your time here. Go home!

This may not be a striking story for those who engage in missionary work
in Asia from Japan to Pakistan. The point of irritation in the conversation
was not really a matter of language. My poor language only intensified the
already existing dissatisfaction. She was annoyed at me for looking at her
in my own terms. She felt that she was only an object of my religious conquest. I had a message for her, but I did not think of the possibility that she
might have a message for me. She would become real when she listened to
me! She noticed this imperialistic one-sidedness and rejected me with
unusually vehement language.

    Through this experience I discovered something more basic than the
religious conviction of a Buddhist. I was confronted by my neighbor who is
not *maya* (illusion), but very real. Dr. John Baillie clearly expresses what I
mean by the "reality" of my neighbor:

> The test of reality is the resistance it offers to the otherwise uninhib-
> ited course of my own thinking, desiring and acting. Reality is what I
> "come up against," what takes me by surprise, the other-than-myself
> which pulls me up and obliges me to reckon with it and adjust myself
> to it because it will not consent simply to adjust itself to me.[1]

I believe that every word used here in the context of the "sense of the presence of God" can be directly applied in expressing "the sense of the presence
of the neighbor." Our sense of the presence of God will be distorted if we fail
to see God's reality in terms of our neighbor's reality. And our sense of our
neighbor's reality will be disfigured unless seen in terms of God's reality.

    When his neighbor becomes one whom he "comes up against," a mis-
sionary realizes that he is sandwiched between Christ's saving reality and
his neighbor's "other-than-myself" reality. He then needs to undertake two
kinds of exegesis: exegesis of the Word of God, and exegesis of the life and
culture of the people among whom he lives and works. These two exegeses
are closely interrelated, and his whole existence is entangled in them.
Called to remain in this sandwiched situation, as it were, he retains his missionary identity.

    By submitting and committing himself to the Word of God, he tries to
communicate the message of the *real* Christ to his *real* neighbors. The sand-

---

1. John Baillie, *The Sense of the Presence of God*, Oxford University Press, 1962, p. 33.

wiched missionary is not merely sitting, like a slice of good Swiss cheese, between Christ and his neighbors. According to words of the Lord: "As thou didst send me into the world, so I have sent them into the world" (Jn. 17:18). He is "in motion." He has a definite direction to go "into the world." With a deep sense of solidarity with his Buddhist, Hindu, Islamic or animistic neighbors whom he meets in the world, he takes the questions asked by them to the enlightenment and judgment of the Word of God. The questions asked are real questions, since they come from real neighbors. Theology has become no longer a private affair but a matter that involves the human community. From "philosophy asks questions and theology answers," he now moves on to see that "his neighbor asks the questions and he seeks the answers in Christ." He makes distinctions between "philosophy and neighbor" and "theology and Christ." Philosophy neither sweats nor hungers nor feeds water buffaloes. But his neighbor does! Theology can become a religious crossword puzzle. But his Christ cannot be reduced to a game. Neighbor and Christ "resist the otherwise uninhibited course of his thinking."

Our neighbors are not concerned with our christology, but they show, from time to time, their interest in our "neighborology." Not "You shall love the Lord your God with all your heart, and with all your soul, and with all your might" (Deut. 6:5), but "You shall love your neighbor as yourself" (Lev. 19:18) will speak to them. "And being in an agony he prayed more earnestly; and his *sweat* became like great drops of blood falling down upon the ground" (Lk. 22:44) may make no impression on them, while "in the *sweat* of your face you shall eat bread" (Gen. 3:19) is of their own experience. In this context, "He who does not love his brother whom he has seen cannot love God whom he has not seen" (I Jn. 4:20) carries a special significance for us, because its order is "neighbor-God." It does not read: "He who does not love God whom he has not seen cannot love his brother whom he has seen."

It is imperative, then, for us to learn how to look at our neighbors. Let me quote from Dr. Emil Brunner:

> The legalistic type of person finds it impossible to come into real human, personal contact with his fellow-man. *Between him and his neighbour there stands something impersonal, the "ideal," the "Law," a programme, something abstract which hinders him from seeing the other person as he really is,* which prevents him from hearing the real claim which his neighbour makes on him. To the legalistic person, the person who acts according to principle only, the other man is only a "case," just as for the judge (in a court of law) the accused is simply a particular "criminal case." He deals with him according to some abstract ruling, not according to himself, not according to his unique being which can never be repeated, not as a person to be met "here and now."[2]

---

2. Emil Brunner, *The Divine Imperative*, Lutterworth Press, 1937, pp. 73ff. My italics.

We must discipline ourselves to see our neighbor immediately and straight-forwardly. If we have some artificial cushions — and one of them can be our own "neighborology" — between us and our neighbor, we fall into a dangerous pit of legalism. We must know the difference between *the legalistic I* and *the missionary I.* The former is the I who does not want to accept the real claim which his neighbor makes on him. The latter is the I who is sent to live in the midst of the reality of his neighbor, and his Christian existence hangs on the claim his neighbor makes on him. Jesus Christ, faced by the reality of his neighbor, accepted the claim the neighbor made on him. His confrontation with his neighbor was "uncushioned."

> And there was a woman who had had a spirit of infirmity for eighteen years; she was bent over and could not fully straighten herself. And when Jesus saw her, he called her and said to her, "Woman, you are freed from your infirmity."
>
> And he laid his hands upon her, and immediately she was made straight, and she praised God. But the ruler of the synagogue, indignant because Jesus had healed on the sabbath, said to the people, "There are six days on which work ought to be done; come on those days and be healed, and not on the sabbath day." Then the Lord answered him, "You hypocrites! Does not each of you on the sabbath untie his ox or his ass from the manger, and lead it away to water it? And ought not this woman, a daughter of Abraham who Satan bound for eighteen years, to be loosed from this bond on the sabbath day?" (Lk. 13:11-16).

The uncushioned neighborology of Christ cuts like a knife through the cushioned neighborology of the ruler of the synagogue.

Why should we consider neighborology at this moment in Southeast Asia? Has it not been with the Christians since the beginning of the church, and haven't we argued it back and forth quite enough in the course of church history? We want, however, to make a point that "neighborology" is, in fact, the best vessel to convey Christ. We want to insist on this, our missionary experience in Southeast Asia.

I said earlier that our neighbors in Asia are not interested in christology, but can be concerned with our neighborology. This means that our neighbors in Asia are ready to hear our message of Christ if we put it in "neighborological" language, though they would reject Christ if we were to present him in christological language.

In order to be able to present Christ in "neigborological" terms to our neighbor we must learn, first of all, to see him, whether he be Buddhist, Hindu, Moslem, animist, Communist, nationalist, revolutionary, intellectual or uneducated, as someone whom we "come up against" and by whom we are placed in the "sandwiched" position. We must try to build our neighborology upon our direct experience with our Asian neighbor, being guided by Christ who is the "un-cushioned" *neighbor* to us all in Asia today.

CHAPTER 8

The Wrath of God in a Culture of Tranquility

- In a land with a tranquility ideal, the biblical message of the wrath of God is a scandal. An angry God? What a message! Disciplined monks are free from wrath, the anti-*Nirvanic* emotion! What is the matter with this God?
- The message of the wrath of God has a special mission in the land with a tranquility ideal, because it will "historicize" the message of God's salvation in Christ. God is involved in history, therefore he cannot be tranquil.
- The wrath of God placed in the context of the culture of the tranquility ideal has a tremendous proclamational (*kerygmatic*) value, since it can indicate how radically God is involved in history. And what is this divine involvement in history? It is the love of God (*agape*).

PROBLEM: THE WRATH OF GOD OBSCURED BY THE IDEAL OF NO-PATHOS (*APATHEIA*)

Lactantius, the Christian apologist active in the early fourth century, wrote a treatise called "On the Wrath of God" (*De ira Dei*). In this remarkable book he attacked the Epicureans and the Stoics who held the view that God is *without passion* (*apatheia*) and cannot be moved to wrath. Lactantius insisted that *God can be moved to wrath.* He said that God is righteous and acts juridically, rewarding the good and punishing the evil. God's wrath is the act by which God punishes wrongdoers. Here Lactantius rendered a great apologetic contribution in distinguishing the image of the biblical God from the predominant philosophico-religious piety of his day. The God of the Bible is not the highest good (*summum bonum*), tranquil, absolute, no-pathos. It is possible for God to have wrath, a radically per-turbed mind. The righteous God is *perturbed* by human unrighteousness.

This insight of Lactantius, voiced against the ancient Stoic ideal of life, needs to be spoken once again against popular Christian piety in Thailand today. Prevalent religious sentiment in Thailand, including that of Christians, is unwittingly under the influence of the doctrine that would hold a perturbed soul to be an obnoxious hindrance to the realization of the higher quality of religious life. The call to no-pathos is not a monopoly of Stoicism. It had been issued by the Gautama Buddha before the time of Stoicism, and is a cardinal teaching of Thai Theravada Buddhism. The biblical message of the wrath of God is, as it was to the Stoics, a stumbling block to the spiritual and intellectual climate of this "Asokan" Stoic country. Perturbation of soul is to be eschewed. So the Christian doctrine of the wrath of God, the divine loss of tranquility, perturbation of soul, has been soft-pedaled or avoided.

When the wrath of God was branded a perturbation of soul and ignored, some vital message, specifically for Thailand, contained in the doctrine of the wrath of God was lost.

In his work *The Theology of the Pain of God*,[1] Kazo Kitamori, the Japanese theologian, has contributed the penetrating insight that the love of God is distorted and made superficial when it is divorced from the wrath of God. Kitamori's warning that the wrath of God has a place in the love of God sheds light on the Thai theological situation today. But Kitamori's insight into the Christian misunderstanding of the love of God divorced from the wrath of God, though an extremely important one, cannot be directly applied to the problem in which we are involved in Thailand.

Luther, the giant proponent of the theology of the triumph of grace, restored the critical reality of the wrath of God to Christian life and theology. The wrath of God re-interpreted by Luther (for instance, "the strange work of God, *opus alienum dei*" or one's agonizing experience of it: *Anfechtung*),[2] by refusing to come under the control of the natural intellectual apprehension of Aristotelianism, shook the foundation of the scholastic captivity of God. This great Reformation discernment that the wrath of God contradicts our domestication of God supplies us with a helpful hint for an examination of the Thai theological situation.

The Thai mind tends to identify God with an absolutistic idea beyond history (a timeless, apathetic God). But the wrath of God has a unique power to historicize God. In short, if God can truly be moved to wrath, God cannot be a timeless, apathetic God beyond history, but God must be God in history ("Thou" in history), in the sense of the drama described in the Bible. The God in history who can be meaningfully moved to wrath cannot be domesticated. The God who is severed from history cannot be meaningfully moved to wrath but can be domesticated. The wrath of God is the critical expression of God in history.

Thai theology, bolstered by an indigenous ideal of *apatheia*, tends inadvertently to neglect "God in history" by reducing the wrath of God to a matter of minor significance.

---

1. John Knox Press, Richmond, 1965; SCM Press, 1966, pp. 183ff.
2. See p. 53, n.1.

TWO LEITMOTIFS OF THAI NO-PATHOS RESPONSIBLE FOR "NEGLECT OF HISTORY"

More specifically, how is it that when the wrath of God is underrated by the no-pathos ideal, the sense of history also loses seriousness? To deal with this question we must examine the structure of Thai no-pathos.

The Thai version of no-pathos derives from at least two dominant sources: (*a*) Buddhism, and (*b*) Nature.

Influence of Buddhism

According to *Udana*,[3] as in any other document of Pali Buddhism, the life of spiritual imperturbability (*passaddhi, santi*) is the ideal for every monk. "The one who has crossed over (the swamp of desire)," *Udana* reads, "crushed down the thorn of lust, and destroyed delusion, will not tremble again (if touched) by joy or pain" (22). "The monk who has subdued the thorn of lust remains unmoved like a mountain peak (in a storm) by insult, punishment and imprisonment" (23). These passages indicate a no-pathos piety similar to that of the Stoic Wise. But Buddhism and Stoicism differ decisively in the way in which this envied state of the imperturbable soul is to be reached.

Udana urges us, if we want to possess the sacred land of imperturbability of soul, to *step out* of all *karmic* chains once and for all. So far as we are bound by the inexorable law of causality, that is to say, so far as we are within time and existence (history), we are inescapably bound by the power of perturbation. The thirtieth Word of *Udana* reads:

> Humankind is attached to existence, is afflicted with existence, and even moreover rejoices in existence. Of what one rejoices in, that leads to fear. Of what one is afraid, that is miserable. Indeed one leads this holy life in order to escape completely from existence. . . . Truly, this suffering arises in dependence on (*karmic*) accumulations. If all attachment (by means of wisdom) is destroyed, (no further) suffering grows up. . . . The complete destruction of thirst and the complete cessation of lust mean the realization of extinguishment (i.e., *Nibbana*).

This final *stepping out* of all that is historical is accomplished by the realization of the radical "no-self" (*anatta*). No-self is the perfect state of no-pathos. How, indeed, can "no-self" be perturbed?

The Buddhist no-pathos, which is based on the doctrine of no-self, goes one decisive step further than that of Stoicism. Stoicism teaches us to keep

---

3. Udana, *80 Inspiring Words of the Buddha (in Sutta Pitaka, Khuddaka Nikaya). A New Version by Bhadragaka*, Bangkok, 1954.

"the six sense-spheres of contact under control" (*Udana 25*), but it does not teach to forsake "the organizing forces of existences" (*Udana 51*). The Stoic doctrine of no-pathos is guided by the same principle as that which governs the cosmos, namely, that the rule of *logos* (*ratio*, reason) within us leads us to the imperturbable life. An inner "orderliness" is the state free from perturbation of soul. *Udana* advocates the ultimate annulment of order itself by *stepping out* of it once for all, which amounts to no-self. Buddhism promises the transcendental metaphysical solution, while Stoicism offers a pyschological immanental solution.

The former finds the final solution *outside* history (*logos* and time), the latter, *within* history (*logos* and time). This difference may illustrate one of the most critical points of difference between the Buddhist (anti-historical) East and the Christian (God in history) West. Generally speaking, Christianity, which proclaims the Incarnate Word (*logos*), can accommodate the Stoic ethos, but finds difficulty in getting along with Buddhism's "will to devaluate history."

The Buddhist no-pathos fosters neglect of history because it teaches that only through the ultimate flight from history (*anatta*) can we achieve the desired state of no-pathos.

Influence of Nature

How does nature influence the Thai mind toward escape from history?

From time immemorial nature has impressed humankind with the view that the flow of time is cyclical. This is nature's interpretation of history which is human and universal. Bishop Newbigin writes:

> The dominant patterns of our own experience are cyclical, not linear. The cycles of days and weeks and years, of vegetable and animal life, of human birth, growth, old age and death, all naturally suggest an interpretation of history in cyclical terms. Indeed human institutions and civilizations apparently go through the same cycle of birth, growth, decay and death.[4]

The cyclical flow of time is strongly felt in agrarian Thailand, where the people live in close contact with nature. There are cyclical "biocosmic rhythms"[5] which govern Thai spiritual and cultural life. In Thailand, benevolent nature circles without disruption *ad infinitum* with a cosmic regularity. Thailand has rarely experienced tidal waves, volcanic eruptions, earthquakes, tornadoes, storms, severe cold, drought, or avalanches. Nature is not "perturbed." It is seldom moved to wrath. Time glides on without

---

4. Lesslie Newbigin, *A Faith for This One World?*, SCM Press, 1961, p. 19.
5. Cf. Mircea Eliade, *Cosmos and History: The Myth of the Eternal Return*, Harper & Row, New York, 1954, p. 52.

encountering serious moments of crisis or decision. Nature, in Thailand, is an efficient teacher of optimism toward life.[6] It allows humans not to be disturbed. Thus the benevolent nature of Thailand has an anti-historical intent. That is to say, nature, represented in the image of a perpetual flow of time in a circle, neglects history where the kind of situation which causes perturbation of soul is certain to arise. In spite of critical political changes, the advent of technology, and rapid Westernization of metropolitan sub-urban life, the Thai mind is basically more cosmos-oriented than history-oriented. The cosmos-oriented human does not grasp the seriousness of the crises. Crises, when interpreted in the framework of nature's cyclical time, lose their seriousness. "Cyclical time" is the image of no-pathos translated into the language of time.

Nature influences humankind to neglect history because the sense of history is too serious for nature, and disrupts its essential message: "All is cyclical and reversible, therefore do not be perturbed! Stay on the side of no-pathos."

These two dominant sources of Thai no-pathos, the desire for the ultimate flight from history to the realm of no-self, and the inclination toward undisrupted cyclical outlook of life, join hands in inducing humankind to adopt a habit of thought which *neglects history.*

THE WRATH OF GOD V. THEOLOGY THAT "NEGLECTS HISTORY"

A theology of neglect of history is the theology of God who *stepped out* of history (God of oriental deism) and who therefore cannot meaningfully be moved to wrath.[7] It is also the theology of God who is held captive in the continual cyclical flow of cosmic time and cannot meaningfully be moved to wrath. It is obvious that theological thinking cannot be put into crisis by the God of oriental deism and by the charm nature creates by being distanced from history. The theology that neglects history is basically an unperturbed theology.

The theology that neglects history can be demonstrated by three distinct points in theological thinking.

First, the theology of neglect of history is not fully aware of the problems relating to revelation and reason. The perennial dilemma of Western theology, the tension between revelation and reason, is scarcely a ripple in a

---

6. Ibid., p. 102.
7. Deism "in general held that there is a universal religion which is in accord with reason. All that is best in Christianity, so the Deists were prone to say, is older than Christianity and is completely in accord with reason. This universal, rational religion includes belief in God as the great Architect of the universe. He created the world, planted reason in *man*, gave him the moral law, and governs the universe by laws which are in accord with reason. God is to be revered and is to be honoured by a life which observes the moral law" (Kenneth S. Latourette, *A History of Christianity*, Eyre and Spottiswoode, 1954, p. 984).

culture where the will to devaluate history rules, consciously or unconsciously, through the no-pathos ideal. How can one be disturbed by the problem of revelation and reason when history, the *locus* of revelation and reason, is under the pressure of the history-neglecting forces of no-self and cyclical piety, and is thus deprived of its seriousness? The theology that ignores history is a stratospheric flight over the mountains of revelation and reason to a final answer! It wants to be enlightened without being entangled in history, the *locus* of revelation and reason. In this sense, the Thai theology that neglects history produces a lazy faith.

Second, the theology of neglect of history is scarcely capable of perceiving the deep existential meaning of the "strange work of God" (*opus alienum dei* — Isa. 28:21) in Christian life and theology. Christian faith is, in its depth, inevitably confronted by the tormenting question of the strange work of God. The strange work of God is neither superhistorical nor supernatural work, but the work which is experienced *within history*, as the forsaking of Christ by God that took place in the historical crucifixion. When the strange work of God is approached by the mind of anti-historical flight and cyclical continuity, it loses its grave significance.

The theology of neglect of history does not want to give serious consideration to history as the *locus* of the *overcoming* of *Anfechtung*. Quickly passing over the strange work of God, it comes to the God of proper work (*opus proprium*). In this speedy transition, the moralism dominant in Thai Christian life finds its encouraging support. The God who is severed from the critical sense of the strange work of God is the reasonable God of moralism characterized by the motif of continuity. In fact, however, God without strange work is, as Luther testifies, God without proper work. The theology of neglect of history dissolves the existential tension between the strange work and proper work of God and at the same time makes God understandable to humankind. It teaches an oriental version of *Christianity Not Mysterious*.[8]

Third, the theology of neglect of history fails to see the qualitative difference between God and humankind. How can it know this crucial difference if it is not consciously involved in history, the *locus* of the particular encounter which takes place between "I and Thou?" This fault is reflected in the use of analogy in Thai theological thinking. In the history-neglecting theology, the analogy works in the framework of circular continuity. That is to say, there is no disruption between finite and infinite. We must resort to analogy when we speak of God, but in doing so we are confronted by the God who constantly perturbs our use of analogy. This paradoxical burden in theological thinking is not sufficiently understood by the theology that neglects history.

The three observations above exemplify the theology of the neglect of history in operation. The contention of this study is that the wrath of God (not a timeless doctrine of the wrath of God) attacks the root of this theology of the neglect of history which sprang chiefly from the two sources of

---

8. The Deist John Toland (1670-1722) published *Christianity Not Mysterious* in 1696.

the dislike of perturbation of soul. How can the wrath of God "historicize" God in the midst of the subtle influence of the no-pathos theology that is characterized, for instance, by stratospheric flight, *Christianity Not Mysterious*, and God who is continuous with humans? Does not the love of God also "historicize" God and stand against the theology of the neglect of history? And perhaps more creatively?

The answer is that in Thailand, where the gospel of Christ is encircled by the spirit of tranquility of soul, the openly contradictory force of God's perturbation of soul, the wrath of God, is needed in order to break through the front line of the anti-historical theological construction. The love of God, very often lost in "cheap love," lacks the disturbing and critical imagery which the wrath of God carries. It also lacks the impact which is needed to awaken the mind captivated by the theology of the neglect of history.

A head-on collision between Thai tranquility theology and the wrath of God presents an opportunity for a fresh and more relevant study of the doctrine of the wrath of God. Granted that there is a danger of falling into naive anthropopathism, it is essential to preach on the wrath of God boldly to the Thai audience, historicizing God in the way the Bible does.

According to Dahlberg, the wrath of God is "the Deity's threatening with annihilation the existence of whatever opposes his will and purpose or violates his holiness and love."[9]

It must be made clear that the wrath of God is provoked by the *historical* violation of God's "holiness and love," as for example:

> Remember and do not forget how you provoked the LORD your God to wrath in the wilderness; from the day you came out of the land of Egypt, until you came to this place, you have been rebellious against the LORD (Deut. 9:7).

The biblical passages of the divine perturbation of soul must be read with the insight that the God who *stepped out* of history or the God who is captive to *cyclical* motion cannot be meaningfully moved to wrath. To quote only a few out of innumerable places referring to the wrath of God, we have:

> They have stirred me to jealousy with what is no god;
>   they have provoked me with their idols.
> So I will stir them to jealousy with those who are no people;
>   I will provoke them with a foolish nation (Deut. 32:21).

> Ah, Assyria, the rod of my anger,
>   the staff of my fury!
> Against a godless nation I send him,
>   and against the people of my wrath I command him,

---

9. B. Dahlberg, "Wrath of God," *Interpreter's Dictionary of the Bible* IV, Abingdon Press, 1964, pp. 903-08.

to take spoil and seize plunder,
    and to tread them like the mire of the street (Isa. 10:5,6).

"You only have I known
    of all the families of the earth;
therefore I will punish you
    for all your iniquities" (Amos 3:2).

These passages speak emphatically of the fact that God's wrath has *historical* and *covenantal* reasons. That is to say, history is the *locus* of God's perturbation of soul. God can be the highest good, the tranquil no-pathos if God is not involved in the history of salvation. This God in history perturbs the theology that neglects history with its three distinctive offsprings, stratospheric flight, *Christianity Not Mysterious*, and God who is continuous with humans. It does so by making history seriously *real.* The stratospheric flight is grounded because history has forced it to realize the irresponsibility of such flight over revelation and reason. Christianity becomes "mysterious" once more by the historical interpretation of the "strange work of God," and God is no longer continuous with humans because of the unique quality of the encounter which takes place in history between "I and Thou."

CONCLUSION

The wrath of God contradicts the theology of the neglect of history, the theology under the influence of the Thai no-pathos ideal (the "*anatta*-istic" flight from history and the naturalistic aversion for the seriousness in history) by insisting upon the fundamental relationship between the wrath of God and history. *God can be moved to wrath because God is God in history.* Or, only God in history can be meaningfully moved to wrath.

Once the defenses of an apathetic Thai theology have been broached by the assertion of the historicity of the wrath of God, then they need to be deepened and substantiated by the sense of the presence of God who came into history in person, Christ, the God incarnate who was not *Christos apathes* (Christ without pathos).

CHAPTER 9

Ten Key Theological Issues Facing Theologians in Asia

- Theology is a reflection on history in the light of the Word of God.
- Ten issues: interdependent world; the Bible; proclamation, accommodation, and syncretism; people of other faiths and ideologies; the West; China; the haves and have-nots; the animistic world; spirituality; doctrinal clarity.

Theology is a reflection. It is an intelligent reflection inspired by the Holy Spirit of God. "But the Counsellor, the Holy Spirit whom the Father will send in my name, he will teach you all things, and bring to your remembrance all that I have said to you" (Jn 14:26). The Holy Spirit comes to us in the name of Jesus Christ. Jesus Christ is the Lord of history, of "all creation" and the church (Col. 1:15-20). The Holy Spirit which "will teach you all things, and bring to your remembrance all that I have said to you" is not an ahistorical Spirit, but a Spirit concerned and involved in history. The Holy Spirit is an intelligent historical Spirit who "will teach you all things." The spirit will teach us about the love of God and the way it works in this very concrete history. What is happening in the Indochinese peninsula — its spiritual turmoil, political confusion; the international brutality which disrupted millions from achieving their human fulfillment; their search for the meaning of nation, community, family, and individual — is the context in which the Holy Spirit will bring to us "all that I have said to you."

Theology is a reflection. Reflection on what? *History in the light of the Word of God.* The Word here must be understood in the solemn theological message of John 14:26. Theology is an intelligent and spiritual reflection on history in its fundamental relationship (the God of the covenant creates and rules history) to the Word of God. It is understanding God's understanding of history and humankind in the illumination of John 14:26. In this way we find our spirituality enlightened. To engage in theology in the historical context does not mean then that the context, whatever

76

it is, is there as something unchangeable and beyond our control. Context is something which must be constantly challenged and forced to change. ". . . At the name of Jesus every knee should bow, in heaven and on earth and under the earth . . ." (Phil. 2:10). To engage in theology within the given historical and cultural context is to engage in intelligent and spiritual examination of "spirits" at work in the world. "Beloved, do not believe every spirit, but test the spirits to see whether they are of God" (I Jn. 4:1). One of the significant events in recent Christian literature is Dr. W. A. Visser 't Hooft's *Memoirs*. What makes the reading irresistibly absorbing and remarkably refreshing? It is a story of a man who has *lived* with sharpened theological awareness in the given historical context and *challenged* the context in intelligent and spiritual ways as inspired by the Holy Spirit. He constantly examined the "spirits." He lived a theological life ever hopeful, emancipating and community building. I don't think the ecumenical movement was his idea. It was the message he heard as the Holy Spirit brought to his remembrance "all that I have said to you." He was, with countless others, reminded of the mind of Christ who seeks the unity of the church.

We live in Southeast Asia. We belong to the community of believers. There is no private theology. Our theology is a community production. Together we are reminded by the Holy Spirit of "all that I have said to you." Together we say, "Out of the depths I cry to thee, O Lord" (Ps. 130:1).

With this meditation I wish to proceed.

INTERDEPENDENT WORLD

The world is tragically divided in all directions. Ours is a broken world. It is badly broken, yet it is interrelated. Humankind experiences today actions and reactions of all kinds from one corner of the world to another with electric speed. This interrelated world is not an interdependent world. It is not the world in which each part helps another for the good of the whole. The despairing dimension of human suffering is taking place when interrelatedness is exploited only for the privileged and therefore the way to realize an interdependent world is hopelessly blocked.

Who is Jesus Christ in this perspective (christology)? How do we relate the unity of the church with the unity of humankind (ecumenical movement)? What is the relationship between unity and interdependence? Is there unity among the churches? In what way? Is there unity of humankind? In what way? What is the role of historical Christianity in the effort to achieve the unity of humankind? How can the variety of Southeast Asian cultural heritages (e.g., Indonesian *adats*) and historical experience (colonialism, ethnic conflicts and enrichment, economic poverty, and so on) be mobilized to strengthen expression and action in the name of Jesus Christ toward the making of an interdependent world (I Cor. 12:12-26)?

THE BIBLE

Is the Bible the Word of God? In what sense? How should the authority of the Bible be understood? What *kind* of authority is it? Is it an exclusive, infallible authority? Is it the authority of divine love? Does its authority simply reflect the authority of Jesus Christ, crucified and risen? With what authority does the Bible speak to us about the message of hope and judgment today? What is the relationship between the human situations depicted in the Bible and our own situations today? How do we communicate the authority of God proclaimed in the biblical human situations to our lives today? How do we introduce the Bible to Asians? How can we most effectively increase communication between the Asian mind and the mind of the Bible?

PROCLAMATION, ACCOMMODATION, AND SYNCRETISM

Christians proclaim Jesus Christ. With what theological understanding do we speak of the relationship between "humanization" and the proclamation of the gospel? Is it "either/or," as is sometimes suggested? What is our evaluation of "humanization" in the light of Jesus Christ? How do we understand proclamation in the light of Jesus Christ? How do we understand the Great Commission in the light of Jesus Christ?

In the proclamation of the gospel, at what point does accommodation become syncretism and at what point does proclamation become iconoclasticism of the cherished cultural values of Asians? Are our church structures the best possible structures in our historical-cultural contexts?

FOLLOWERS OF OTHER FAITHS AND IDEOLOGIES

What are the meaningful and edifying theological interpretations of the commitments and destiny of people of other living faiths and ideologies?

(*a*) What is the unique quality of the Christian "abundant life" in the world of other living faiths and ideologies? How do we express it and communicate it? How is the "abundant life" experienced by people of other living faiths and ideologies related to the Christian "abundant life?" Is dialogue possible? And if so, on what theological basis? Christians experience frustration and despair. People of other living faiths and ideologies also experience frustration and despair. In what way do the frustrations and despair experienced and expressed by Christians and people of other living faiths and ideologies find their place in Jesus Christ? On what theological basis should we share our frustrations, judgment, and hope?

(*b*) The world demands from us concrete demonstration of mercy. Has Christianity, both yesterday and today, shown itself to the world as the religion of mercy? What is the theological basis for articulating the importance of "showing mercy" in the world in which we live today? How is mercy shown by those of other faiths and ideologies related to mercy shown in the name of Jesus Christ? Is mercy found only in Jesus Christ? What kind of mercy is it that the Bible is trying to communicate to us? If mercy is found "outside" the name of Jesus Christ, what is the meaning of "no other name," "and there is salvation in no one else, for there is no other name under heaven given among men by which we must be saved" (Acts 4:12)? What is the *uniqueness* of God's mercy demonstrated in his Son, Jesus Christ?

(*c*) In the documents of Vatican II we read:

> Those also can attain to everlasting salvation who through no fault of their own do not know the gospel of Christ or His Church, yet sincerely seek God and, moved by grace, strive by their deeds to do His will as it is known to them through the dictates of conscience. Nor does divine Providence deny the help necessary for salvation to those who, without blame on their part, have not yet arrived at an explicit knowledge of God, but who strive to live a good life, thanks to His grace.[1]

What is the practical implication of this? What are our local and concrete theological comments on this? Does this address people of other living faiths? What is the pastoral as well as the evangelistic implications of this in Southeast Asia?

(*d*) What is the theological understanding of the relationship between proclamation and dialogue? There are many ways of proclaiming the gospel. One of critical importance is through life itself — the way they live. Theology must become theology-lived or lived-theology. What is our theological understanding of our own tragic division between theology and life? How do we read our own church history in this light?

THE WEST

What is the West to Asia? Historically the West has been both "gun" (wounding) and "ointment" (healing) to Asia. The West's influence upon Asia for the last four hundred years has been substantial. The massive effect of modernization is a process of Westernization. This shaking of the foundations in Asian life by the West's mental and scientific-technological impact is a great event in the history of humankind. Theology in Asia cannot be meaningfully contextualized without addressing itself to the theme of the "gun and ointment" relationship between the West and Asia. What is the spirit and mind of the West which gave the world super-production and super-destruction?. Will the West become more "gun" than "ointment" in the future of Asia? Will not the West need Asian ointment? What is Asian ointment? How does Christ, God's anointed, the Word which was from the beginning, speak to us in this historic context?

---

1. *Dogmatic Constitution on the Church*, 16.

CHINA

China is a nation of great antiquity and a rich heritage of civilization. The concept of the unity of humankind (Christian or otherwise) suffers a crippling lack of reality when China is viewed only in the terms set by the Christian West. The place of the West as the sole possessor of the scale of value judgment as to what is good for humankind is now seriously disputed. In 1949 Mao Tse-tung realized a great proletarian revolution which affected substantially the lives of 800 million people on the mainland. 1949 then saw the birth of a new nation replacing the old nation. Is Mao Tse-tung a Cyrus (Isa. 45:1-7)? Is it possible that Ho Chi Minh is the Lord's anointed? What is the reconciling intention of God (II Cor. 5:18-21), who is history-concerned, historically staged through *men* such as Gandhi, Nehru, Mao, Ho, and Sukarno? How do we read the signs of the times? Will the study of Mao-China have something critically important to say to the question, "Who is Jesus Christ?" Is not the present reality of China "a great theological reality?" What would be a reappropriation of the central message of the Christian faith in the light of China in particular, and of Asia in the process of radical changes in general? Is not Christ there, hidden or revealed? What is it that we understand when we speak of the presence and work of God in history?

We have seen the spectacle of history in Vietnam, namely, that the world's mightiest nation was forced to acknowledge defeat through the resistance put up by one tiny Asian country. B52s bombers and genocidal strategies were unable to mold the history of Indo-China as the leaders of the powerful nation intended. This astonishing experience in the eyes of every single Asian (and, of course, in the eyes of all people on the planet) must find responsible Asian theological expression. What is it?

THE HAVES AND HAVE-NOTS

Our planet is divided into two sections of humanity: *the haves and the have-nots*. Christian nations are in the "have" zones. The ever-widening gap is creating bitterness of tragic proportions on the side of the have-nots. Christian nations represent the global power of the *status quo*. The nations in which Christianity is not dominant are generally nations struggling against international exploitation and aspiring for the establishment of global justice. The "have" Christian nations exercise tremendous power (political, military, economic) to suppress the tide of aspirations of the struggling peoples of Asia. This, however, is not the whole story. We must not forget the scandal of the Asian rich (sometimes super-rich) exploiting Asian poor consistently and ruthlessly. In such a concrete historical context, what would Asian theologians say?

ANIMISTIC WORLD

How do we meet the challenge to present the gospel of Christ to the people living in the animistic world, and to people moving from the animistic world to an urban setting? What is the relationship between *spirits and the Holy Spirit?*

SPIRITUALITY

Humans are created in the image of God. That we are spiritual does not mean we have a ghostly existence. Our spiritual life is not an isolated life. It participates in the spiritual value upheld in the community in which we belong. Our spirituality is a corporate experience. Each nation, each ethnic group has, because of its particular history, its own accent in the realm of spirituality. Critical theological appreciation of our spirituality, both in general and specific manifestations, is urgently needed. The Holy Spirit illuminates and judges our Asian spirituality. Theology is asked to articulate this illumination. Our spiritual value and our social value will be enlightened by this theological effort toward achieving Christ-like spirituality, one ever creative and hopeful.

DOCTRINAL CLARITY

There are persistent theological questions which must be answered. Here are some classic questions, for example, taken from the experience of the Jesuit Luis Frois who propagated the gospel in sixteenth-century Japan. He was surrounded by the Japanese, who pressed for doctrinal clarity.

(*a*) Satan has fallen out of the grace of God. Yet Satan retains and enjoys greater freedom than ours in deceiving us. Indeed, Satan can bring humans to the possibility of eternal damnation. Why?

(*b*) If God is love, God should have created us to be incapable of committing sin. Why did God not so create us?

(*c*) God has endowed us with freedom. If this is so, why did not God warn the first *man*, when he was tempted by the Serpent, that he might be deceived? If God had done so, that man could have exercised his freedom to choose.

(*d*) If human spirituality is, in its essence, created untainted and holy, why then can this sacred spirituality be corrupted by original sin working in the bodily existence of humans?

(*e*) Why does not a good person necessarily prosper? Why is it possible that the wicked prosper and are at peace?

(*f*) If there is a God of great love, as Christianity proclaims, why is it that God kept the gospel from the Japanese people for so long?

CHAPTER 10

Theological Re-Rooting in the Theology of the Pain of God

- The subject of the chapter is theological problems related to the process of indigenization and accommodation. This is a case study of Kitamori's work.
- Theological re-rooting is a process of re-rooting theological thought from one cultural zone to another, one period to another period, one history-consciousness to another history-consciousness. This process is one of great complexity. Re-rooting of theology must be guided by theological principle. It is in the light of this observation that this chapter is called "theological re-rooting," instead of the re-rooting of theology.
- In the fusion of the two Japanese words, *tsutsumu* and *tsurasa*, Kitamori finds the powerful "agent" concept which can re-root the Christian message in the Japanese culture mind. *Tsutsumu* means to enfold, to enwrap, and *tsurasa* means to feel pain in one's deep personal life for the sake of others — vicarious suffering! — at the same time refraining from revealing how deeply one suffers. All pain is kept to oneself for the happiness of others.
- Wherever and whenever people suffer for the sake of another, they analogically participate with the one who suffered on the cross. Human pain must be seen christologically. When it is seen thus, it provides a useful re-rooting agent. The analogy of suffering (*analogia doloris*) has a high potentiality in the process of theological re-rooting.

It was soon after the Second World War when *Theology of the Pain of God* appeared (1946). The Japanese nation was then deeply troubled, paralyzed, and "in pain." "The present is an age of pain. If our age is not to be called a 'time of pain' for what period of history can the term be appropriate?" (p. 85). *Theology of the Pain of God* spoke the message of God who

82

"resolves our human pain by his own, to the broken nation and her shaken people" (p. 20).

At the outset of my reflections on the book, I wish to emphasize the point that the book speaks the language of conviction, commitment, and firm faith.

> My prayer night and day is that the gospel of love rooted in the pain of God may become real to all men. All human emptiness will be filled if this gospel is known to every creature, since the answer to every human problem lies in the gospel. Therefore I pray, "May thou, O Lord, make known to all men thy love rooted in the pain of God." The greatest joy and thanksgiving comes from the knowledge that this prayer is being granted and that step by step this gospel is becoming real to mankind (p. 150).

The gospel interpreted in terms of "the love rooted in the pain of God" has the burden of being "the prince of all other doctrines." What *sola fide* was to Luther, "the love rooted in the pain of God" is to Kitamori. The theology of the pain of God describes "the heart of God most deeply," following Jeremiah and Paul (p. 20).

What is this "love rooted in the pain of God?" According to Kitamori, there are three orders of love in God.

(*a*) The first order of love of God is simply named "the love of God." "This love of God pours *immediately* on its object without any hindrance" (p. 17). God loves his Son without any hindrance since the Son is "worthy of receiving it" (p. 117). "Both Christ and man were originally objects of God's love of the first order, but now only Christ is its object. Man has now fallen away from this kind of God's love . . ." (p. 118). "This type of God's love may be characterized as smooth, flowing, and intense" (p. 118). It is the love of the Father pouring upon "the two sons" before that tragic event; "the younger son collected all his belongings and went off to a foreign land."

(*b*) Has God given up loving the fallen humankind? "God did not repulse those who should be repulsed. God *embraced* them . . . 'How can I give you up, O Ephraim! How can I hand you over, O Israel! . . .'" (p. 119). Here the first love which is "smooth, flowing, and intense" becomes the pain of God. "The 'pain' of God reflects God's will to love the object of God's wrath" (p. 21). Fallen humanity is the object of God's wrath. "This wrath of God is absolute and firm" (p. 21). Kitamori quotes Theodosius Harnack's *Luthers Theologie* and indicates the presence of a painful "against" between "God in his will of wrath and God in his will of love" (p. 45). At Golgotha, *da streydet Gott mit Gott* (God is fighting with God — Luther's words) (p. 21). "The fact that this fighting God is not two different gods but the same God causes pain. Here heart is opposed to heart within God"

(p. 21). Kitamori often illustrated the pain of God, in his classroom informal talks, as a piece of fine silk cloth wrapping heavy sharp augers. This superbly Japanese image depicts, in a nutshell, the essential structure of the pain of God.

(c) First, there is "smooth and flowing" love. Second, the first love becomes pain, since it refuses to repulse the object of wrath. Third, embracing fallen humanity, the second love transcends human obedience and becomes the love rooted in the pain of God. The love here is no longer *immediate* flowing love of the first order, but the love *mediated* by the pain of God. The initial flowing love is recovered now on the *mediated* basis. "My heart is troubled" (Jer. 31:20) stands at the center of the second order. This "troubled heart" now in the third order becomes "yearning heart" and "compassionate heart" (Isa. 63:15; p.121). The love of God is deeply troubled, yet it has become the love rooted in the pain of God, "yearning heart."[1] "But while he was yet at a distance, his father saw him and had compassion, and ran and embraced him and kissed him." This is the love rooted in the pain of God. This is the love *mediated* by the tragic pain of having had his son in a foreign country. The third order of love is not free from pain. It constantly carries pain within itself. "The three orders of love are seen inclusively in the one order — the 'pain of God'" (p. 122). This is why Paul confesses "For I decided to know nothing among you except Jesus Christ and him crucified" (p. 123).

The intention of this paper is not to give a full survey of *Theology of the Pain of God*, but rather to ask questions related to "theological re-rooting." I have just described the heart of Kitamori's theology. We now have a working basis on which to proceed.

Re-Rooting of "God Is Fighting with God" in a Japanese Cultural Milieu

Obviously Kitamori is deeply influenced by Luther. Perhaps the most decisive theological illumination that came from Luther is the one at Golgotha, "God is fighting with God." This powerful formulation of Luther, the head-on conflict between the wrath of God and the love of God within one God, has supplied the fundamental theological framework for the theology of the pain of God. Kitamori says that the cause of this grave conflict is that God is determined *to embrace* (*tsutsumu*) the sinful and rebellious reality

---

1. "Is Ephraim my dear son, is he a pleasant child? For since I spake against him, I do earnestly remember him still: therefore my bowels are troubled for him: I will surely have mercy upon him, saith the LORD" (Jer. 31:20, AV); "Look down from heaven, and behold from the habitation of thy holiness and of thy glory: where is thy zeal and thy strength, the sounding of thy bowels and of the mercies towards me? Are they restrained?" (Isa. 63:15, AV). These are the basic texts for Kitamori's theology. Cf. pp.151-62, where his exegesis is given.

which God "ought not to forgive or to enfold" (p. 21). Through this single verb *tsutsumu*, the total impact and message of "God is fighting with God" is re-rooted to the Japanese understanding.

The crucial word here is *tsutsumu*. Why does it display such a high re-rooting value in the context of the theology of the pain of God? In the pantheistic Japanese culture, where people enjoy and appreciate the moral surrounding as a hazy and charmingly simple totality, the verb *tsutsumu* carries a certain significant place of honor. *Tsutsumu* means the natural (non-argumentative) desire to *tsutsumu* desirable and undesirable, clean and dirty, right and wrong. "God causes his sun to rise on bad men as well as good, and his rain to fall on honest and dishonest men alike" (Matt. 5:45) might be the golden text for the Japanese *tsutsumu* mind. But exactly here the Japanese pantheistic, demarcation-erasing, mind misrepresents the mind of God. *Tsutsumu* in its natural meaning cannot bring humanity to the core of the biblical message.

At this point Kitamori invites us to see the other side of *tsutsumu* in the Japanese culture. When *tsutsumu* is combined with *tsurasa*, the fusion of the two concepts yields an outstanding re-rooting value. What is *tsurasa*?

> *Tsurasa*, the basic principle in Japanese tragedy, is realized when one suffers and dies, or makes his beloved son suffer and die, for the sake of loving and making others live. Even though he tries hard to conceal and endure his agony, his cries filtering through his efforts are heard. When the Japanese playgoers hear these cries, they shed tears speechlessly. It is correct to say that nothing moves the mind of the Japanese as deeply as these spectacles (p.135).

For the sake of loving and making fallen humanity live, the Father let the Son suffer and die. The Father then becomes the God of *tsurasa*. God suffers without fully letting us know how deeply God suffers. The *tsurai* (adjective) God is the One who contains the painful conflict within Godself because of the humanity whom God loves and from whom this conflict comes. In order to make others live, the Servant of the Lord silently takes the conflict between God and God's people into God's own heart and endures it. This is the *tsurai* situation! If one decides not to *tsutsumu* ("to enfold" or "to get involved"), there will be no possibility of *tsurasa* (to experience the painful inner dilemma caused by one's concern for others). Here is a Christian meaning of *tsutsumu*. *Tsutsumu* without *tsurasa* is a superficial *tsutsumu*, while *tsutsumu* with *tsurasa* is "Christian" *tsutsumu*. The latter precipitates the former into crisis. Yet, the former functions as useful ground for the re-rooting. Because it is on the soil of the former, the latter can meaningfully operate. When *tsutsumu* deepens itself by the *tsurasa* quality, the pantheistically oriented *tsutsumu* principle is transformed to the one which has dual significance. The concept of *tsutsumu* is now "amphibious;" it can walk on the dry land of the traditional Japanese cultural value and at the same time it can swim in the sacred water where the Christian value is hidden. For this amphibious quality, *tsutsumu* becomes an amazingly efficient re-rooting agent.

In short, "embrace and endure *tsurasa*" or "embrace in spite of *tsurasa*" is a dynamic correspondence to what Luther meant by the equally striking expression, "God is fighting with God." Thus it is possible to translate Luther's "God is fighting with God" as "there God was *tsurai* with God!"

One more point deserving our attention is about the cultural basis as the possibility of theological re-rooting. It is a providential coincidence that between the Japan of Kitamori and the Germany of Luther there existed a similar cultural feeling which gave a common re-rooting basis. Theological expressions are relevant and persuasive when they are constructed with the raw materials of the local cultural life. "God is fighting with God" cannot be conveyed to the Japanese mind if the Japanese mentality does not share a certain degree of similarity with the culture from which Luther worked out this explosive formulation. There is a possibility that while the Japanese Kitamori's reading of Jeremiah 31:20 and Isaiah 63:15 suggested the direction toward a theology of the pain of God, the Samoan or the Burmese theologian may not voice the similar theological note, since Samoan "cultural emotion" may be quite different from that of the Japanese.

The question is this: how decisive is the role of any given culture, be it Japanese, Samoan, or Burmese, in the re-rooting of theological truth? Is it true that the message of the love rooted in the pain of God can be relatively easy to introduce to a Japanese audience, since they understand *tsurasa*? How do we understand the relationship between the love rooted in the pain of God and the culture which does not give serious attention to the spiritual value of *tsurasa* and *tsutsumu*? Are they simply handicapped in their capacity for appreciating the gospel of Christ? It is hard to suppose the existence of any culture which rejects the concept of *tsurasa* or *tsutsumu* altogether. But there must be varieties of intensity with which its people regard these two values. In a culture where the sense of *tsurasa* and *tsutsumu* is weak, perhaps, we must find another "amphibious" agent in order to accommodate the love rooted in the pain of God. With this observation in mind, we proceed.

Re-Rooting of the Gospel of Jesus Christ for the Japanese Mind

Kitamori's fundamental concern is, of course, to re-root the gospel of Christ for the Japanese mind. Theological re-rooting is a thoughtful attempt to translate the inner meaning of the message of Jesus Christ from one cultural milieu and root it in another. Theological re-rooting, further, is burdened with a particularly difficult assignment, since it must, in each attempt of rooting, show forth a fresh aspect of the "unspeakable gift of God" (II Cor. 9:15) and thus must deepen the meaning of the gospel for the understanding of the people in whom it is intended to re-root. Each step of re-rooting must be an experience of the new depth and wealth of the gospel! This is because, in my judgment, the gospel reveals its hidden energy just at the very point and process of re-rooting.

Theological re-rooting is highly *interpretative* work. It has to do with the inner meaning (interpreted meaning) of the message concerning Jesus Christ.

The love rooted in the pain of God is, according to Kitamori, the inner meaning of the message of Jesus Christ. This love was the origin of the history of the people of Israel; it was manifested in a supreme manner in the work and life of Jesus Christ, and it became the source of the amazing inspiration for the apostles and the church they founded. The love rooted in the pain of God runs through the total story of God's involvement with humankind. Theologians in the past talked about the love of God. In an edifying way they discussed the relationship between the wrath and love of God. But their discussions were still unsatisfactory from the viewpoint of Kitamori, since they had not arrived at the theological concept of "pain of God." For him the meaning of the message of Jesus Christ reaches its innermost essence (pp. 44ff.) in the theological concept of the "pain of God."

The love rooted in the pain of God is an interpreted gospel (*kerygma*). The church cannot function simply on the level of the flat text of the Bible. Interpretation immediately suggests the person of the interpreter. Every interpreter of biblical texts lives in his or her historical context, Luther in sixteenth-century Germany and Kitamori in twentieth century Japan. They read the Word of God *de profundis* in each historical and cultural context. Then they are struck by certain passages of the Bible, Luther by Romans 1:17 and Kitamori by Jeremiah 31:20 and Isaiah 63:15. Kitamori is caught and arrested by these passages *in a special way*. "Ever since this strange word struck me, I have meditated on it night and day" (p. 151). Here the freedom of God and freedom of person met, since there is no reason why these two passages *must* come to Kitamori as they did. At the meeting of these two freedoms the conviction of a theologian emerged.

At the very point of this "discovery of the gospel" theological re-rooting begins. Kitamori speaks of God's love. The Christian concept of love is, at the beginning of his theological journey, fused with the Japanese spiritual value.

The Christian proclamation seeks re-rooting whenever it comes to a new land. This is basically affirmed by the historical event of incarnation ("the Word became flesh"). Incarnation means in-culturation and in-localization. The potential "amphibious agent" waits to be discovered by the right theologian at the right time. The discoverer discerns the hidden quality of "amphibious-ness" among the ordinary-looking spiritual and cultural values. The two ways run simultaneously on some fortunate occasions. For instance, the *tsurasa* truth illumines the gosel and the gospel penetrates the *tsurasa* truth. *Tsurasa* and gospel become inseparable! What takes place is dialogue between the *inner* meaning of the event of Christ and the *inner* feeling of the Japanese people. In this meeting of the two *inners*, as it were, re-rooting establishes itself.

Is the Analogy of Suffering (analogia doloris) a Comprehensive Re-Rooting Principle?

Tsurasa illumines the gospel. Gospel penetrates *tsurasa*. This correlation between the two is the major contribution of Kitamori's work. The Japanese quality in his theological thinking is prominent at this point. Kitamori refers to the profound religious conviction expressed by the prince Shotoku, and through the prince's thought invites us to the deeper understanding of the love rooted in the pain of God. The enlightened prince says, "Sickness is healed by sickness." According to Kitamori, this is a profound religious understanding comparable to the biblical position: "Wound is healed by the wound." The prince's interpretation is limited. "There can be no inflexible wrath of the absolute in Buddhism, as long as it does not have the God of the first commandment. An absolute being without wrath can have no real pain" (p. 27).

Does Kitamori mean that in Buddhism there may be pain but no real pain? But how should one understand the "Buddhist understanding of pain" or the "Buddhist experience of pain" in the light of "theologically-interpreted-real-pain?" How can pain, the *real* pain, which exists outside recognition of the pain of God, be given its proper theological value? What does Kitamori mean by *real* pain? Is *real* pain only the pain of God which is *tsurai* love? Is human pain not quite real? Again, what is the theological estimation of human pain outside the analogy of suffering (p. 56)?

> Our human pain is by itself dark, meaningless, and barren. Man's pain is the wrath of God. . . . All kinds of pain experienced in this world remain meaningless and fruitless as long as they do not serve the pain of God. We must take care not to suffer human pain in vain. . . . By serving as witness to the pain God, our pain is transformed into light (pp. 52f.).

Is there any human pain, be it of a Buddhist, a Muslim, an animist, or a communist, which is *not* serving as witness to the pain of God in one way or another? Are all the pains suffered by the Sinhalese Buddhists in the past "dark, meaningless and barren?"[2] When does our human pain serve God's pain?

> To follow the Lord of the cross is to serve the path of God. Thus, to follow the Lord of the cross, bearing one's own cross, is to serve the pain of God by suffering pain oneself. . . . "Those who do not serve the pain of God by their own pain are not worthy of God's pain" — this is the absolute declaration (p. 50).

---

2. See *The Revolt in the Temple*, ch. 3.

While pursuing the theological value of human pain, we are given this striking paragraph:

> In the pain of God is his power which completely conquers the dis-
> obedience so deeply embedded in all human activities. In the analogy
> of pain, *man's* pain serves the pain of God, who completely conquers
> our wilfulness, illusions, and disobedience. *God accepts our service by
> resolving our disobedience.* Thus *man's* pain serves the pain of God by
> receiving such *status* that it can never fall into disobedience (p. 56).

Does this mean then that all human "meaningless and fruitless" pains deriv-
ing from disobedience are made to serve the pain of God? Does this mean
that all kinds of pains are, without condition, *embraced* by God's pain, since
Christ died for us *while we were still enemies* (Rom. 5:10; p. 92)? Embraced by
the pain of God now, are the human pains outside analogy of suffering
made meaningful and fruitful? Or is Kitamori saying comprehensively that
there is no human pain which is *outside* the analogy of suffering, since *outside* is brought *inside* by the love rooted in the pain of God? Even the people who consciously reject the analogy of suffering and thus refuse to be
related to the love rooted in the pain of God — are they "completely con-
quered" because Christ died for us while we were still "dark, meaningless
and barren?" I understand him to affirm this.

Is not this theology of the analogy of suffering a most comprehensive
accommodational principle? Wherever and whenever human pain exists,
a person who is involved in pain is, repentant or not, embraced by the
tsurai love of God. Does the God of Kitamori embrace too much? Yes, it
does. But it does so *christologically*, that is, in the light of the Son who was
crucified *outside* the city!

PART III

Interpreting Thai Buddhist Life

CHAPTER 11

Buddhist, Not Buddhism

- Perhaps we pay undue attention to *ism*, and in contrast, too little attention to *ist*. It is obvious that the study of Buddh*ism* demands less concentration and energy than the study of the living person called a Buddh*ist*.
- We must study Buddh*ism*, of course, if we wish to understand the Buddh*ist*. Our ultimate interest must lie, however, with understanding the Buddh*ist* and not Buddh*ism*. What matters for the Christian gospel is not Buddh*ism*, but the Buddh*ist*.

For eight years I lived in Thailand, a land of Theravada Buddhism. Thai Buddhism is, perhaps, the purest form of Buddhism practiced in the world today. Have you been to Bangkok? If you have, you must have seen some of the 240,000 monks of the kingdom on the streets of that bustling modern city. The monks live as though no change had taken place in the world for the last 2,500 years!

When I first went to Thailand, I had a rather negative view of Buddhism there. I felt that Buddhism did not have much of a future and was probably passing out of the thoughts of many millions in Southeast Asia. Since life had become increasingly modernized and secularized, that ancient religion of "detachment" and "tranquility" was bound to diminish. So I did not pay much attention to it.

However, after three years had passed, I had to revise my view of Buddhism in Thailand. As my relationship with Buddhist friends increased and my language comprehension grew, I came to realize that what really matters is not a set of doctrines called Buddhism, but *people* who live according to the doctrine of the Buddha, or I should say, who are trying to live according to the doctrine of the Buddha. Accordingly, my interest shifted from Buddhism to Buddhist people.

Soon I found that the study of *ist* is far more interesting and exciting than that of *ism*. I carefully observed Buddhists, and to my surprise found many similar things between them and myself. One day I said to myself: "We are just alike. We want money. We want position. We want honor. We

93

are both concerned about ourselves. We are failing to practice what the Buddha or Christ commanded. We are quick in judging others and very slow in judging ourselves!" Comparisons on the level of Buddh*ist* and Chris-*tian* often produce an embarrassing result. On the contrary, we can be well sheltered when we engage in the comparison between Buddh*ism* and Christ*ianity*. Here Christians frequently launch into "the defense of the right doctrines" so passionately and energetically that they become Chris-*tianity* and cease to be Christ*ians*.

One can study Buddhism in school. Some will even study the Pali language in order to read the original Buddhist canon. One must not minimize the importance of understanding the ancient document of faith. But, again, here is something we must not forget: Buddhism does not feel hungry even if it does not eat for many centuries. Buddhism does not sweat even if it is placed under the hot tropical sun. Buddhism does not want to sell a bicycle and buy a motorcycle instead. Buddhism does not suffer from flood and drought. A Buddhist, on the contrary, is different. He or she complains, laughs, grieves, sweats, suffers, thirsts, and hungers.

A Buddhist is a person. A person does not cease to be a person. A person does not become either an angel or a devil. By the grace of God, he or she remains a person with many needs and drives: emotional, physical, intellectual, spiritual — all combined in a wonderful kind of unity. This "wonderful kind of unity," however, becomes from time to time seriously sick. Then the person is paralyzed, becomes *homo aeger* (a sick person), says Augustine. Yet that sick person is unusual, wonderful, and inspiring! What great complex creatures these human beings are! Because we are so complex, we have always been a puzzle to ourselves. It is easier for us to understand a lion or an elephant than to understand ourselves. There are many doctrines, both helpful and harmful, about human beings. But even the best of all doctrines is not identical with the living person whom we see every day everywhere. If one of the doctrines on human beings had been adequate to explain it, then the "incarnation" would not have been necessary. Instead of the costly incarnation, God becoming human being, and dwelling amongst us, God might just as well have sent some wonderful doctrine about human beings. The best of all the good doctrines cannot compete with the one fact of God's incarnation in Jesus Christ.

Now human beings are, according to the Bible, the "image of God." This is a great doctrine about human beings. Whenever the church opens her mouth on the issue of the "human dignity," this doctrine has been the point of departure. But this doctrine, in short, must not remain simply a doctrine. It must become integrated into our appreciation of people with whom we come in contact every day. The "idea" of ice tea will not quench our thirst. It is, no doubt, a good theory for quenching our thirst, but theory cannot become effective until it is acted upon. When the "idea" of ice tea becomes actualized in ice cubes and a brown-colored liquid called tea, then it can be drunk and will stop our thirst. So it is with the doctrine of the "image of God." It has to become, in each given situation, some sort of "ice cubes and brown-colored liquid." That is to say, it must be actualized within human relationships if it is to display its dynamic and real power.

We are bound by all kinds of doctrines. Our interest is always on the side of *ism* rather than *ist*. Excessive interest in *ism* brings forth a disastrous situation which may be called the tyranny of doctrines. We tend to look at other persons through "doctrinally trained" eyes. So we become experts in quick pronouncements of judgment upon others. When "doctrinally trained eyes" say, "Now, master, this woman has been caught in adultery, in the very act. According to the Law, Moses commanded us to stone such women to death!" (Jn. 8:4), "incarnate eyes" look in a *different direction.* "Jesus stooped down and began to write with his finger in dust on the ground" (v. 6). *Ism* and *ist* are related. Don't let *ism* walk alone!

CHAPTER 12

Cool *Arhat* and Hot God

- "Anyone, Malunkyaputta, who should say 'I will not lead a religious life with the Lord until the Lord explains to me whether . . .' that person would die, Malunkyaputta, without its being explained."
- Ideal of the *apatheia*-person: "We must understand that we do not take food because it tastes good, but in order to cure pain and satisfy hunger. When we eat to satisfy hunger, even though the food is not good, it will satisfy the hunger. Suppose we take food for the sake of its flavor without further consideration, if it is not good, then aversion will occur. On the other hand, if it is good, then greed will occur."
- Principle of "homelessness":
  > A den of strife is household life,
  > And filled with toil and need;
  > But free and high as the open sky
  > Is the life the homeless lead.
- The "hot" God. Why is God hot? Because God is the God of covenant. The biblical concept of covenant is fundamentally a "hot" concept.
- Jesus Christ restores and strengthens "I."
- Placing of *dukkha*, *anicca*, and *anatta* in the theology of covenant between Israel (church) and God; namely, Hebraization of *dukkha*, *anicca*, and *anatta* will give us a helpful theological starting point in the culture of Thailand.
- Japanization or Filipinization of *dukkha*, *anicca*, and *anatta* cannot produce the critical dimension that Hebraization is able to create.
- The hot God does not reject the cool person. God warms the cool person by accepting the person's *dukkha*, *anicca*, and *anatta*.

2512 Buddhist Era
Bangkok, Thailand

Dear Elder Malunkyaputta,

For some years your name has been familiar to me. And often I have tried to form your image in my mind. Today — what a hot and humid day it was! — as I was sitting next to a saffron-robed monk in the public municipal bus, as I was walking in the busy shopping center of Bangkok, as I was taking a refreshing cold shower in my lodging, my thoughts went out to you. I know you are no longer available to me. You are gone! "Too bad," I said to myself, "I cannot meet the Elder and talk with him personally! I know several quiet air-conditioned coffee rooms in Bangkok!"

You may ask, why am I interested in you? Well, my answer is simple. You remember *The Parable of the Arrow* told by your great Master, the Buddha. Who occasioned the parable? It was *you*! I think you have contributed greatly to the spiritual life of humankind by being the cause for the Enlightened One to speak his wise words. You framed an interesting query in your mind:

> These theories have been left unexplained by the Lord, set aside and rejected, whether the world is eternal or not eternal, whether the world is finite or not, whether the soul (life) is the same as the body, or whether the soul is one thing and the body another, whether a Buddha (Tathagata) exists after death or does not exist after death, and whether a Buddha is non-existent and not non-existent after death. . . .

You then resolved: "If the Lord does not explain to me, I will give up the training, and return to a worldly life." Why are all these *whethers* . . . so important to you? Were you really interested in finding out the answers to these questions? Or were you representing the kind of religious and philosophical questions your age asked? You, anyway, approached the Buddha with these "serious" questions and the Buddha answered you and us all:

> Anyone, Malunkyaputta, who should say "I will not lead a religious life with the Lord, until the Lord explains to me whether . . ." that person would die, Malunkyaputta, without its being explained.
>
> It is as if a man had been wounded by an arrow thickly smeared with poison, and his friends, companions, relatives and kinsmen were to get a surgeon to heal him, and he were to say, "I will not have this arrow pulled out, until I know by what man I was wounded, whether he is of the warrior caste, or a brahmin, or the agricultural, or the lowest caste." Or he were to say, "I will not have this arrow pulled out until I know of what name or family the man is . . . or whether he is tall, or short, or of middle height . . . or whether he is black, or dark, or yellowish . . . or whether he comes from such and such a village, or town, or city . . . or until I know whether the bow with which I was wounded was a chapa or a kondanda, or until I know whether the

bowstring was of swallow-wort, or bamboo-fibre, or sinew, or hemp, or of milk-sap tree, or until I know whether the shaft was from a wild or cultivated plant . . . or whether it was feathered from a vulture's wing or a heron's or a hawk's, or a peacock's, or a sithilahanu-bird's . . . or whether it was wrapped round with the sinew of an ox, or of a buffalo, or of a ruru-deer, or of a monkey . . . or until I know whether it was an ordinary arrow, or a razor arrow, or a vekanda, or an iron arrow, or a calf-tooth arrow, or one of a karavira lead." That man would die, Malunkyaputta, without knowing all this.

The Master then proceeded to his conclusion with amazing effectiveness and firm conviction:

It is not on the view that the world is eternal, Malunkyaputta, that a religious life depends; it is not on the view that the world is not eternal that a religious life depends. Whether the view is held that the world is eternal, or that the world is not eternal, there is still re-birth, there is old age, there is death, and grief, lamentation, suffering, sorrow, and despair, the destruction of which even in this life I announce. . . . Therefore, Malunkyaputta, consider as unexplained what I have not explained, and consider as explained what I have explained. And what, Malunkyaputta, have I not explained? Whether the world is eternal I have not explained . . . . And why, Malunkyaputta, have I not explained this? Because this, Malunkyaputta, is not useful, it is not concerned with the principle of a religious life, does not conduce to aversion, absence of passion, cessation, tranquillity, supernatural faculty, perfect knowledge, Nirvana, and therefore I have not explained it. And what, Malunkyaputta, have I explained? Suffering have I explained, the cause of suffering, the destruction of suffering, and the path that leads to the destruction of suffering have I explained. For this, Malunkyaputta, is useful, this is concerned with the principle of a religious life; this conduces to aversion, absence of passion, cessation, tranquillity, supernatural faculty, perfect knowledge, Nirvana, and therefore have I explained it. Therefore, Malunkyaputta, consider as unexplained what I have not explained, and consider as explained what I have explained.[1]

The parable ends with this note: "Thus spoke the Lord and with joy the elder Malunkyaputta applauded the words of the Lord." I would have, dear Elder, applauded the words of the Lord as much as you did were I there with you!

Dear Elder, you have asked many "whethers. . ." You might have been a philosopher-monk. But your Master, if I understand him correctly, pointed out to you *the real issue*, namely, while your intellect is asking such "pene-

1. Mircea Eliade, *From Primitives to Zen*, Collins, 1967, p. 570.

trating" inquiries, your very life is submerged deep in *unsatisfactoriness* (*dukkha*). Why do you, "the man shot by a poison arrow" (*indukkha*), engage in discourse ". . . until I know whether . . .?" Why do you ask "non-crisis" questions while you are yourself caught in crisis? How can you free yourself from the *primary* reality that "you are shot?" Don't you realize that while you are exhibiting your supreme quality of *homo sapiens* by asking these "metaphysical questions," your very existence is in misery and sick (*homo aeger*)? Why have you arranged some distance between your intellect and your existence? Don't you see how disastrous is this "some distance" to you personally? "That man would die, Malunkyaputta, without knowing all this!" Why will he die? Obvious! It is because he is, to use another image, discoursing on "how to dry himself while he is drowning!"

Dear Elder, this parable has left a deep impression upon me. I learned that what was really wrong with the man shot by a poison arrow was that he, in spite of the reality that poison was circulating in his body and destroying his life, kept his faculty of understanding apart from his dying existence. His life was in a critical condition, but his reasoning was sitting on a comfortable couch and asking a chain of not *useful* questions! This strange *distance* between existence and understanding is fatal because it prevents him from asking *useful* questions, the questions which are in accord with the "principle of religious life." That harmful distance is a harmful misdirection. His questions are directed to a *useless* subject!

Sincerely yours,

THE IDEAL OF THE *APATHEIA*-PERSON

What is the useful subject with which we should totally involve ourselves? It is *dukkha* (unsatisfactoriness, suffering). "Suffering have I explained, the cause of suffering, the destruction of suffering, and the path that leads to the destruction of suffering have I explained. For this, Malunkyaputta, is useful, this is concerned with the principle of a religious life." *Dukkha* is the theme of the Buddha's primary truth. "Whether the view is held that the world is eternal, or that the world is not eternal, there is still re-birth, there is old age, there is death, and grief, lamentation, suffering, sorrow and despair!" One may extend this saying by adding that ". . . whether the view is held that there is a Creator God who rules the history of humankind, the Incarnate God who was dead and risen for the sake of humankind, and in this Man *agape* is revealed to humankind . . . there is still re-birth, old age. . . ." John Baillie coined an amusing expression when he explained that character of *reality* as "that which is-ly is."[2] In spite of all "whethers . . ." the *dukkha* "is-ly is!" The Enlightened One realized the "is-ly is-ness" of *dukkha* and interpreted it with his penetrating insight. And he came to know the way for us to escape from *dukkha*. Let us listen to the heart of the

---

2. John Baillie, *The Sense of the Presence of God*, Oxford University Press, 1962, p. 32.

Buddhist doctrines and life, the Four Noble Truths, and the Eightfold Paths which explicate the *dukkha* which "is-ly is."

> What now, O monks, is the noble truth of *Suffering?* Birth is suffering, old age is suffering, death is suffering, sorrow, lamentation, pain, grief and despair are suffering.
>
> But what, O monks, is the noble truth of the *Origin* of suffering? It is that Craving which gives rise to fresh rebirth and, bound up with pleasure and lust, now here, now there, finds ever fresh delight. It is the Sensual Craving, Craving for Existence, Craving for Self-Annihilation.
>
> But what, O monks, is the noble truth of the *Extinction* of suffering? It is the complete fading away and extinction of this craving, its forsaking and giving up, liberation and detachment from it.
>
> But what, O monks, is the noble truth of the path leading to the extinction of suffering? It is the noble *Eightfold Path*: (i) right understanding, (ii) right thought, (iii) right speech, (iv) right bodily action, (v) right livelihood, (vi) right effort, (vii) right mindfulness, (viii) right concentration.[3]

The youth group of the Singapore Buddhist Union composed this song explaining the Four Noble Truths to young people today. They sing it with guitar and Chinese flute accompaniment.

> First Noble Truth
> Is Sorrow
> Be not mocked by the life ye prize
> Only its pains abide
> Its pleasure like the birds that fly
>
> Chorus: The Four Noble Truths
>   The Four Noble Truths.
>
> Ache of birth
> Ache of helpless days
> Ache of hot youth ache of manhood's prime
> Ache of chill years choking of death
> The babe is wise weepeth being born
>
> Second Noble Truth
> Sorrow's Cause
> What grief springs of itself?
> And springs not of desire?
> Passion's quick spark of fire

---

3. *Digha-Nikaya* 22 (Naha-Satipatthana-sutta).

Lust of things
Craving
Eager you cling to shadows and dreams
Sense-struck again the sodden self
Karma returns with new deceits

Third Noble Truth
Sorrow's Ceasing
Peace goes to those who conquer love of self
To tear the deep root passion
To still all our inward strife

Perfect Service
Duties done
Charity and soft speech
These riches shall not fade
Nor will any death dispraise

Fourth Noble Truth
Is the Way
Is open to all who seek
Plain to all feet to tread
Noble Eightfold Path goeth straight

My brothers
My sisters
Tread the Noble Eightfold Path
Suffer not and be at peace
Come to the lovelier verities
May all beings be well and happy

No one can become a Buddhist unless one is committed to this particular formulation of the primary truth of *dukkha*, and is at least sincerely trying to realize these Four Noble Truths in one's life.

"O Monks, when one's turban is ablaze or one's head is ablaze, what should be done?" The monks answered, "Lord, when one's turban is ablaze or head is ablaze, for the extinguishing thereof, one must put forth extra desire, extra effort, extra endeavour, extra impulse, extra mindfulness, extra attention." "Monks," rejoined the Buddha, "it is just such an extra desire, effort, endeavour, impulse, mindfulness and attention that one should put forth for the comprehension of the Four Noble Truths."[4]

---

4. *Kindred Sayings* V (Pali Text Society), p. 372.

The one with "extra desire, effort, endeavour, impulse, mindfulness and attention" trying to end one's *dukkha* is already in the *sotas* (stream), the stream of emancipation toward the ultimate emancipation in *nirvana*.

> Whenever, O monks, the noble disciple, according to reality has understood the arising and vanishing of these five faculties (feelings), as well as their enjoyment and misery, and the escape therefrom, then, it is said of this noble disciple that he has entered the Stream (*sotapanna*), for ever escaped the states of woe and is assured of final enlightenment.[5]

One enters into *sotas* from outside-*sotas*. Then, one gradually goes up the ladder of perfection toward the final state of the *arhat*-ship (*arhat*, worthy one). *Arhat*-ship comes at the end of a great spiritual odyssey from the state of outside-*sotas*.

> Mankind is attached to existence, is afflicted with existence, and even, moreover, rejoices in existence. Of what one rejoices in, that leads to fear. Of what one is afraid, that is miserable. Indeed one leads this holy life in order to escape completely from existence. I declare that all those ascetics and Holy Priests who proclaim release from existence through (the view of a permanent self-) existence all of them will not attain release from existence. Again I declare that all those ascetics and Holy Priests who proclaim release from existence through (the view of self-) annihilation, all of them will not attain release from existence. Truly, this suffering arises in dependence of (*kammic*) accumulations. If all attachment (by means of wisdom) is destroyed, (no further) suffering grows up. Look at this whole world in which the created beings are entangled (in the net) of ignorance. Though entirely trapped in existence, yet they rejoice in existence. For, whatever forms of existence there are, all of them, everywhere and in every respect, are changeable, miserable and subject to dissolution. Whoever perceives this truth with perfect wisdom according to reality, abandons thirst for existence and in (the view of self-) annihilation he is not interested. The complete destruction of thirst and the complete cessation of lust mean the realization of extinguishment (i.e. *Nibbana*). For such a monk who, freed from attachment, has become extinguished, there is no further re-existence (for him). He has over-powered and defeated the Evil One in the struggle. Such a one has escaped all (the various forms of) existence.[6]

The primary truth about humankind is that it "is attached to existence, is afflicted with existence, and even, moreover, rejoices in existence." The

---

5. *Samyutta-Nikaya* XLVIII.30.
6. *80 Inspiring Words of the Buddha. From the Udana* # 30, Bangkok, 1954.

aim of the "holy life" is "to escape all the various forms of existence." Why? "Whatever forms of existence there are, all of them, everywhere and in every respect, are changeable, miserable and subject to dissolution."

> We say that the Buddha discovered *lokuttaratnam* (the Truth that releases from the world). Therefore Buddhism is the teaching that one should cast off suffering, get beyond suffering, the one thing one can count on in the world, and so not create and bear suffering. . . . The mind that thus transcends the world is called *lokuttarachit*.[7]

The *arhat* is, then, an *apatheia*-person. The *arhat* must become apathetic to existence including oneself.

> When objects make contact with the eye, observe and identify them, and know what action has to be taken with whatever is seen. But do not permit like or dislike to arise.[8]

The one who does not "permit like or dislike to arise" is the ideal person. This ideal person is an *apatheia*-person. On the occasion of the Royal Ceremony at the Cremation of His Holiness the Late Patriarch, Somdech Phra Ariyavamsagatanana Nanodayamahathera in 1965, the Buddhist University in Bangkok published a book entitled *The Development of Insight*. This book urges us to eliminate the illusion of "I" by the development of the Buddhist insight.

> We never feel the sound as being "I." Therefore, the craving and wrong view do not exist in sound. For this reason, it is not necessary to be mindful of the sound. Whenever craving, conceit and wrong view exist, that is the place where we will have to eliminate them by mindfulness. Accordingly, we must be mindful of hearing when we hear. We must also know that hearing is a mental state, otherwise we mistake the hearing as "I" hear. We must be mindful of hearing so that we may eliminate the illusion of "I" or "Self" from the hearing. Hence it is of extreme importance to realize that when we hear or see, it is the mental state which hears or sees. Should we be aware only that we are now seeing or hearing, and do not realize that it is the mental state which is seeing or hearing, we will not be able to realize the true nature of phenomena. In other words, in order to realize nature clearly, when we see, we have to be mindful of that mental state which sees because the misunderstanding of the "I" exists there. We must be mindful until we know the truth, and we can eliminate the "I" concept.[9]

---

7. Buddhadasa Bhikku, *Buddhism in 20 Minutes*, a cyclostyled paper prepared and translated by Herbert Grether, 14 Pramuan Road, Bangkok.

8. Buddhadasa Bhikku, *Buddha Dhamma for Students*, p. 7, Sublime Life Mission, Bangkok, 1966.

9. Upasika Naeb Mahaniranonda, *The Development of Insight*, The Buddhist University, 1965, pp. 79f.

When a person says "I" hear or "I" see, that person is still "fettered." That person is a "*patheia*"-person who has not yet realized that it is not "I" but the simple function of "the mental state" that hears and sees. As long as there is "the illusion of 'I' or 'Self,'" we are not free from "*patheia*" or "I" and "Self," or to be precise, from "*patheia*" of the "illusion of I." "*Patheia*" has its home in the "illusion of I." "Mindfulness" and "insight" will emancipate us from "I" and thus from "I-*patheia*." "I" is the contents and subject of suffering. Mental states reacting "apathetically" to inside and outside happenings cannot produce suffering, since there is no attachment and involvement.

> We must understand that we do not take food because it tastes good, but in order to cure pain and satisfy hunger. When we take food to satisfy hunger, even though the food is not good, it will satisfy the hunger. Suppose we take food for the sake of its flavour without further consideration, if it is not good, then aversion will occur. On the other hand, if it is good, then greed will occur. This would mean that we are taking the food to encourage defilements. When food is good, greed, which is a craving or attachment, will occur. When it is not good, dissatisfaction or dislike will occur. We shall be unable to prevent defilements if we have this attitude. To eat without consideration is to create more cycles of birth and death, which is the endless continuation of suffering. Therefore, when we are applying the application of mindfulness as we are going to take food, we must understand the reason at each mouthful; so that when we are eating, it will be solely for the purpose of being free from suffering.[10]

"At each mouthful" one must be mindful to check the invasion of "I" into the mind. I eat simply "to cure and satisfy hunger!" Any other desire will allow "I" (the illusion) to invade and nest within us and concomitantly "*patheia*." Mindful indeed! It is not "a person" into which the "illusion of I" comes! It is an illusion of "I" into which the illusion of "I" comes! It is not really that "I" eat; rather the whole operation of eating is simply the curing of suffering and hunger! And not anything more! Birth and death must be understood as "*apatheia* events."

> And what is aging and dying? Whatever for this or that class of beings is aging, decrepitude, breaking up, hoariness, wrinkling of the skin, dwindling of the life span, over-ripeness of the sense-faculties: this is called aging. Whatever for this or that being in this or that class of beings is the falling and deceasing, the breaking, the disappearance, the mortality and dying, the passing away, the breaking of the *khan-dhas*, the laying down of the body; this is called dying. This is called aging and dying. And what is birth? Whatever for this or that being

---

10. Ibid., pp. 88f.

in this or that class of beings is the conception, the birth, the descent, the production, the appearance of the *khandhas,* the acquiring of the sensory fields: this is called birth.[11]

The persistent power that hinders the formation of this ideal *apatheia*-person is the concept of "I" and "My," as we have seen. Perhaps the most influential and controversial monk in the Kingdom, Venerable Buddhadasa Bhikkhu, writes how the illusion of "my" makes us fail to see the critical state of "being shot by a poison arrow:"

> Now it is usually proclaimed eloquently, also mistakenly and misleadingly, that birth, aging and death are suffering. But birth is *not* suffering, aging is *not* suffering, death is not suffering in a case where there is no grasping at "my" birth, "my" death. At the moment, we are grasping, regarding birth, aging, pain and death as "mine." If we don't grasp, they are not suffering; they are only bodily changes. The body changes thus, and we call it aging; the body changes thus, and we call it death. But we fail to see it as just bodily changes. We see it as actual birth, and what is more, we call it "my" birth, "my" aging, "my" death. This is a multiple delusion because "I" is a delusion to start with; so seeing a bodily change as "my" birth or "my" aging is yet a further delusion. We fail to see that these are simply bodily changes. Now just as soon as we do see these as just bodily changes, birth, aging and death disappear, and "I" disappears at the same time. There is no longer any "I;" and this condition is not suffering.[12]

The *arhat,* the ideal *apatheia*-person, is the man of thorough-going detachment from all involvements. *Arhat* literally means "worthy one" demonstrating "worthiness" in freedom from anger (*akkodhana*), freedom from pride (*anus-sada*), calm (*santo*), freedom from fear (*apetabheravo*), content (*santusito*), freedom from fettering ideas (*samyojaniyehi vippamutto*), does not worry (*na paritassati*), and is happy (*sukhin*).[13] The saving message of the Four Noble Truths may be, then, well expressed in short sentences from the *Dhammapada*:

> O Monk, bail out this boat (i.e. personality, made heavy by a leak)! When emptied, it will move on more swiftly. If you are empty of (cut down) lust and hatred, you will attain extinguishment.[14]

---

11. E. Conze (ed.), *Buddhist Texts through the Ages,* Harper Torch Books, 1964, p. 67.
12. *Buddha Dhamma for Students,* p. 61.
13. Rune Johansson, *The Psychology of Nirvana,* p. 124.
14. Bhadragaka, *The Dhammapada* # 369, *A Collection of Verses on the Doctrine of the Buddha,* Bangkok, 1952.

THE PRINCIPLE OF "HOMELESSNESS"

The "holy life" is life escaping from "all the various forms of existence." For the one who aspires to the ultimate emancipation from the cycle of suffering, life in the home constitutes a fundamental hindrance and temptation. Gautama named his son Rahula by saying, "An impediment (*rahu*) has been born; a fetter has arisen." Home means "home of impediments." One must "go forth" from home to homelessness, from the environment of impediment to the Stream (*sotas*).

> A den of strife is household life,
> And filled with toil and need;
> But free and high as the open sky
> Is the life the homeless lead.[15]

Leaving his home behind, he enters into the life of homelessness. Homelessness is different from nomadic life. The nomads carry their home with them. When they wander, their home wanders too. They do not reject the value of home. According to the *arhat*-orientation, however, home is an anti-value. Home-involvement and home-attachment make us fail to recognize the primary truth of our existence, the *dukkha*.

The arhatic homelessness brought forth the monastic order (*sangha*). The ones who belong to the *sangha* belong to it by negating home. At the center of the *sangha* life stand the 227 Injunctions safeguarding the principle of homelessness for the monks who are in the Stream. The first four Injunctions of the 227 are called "the Defeat." The punishment for the violation of any of the four would entail expulsion from the order (the state of homelessness) which is considered to be a defeat for the monk. The very first of the 227 Injunctions is "sexual intercourse." Sexual intercourse must be categorically rejected in the life of homelessness. Sexuality is a home principle, while asexuality is a homelessness principle. The monk must become asexual. Indeed, he must become neither male nor female, but the "third sex." Sexuality of the third kind, this specific form of asexuality, is congruous, of course, with the ideal of the *apatheia*. Injunction 9 is against a monk arranging a marriage. If he should arrange one, the punishment has to be determined by a formal meeting of the order. Injunction 11 prohibits "building a dwelling for oneself of which a donor is owner without the Order having designated the site." "Dwelling place," as with sexuality, carries special implications for the religion of homelessness. The one who steps out of home, steps out of the normal arrangement of dwelling. He moves into a "homeless dwelling." The monk, the third sex, must be specially careful when he walks through villages (the home-area, sexuality-area):

---

15. Narada Thera, *Buddhism in a Nutshell*, Colombo, 1959, p. 59.

Injunction 150: A monk should not move his hands and feet unnec-
cessarily when going through a village.

Injunction 151: A monk should not move his hands and feet unnecessarily when sitting in a village.

Injunction 152: A monk should keep his eyes lowered when going
through a village.

The monk walks with "his eyes lowered when going through a village"
because of his dedication to the principle of the supreme *arhat*-ship. "His
eyes lowered!" This is a symbolic saying. This "lowering" has the backing of
a great spiritual insight! The *apatheia* principle warns us not to let "each
mouthful" arouse any sense of aversion and greed. The principle of homelessness displays its genuine force when one becomes homeless in history,
that is to say, one "goes forth" from history to "ahistory" ("historylessness").
The homeless man must not feel either aversion or greed with regard to
history. He must not move his hands and feet unnecessarily in history since
he has rejected having a home in and of history. The principle of homelessness is thus not just leaving one's home and getting away from all kinds
of impediments, but it touches a deeper stratum of the *arhat*-ideal, namely,
keeping one's "eyes lowered" at history!

Dear Elder Malunkyaputta,

Let me write you just a brief note. Do you think I have understood the
main point of your Master correctly? I welcome any comment from you! I
think that the ideal of the *apatheia*-person in the "homeless" *sangha* ("keep
one's eyes lowered when going through a village") is the fundamental of
the good news of the *arhat*-ship. There may be many people who may be
called "apathetic." But we are not speaking of just "apathetic" persons. Our
discussion is specific. It is about the specific *apatheia*-person whose life is
defined by the insight of the Four Noble Truths. The *apatheia*-person is a
person of the Four Noble Truths.

How does this *apatheia* person who lives with "his eyes lowered" in homelessness fit in the story of the parable of the arrow? The *apatheia*-person (the
ideal "worthy" person, the *arhat*) is the one who pursues the "useful questions," not asking all kinds of useless "whethers . . ." This person immediately asks friends and relatives to pull out the "poison arrow," the poison
arrow of attachments in "the various forms of existence." And with "extra
desire, extra effort, extra endeavour, extra impulse, extra mindfulness,
extra attention" he has tried and succeeded in extinguishing the "blaze" in
his "turban or head." The strange "distance" between one's "understanding" and "existence" has been overcome since being able to distinguish the
difference between the "useful religious principle" and "useless religious
principle."

Dear Elder, let me write to you again.

THE "HOT" GOD

The Bible speaks of a God who is not *without passion*. God is not an *apatheia* God.

> Then Noah built an altar to the LORD, and took of every clean animal and of every clean bird, and offered burnt offerings on the altar. And when the LORD smelled the pleasing odour, the LORD said in his heart, "I will never again . . ." (Gen. 8:20,21).

Here we read a crude anthropomorphic presentation of God who "smelled the pleasing odour." God is not *arhatic* since God indicates that the smell is "pleasing." An *apatheia* God must be free from the pleasant or painful. From the arhatic point of view, this God needs development of insight!

> You shall not make yourself a graven image, or any likeness of any-thing that is in heaven above, or that is in the earth beneath, or that is in the water under the earth; you shall not bow down to them or serve them; for I the LORD your God am a jealous God, visiting the iniquity of the fathers upon the children to the third and fourth generation of those who hate me, but showing steadfast love to thousands of those who love me and keep my commandments (Exod. 20:4-6).

The second of the Ten Commandments introduces God as an *impassioned* (jealous) God. The reason for God's jealousy is that God has entered into a covenant relationship with Israel. God and Israel are to live in a specially close "attachment." If, therefore, Israel breaks this relationship and shows his love to anyone else, God becomes jealous. There is a covenant rela-tionship (attachment); *therefore* there is jealousy. The strong covenant-awareness of God produces a strong emotion, jealousy! A weak covenant-awareness will produce only the weak emotion of indifference.

God is, moreover, moved to wrath, as we have already seen in another context. God is not *akkadhana* (free from anger). But this does not mean that God is quick to anger.

> "The LORD, the LORD, a God merciful and gracious, slow to anger, and abounding in steadfast love and faithfulness . . ." (Exod. 34:5,6).

The "hot" God heats the cool outlook by placing it in the context of covenant relationship. The life in the covenant relationship is experienced basically not as decaying (direction toward "coolness"), but as healing and renewing (direction toward "hotness").

> Come, let us return to the LORD; for he has torn, that he may heal us; he has stricken, and he will bind us up. After two days he will revive

us; on the third day he will raise us up, that we may live before him. Let us know, let us press on to know the LORD; his going forth is sure as the dawn; he will come to us as the showers, as the spring rains that water the earth (Hos. 6:1-3).

At this point the decay-message and healing-message crash head-on. The healing-message is meaningful as long as it is based on the strength of the covenant-awareness. The covenant-awarness is not, in the tradition of Israel and the church, an ahistorical concept. To be precise, it is this covenant-awareness which has given sharp focus to history-awareness. Theologically speaking, *history is the experience of covenant.* The healing the Bible speaks about is related, directly or indirectly, to God's covenant relationship with Israel and the church.

The God who is engaged in history is the God who is concerned with the restoration of "I" in this history. As soon as history is looked upon as an illusion, the 'I' will be understood likewise as an illusion, and *vice versa.* The "*covenant* God" means the God engaged in history in order to restore the "I". The covenant God purposes not the elimination of "I" but the restoration and resurrection of "I." God is not *nirvana*-oriented, but is history-oriented;

> Thus says the LORD, your Redeemer, the Holy One of Israel: "I am the LORD your God, who teaches you to profit, who leads you in the way you should go. O that you had hearkened to my commandments! Then your peace would have been like a river, and your righteousness like the waves of the sea; your offspring would have been like the sand, and your descendants like its grains — their name would never be cut off or destroyed from before me." (Isa. 48:17-19).

God desires the increase of the people "before me" giving the commandments in order to accomplish the restoration of "I" and nations. "Before me" is the place where all these events of judgment and salvation take place. It is not "*before* nirvana." The ultimate human purpose must be in accord with the ultimate aim of God who is engaged in history.

> Woe to him who builds his house by unrighteousness, and his upper rooms by injustice; who makes his neighbour serve him for nothing, and does not give him his wages, who says, "I will build myself a great house with spacious upper rooms," and cut out windows for it, paneling it with cedar, and painting it with vermilion. Do you think you are a king because you compete in cedar? Did not your father eat and drink and do justice and righteousness? Then it was well with him. He judged the cause of the poor and needy; then it was well. Is not this to know me? says the LORD. But you have eyes and heart only for your dishonest gain, for shedding innocent blood, and for practising oppression and violence (Jer. 22:13-17).

Self-aggrandizement is not self-restoration. "Self" without the knowledge of the Lord is the lost self. It is a restoration of "I" but *not* "before me." "I" build a house with spacious upper rooms, windows and attractive panelling. But this "I" rejects the covenantal rule of God. God desires justice done in this history. The "I" of the "spacious upper rooms" is the "I" heading towards destruction and violence. "I" need restoration and it must be brought "before me." "I" is judged before God. God's judgment concentrates on the restoration, not the elimination, of "I."

In an understanding of the *arhat*-orientation the whole problem begins when "I" begin to think of *my* house, *my* "spacious upper rooms," *my* "cedar panelling." House, spacious upper rooms and cedar panelling, by themselves, have no anti-*arhat* values. But as soon as "*my*" comes in, the flood of "radical evil" flows in. The solution proposed by the *arhat*-orientation is the *panna*-ful (wisdom) insight that "I" is totally an illusion. If there is no "I," where is *my* house, *my* spacious upper rooms and *my* cedar panelling?

This is not, however, the solution proposed by the covenant God. The increase of "I" in the covenant relationship is a manifestation of the blessing of God. "I" is *not* an illusion. If "I" is an illusion, history is, as we have noted, an illusion and God who is engaged in illusion history is also an illusion. "I" "is-ly is." It is there. But it *wills* evil. It refuses to give proper wages. It despises the covenantal life with God. The solution does not lie in the elimination of "I," but in the redirection of *will*. "I am" does not create a problem. "I will" is the root from which evil derives. In the *arhat*-orientation, "I am" is the fundamental problem. To be precise, the *awareness* of "I am" is the source of all unsatisfactoriness. In the theological context of the covenant God, "I am" is not "unsatisfactory" to God. But "I will" becomes "unsatisfactory" to God since "I will" is no longer obedient to God.

The salvation of God increases "I am" and rectifies "I will." Listen to the following story from Mark:

> So they arrived at Bethsaida where a blind man was brought to him, with the earnest request that he should touch him. Jesus took the blind man's hand and led him outside the village. Then he moistened his eyes with saliva and putting his hands on him, asked, "Can you see at all?" The man looked up and said, "I can see people. They look like trees — only they are walking about." Then Jesus put his hands on his eyes once more and his sight came into focus, and he recovered and saw everything sharp and clear. And Jesus sent him off to his own house with the words, "Don't even go into the village" (8:22-26).

Jesus restores sight to the blind man. In the light of the *arhat*-orientation, the restoration of sight is only temporary salvation (*anicca*). As long as the illusion of "I" is there, whether one has sight or not does not essentially matter. In fact, when "I" is gone, then a human being is ultimately free from *both sight and blindness.* In the view of the *arhat*-orientation, to cure the blindness without eliminating "I" is a partial salvation! Jesus' question: "Can you see at all?" is a question which would provoke more "I" rather than effacing it!

"I can see people. They look like trees — only they are walking about." This man is living in the "wrong view" of "I" see. This misunderstanding of "I" see must have been something which Jesus should have healed! Indeed, all other healings will cause more troubles since the man has to become blind again some time! Whether Jesus restores the sight of the blind or not, "there is still rebirth, there is old age, there is death, and grief, lamentation, suffering, sorrow and despair!" in so far as there remains the illusion of "I." According to the *arhat*-orientation there will be no more rebirth, old age, death, grief, lamentation, suffering, sorrow, despair, and blindness for the *anatta* (no-self)!

Under these concepts, Jesus Christ lives with the wrong view. He even increases the wrong view. Every cure which Jesus effects only results in more persons living in "fettering ideas," since his cure reinstitutes the integrity of "I." Indeed, one may say in the light of the doctrine of *anatta*, Jesus Christ is the "arch wrong-viewer." He lives with a strong sense of "I see," "I hear," "I live," "I die," "I give," and "I love." "I" begins to say, "I see," "I hear," "I live," "I die," "I give," and "I love" as "I" when he is touched by the "I see," "I hear," "I live," "I die," "I give," and "I love" of Jesus Christ.

Master, I brought my son to you because he has a dumb spirit. Wherever he is, it gets hold of him, throws him down on the ground and there he foams at the mouth and grinds his teeth. It's simply wearing him out. I did speak to your disciples to get them to drive it out, but they hadn't the power to do it.

Jesus answered them, "Oh, what a faithless people you are! How long must I be with you, how long must I put up with you? Bring him here to me." So they brought the boy to him, and as soon as the spirit saw Jesus, it convulsed the boy, who fell to the ground and writhed there, foaming at the mouth. "How long has he been like this?" Jesus asked the father. "Ever since he was a child," he replied. "Again and again it has thrown him into the fire or into water to finish him off. But if you can do anything, please take pity on us and help us." "If you can do anything!" retorted Jesus. "Everything is possible to the man who believes." "I do believe," the boy's father burst out. "Help me to believe more!" When Jesus noticed that a crowd was rapidly gathering, he spoke sharply to the evil spirit, with the words, "I command you, deaf and dumb spirit, come out of this boy, and never go into him again!" The spirit gave a loud scream and after a dreadful convulsion left him. The boy lay there like a corpse, so that most of the bystanders said, "He is dead." But Jesus grasped his hands and lifted him up, and then he stood on his own feet. When he had gone home, Jesus' disciples asked him privately, "Why were we unable to drive it out?" "Nothing can drive out this kind of thing except prayer," replied Jesus (Mk. 9:17-29).

The father is beset with *dukkha*. His son is epileptic. What a heartache! It may mitigate the father's torment if he can transcend the sound of "foaming at the mouth and grinding of the teeth" as sounds simply coming into his "mental state." But the truth is that the sounds wear on both his son and himself! So the father does not know what to do. "I" brought my son to you! "I" want you to restore "I" to my poor epileptic son. Can he have "I" once more? "Bring him here to *me*," commands Jesus. Then, Jesus studies the history of the disintegration of "I" in this boy. "Ever since he was a child!" Yes, but how about your "I?" How should I restore "I" to your son without doing the same to you? Your "I" is there! "I" see it plainly! But your "I" must say "I" believe! I do not desire to impoverish your "I" in my act of integration of the "I" of your son. In all occasions I want to effect more integration of "I" by the power of the "finger of God" (Lk. 11:20). I want to spark your epileptic "I" by the presence and power of my own "I."

This implies nothing less than resurrection experience: ". . . bystanders said, 'He is dead.' But Jesus took his hands and lifted him up, and then he stood on his own feet." In truth, it is not just a restoration of "I" that was effected. It is reintegration, sanctification, and resurrection of "I" which took place in the presence of Jesus Christ. Resurrection is the subject of prayer. Only God can execute the marvel of "he stood on his own feet."

Then God is the arch wrong-viewer! God tries to effect an extreme opposite of *anatta*, the *resurrection of self*! Is there anything any more diametrically opposed to the resurrection of self than *anatta*?

At the point of the reintegration of this epileptic boy and the resurrection of Jesus Christ, *arhat*-orientation finds the extreme opposite to itself. Chaos and darkness are overcome. A new creation takes place. Jesus' hand is upon the man's blind eyes. That hand restores sight. It is a manifestation of God's covenantal love to us. Our "unsatisfactoriness" to God has been overcome. In Christ, we began to see the glory of God, not as the people who aspire to reach beyond history, but as those who live in history. The crucifixion took place in history. And precisely there we see God's covenantal triumph!

HEATING THE COOL IDEALS OF *DUKKHA, ANICCA,* AND *ANATTA*

The *arhat*-ideal is radically different from the spirituality expressed in the lives of the people of Israel (the Old Testament) and of the church (the New Testament). God rules history. God's direction is not *away from* history (detachment — "eyes lowered"), but *toward* history (attachment — "I have seen the affliction of my people who are in Egypt"). Perhaps this is the basic contrast between Theravada Buddhism and the Judaeo-Christian faith: the two histories, the two eyes.

In order to study the theological significance of this encounter, we may be helped by the covenant read to Israel at the time of Josiah's reformation.

> For you are a people holy to the LORD your God; the LORD your God has chosen you to be a people for his own possession, out of all the peoples that are on the face of the earth. It was not because you were more in number than any other people that the LORD set his love upon you and chose you, for you were the fewest of all peoples; but it is because the LORD loves you, and is keeping the oath which he swore to your fathers, that the LORD has brought you out with a mighty hand, and redeemed you from the house of bondage, from the hand of Pharaoh king of Egypt (Deut. 7:6-8).

God saved the nation, "the fewest of all peoples," from the oppression of Egypt. This is the foundation of the faith of Israel. Israel experienced this. Her God experienced this. Israel experienced it as the one who is saved and God experienced it as the One who saved "with a mighty hand." Israel, "the fewest of all peoples," is a stubborn people (Exod. 32:7-9). They are, as it were, not "worthy ones." They are not really in the *sotas* of salvation and they lack the *arhatic* concentration and dedication.

> Remember and do not forget how you provoked the LORD your God to wrath in the wilderness; from the day you came out of the land of Egypt, until you came to this place, you have been rebellious against the LORD (Deut. 9:7).

Israel is "unsatisfactory" (*dukkha*) to God. This is God's experience of them. Israel's devotion to God is "transitory" and "impermanent" (*anicca*):

> What shall I do with you, O Ephraim? What shall I do with you, O Judah? Your love is like a morning cloud, like the dew that goes early away (Hos. 6:4).

They destroyed themselves (*anatta*) by rebelling against their God:

> I sent among you a pestilence after the manner of Egypt; I slew your young men with the sword; I carried away your horses; and I made the stench of your camp go up into your nostrils; yet you did not return to me, says the LORD (Amos 4:10).

In spite of Israel's "unsatisfactoriness," "transitoriness," and "self-destruction," God remains in a saving covenant with her.

> I will not execute my fierce anger, I will not again destroy Ephraim; for I am God and not man, the Holy One in your midst, and I will not come to destroy (Hos. 11:9).

This is what is meant when it is said that God does not go away from history, but engages in history. God's faithfulness is faithfulness directed into history, even though that history is full of "unsatisfactoriness," "transitoriness," and "self-devastation" as represented by the covenant people, Israel. God "will not come to destroy" the "unworthy ones." Viewed from the side of God's experience of history, humankind is marked by *dukkha, anicca,* and *anatta.* It is to God *dukkha, anicca,* and *anatta.* This theological context changes the meaning of these three marks of humankind radically. *Dukkha* does not simply mean "unsatisfactoriness" of life. It signifies specifically humankind's unsatisfactory commitment and devotion to God. *Anicca,* in the same way, does not mean humankind's realization of its existence as impermanent and transitory. It means that humankind breaks its covenant relationship with God through its changeable and transitory devotion to God. The doctrine of *anatta,* which inspires a person to eliminate "I," the source of all personal troubles, becomes a useful indicator that when the person rejects God's covenantal faithfulness, he or she moves toward destruction and the elimination of oneself. The three basic marks of humankind illuminated by the Enlightened One thus receive new meaning when they are placed in the context of the life of the "fewest of all peoples" God has chosen, this strange nation called Israel. The depth-psychological analysis of humankind given by the Buddha is now historicized. The agent of this historicization is God who is neither *dukkha,* nor *anicca,* nor *anatta.*

> Turn to me and be saved, all the ends of the earth! For I am God, and there is no other. By myself I have sworn, from my mouth has gone forth in righteousness a word that shall not return (Isa. 45:22-23).

When *dukkha, anicca,* and *anatta* are placed, as marks of humankind in the covenant relationship with God, they are historicized. In this theological perspective of God's experience of history — in the context of "turn to me and be saved, all the ends of the earth" — the insight of the Buddha and the message of Israel encounter one another. This point is the point of historicization. "Man is shot by a poisonous arrow" must now be understood in the concept of the broken covenant relationship. When it is so taken up, the incident of wounding by a poisonous arrow will become "useful" for human salvation. That strange "distance" between thought and existence is not, indeed, a useful distance. But that distance must be erased not by the spiritual energy seeking *nirvana,* but by the spirit of engagement in history. The distance must be removed by the principle of "attachment" to history, not by the principle of "detachment" from history. The poison is circulating! The situation is urgent. Urgency to be free from history and urgency to be involved in history are two different kinds of urgencies. The message of Israel is that "urgency" is a history-concept. Urgency can be truly what it is when it is considered within the live relationship of "covenant."

Historicization here, then, means to *bring* the profound insights of the Enlightened One to Israel's experience of history.

This special "bringing," the Hebraization of the Buddha's teaching, is significant in that it will help us to see the radical difference between "detachment" from history and "attachment" to history. And while it engages in this theological operation, it will clarify also the centrality of "God in history," who is the Lord over all doctrines, *dukkha*, *anicca*, and *anatta*, by the power of God's presence and work in history. The strongly historical God can make use of all weakly historical as well as ahistorical thoughts, convictions, and enlightenments. But the reverse is hardly a possibility.

Then God is the One who gives meaning to all people who live in history. God does not reject *dukkha*, *anicca*, and *anatta* but historicizes them by God's historical covenant-relationship. The new meaning to *dukkha*, *anicca*, and *anatta* is to interpret these essential marks of human life as the factors contributing to the elucidation of God who is involved in history. Beyond-history and ahistorical concepts are now placed in the this-history context of God's covenant-relationship. This must be the starting point for our theological response to the *arhat*-orientation. And this *placing does not produce* syncretism. It must be, rather, understood as *participation* of the insights of the Buddha in the Christian understanding of history, namely, that "history is experienced and ruled by the covenant God."

The bringing of *dukkha*, *anicca*, and *anatta* to the spirituality of Israel is called here Hebraization. Before we proceed further, I must make two brief comments on Hebraization.

(1) Hebraization in this context consists of injecting the covenant concept into the Thai indigenous spiritual and religious concepts. In short, Hebraization is "covenantization." There are all kinds of covenants. But here we are speaking of the specific kind of covenant experienced by the people of Israel. Israel's covenant-life is unique in history. It is a theological experience of faith and unfaith, gathering and scattering, salvation and destruction, yet all under guidance of God who rules her history and the world's. Our primary target is to bring the historical experience of the covenant-life of this "fewest of all peoples" to the *dukkha*, *anicca*, and *anatta* concepts, since this is the greatest message of Israel to the Thai people today. And within this context of the appreciation of Israel's experience of history, we are invited to evolve further theological response to the *arhat*-orientation. Our theological response cannot be based on Japanization or Indianization or Filipinization of *dukkha*, *anicca*, and *anatta*. Theological response begins when we bring *dukkha*, *anicca*, and *anatta* to *Israel's* experience of covenant life.

(2) Japanization of *dukkha*, *anicca*, and *anatta* would invite fewer frictions than Hebraization of them. The bringing of *dukkha*, *anicca*, and *anatta* to Japanese spirituality would not occasion radical reversal of the original intentions and message of these three doctrines. It is because the

spiritual and cultural context in which the two live are basically the same. It is like, to use an image, the movement of a fish from salt water to salt water. The fish may notice some unfamiliar scenes and perhaps difference in water temperature, but basically the environment is the same. It is salt water. Without special difficulty fish can live in the new water. But when a fish moves from salt water to fresh water, it immediately realizes the basic (vital) difference in its surroundings. The change is immense. This is what happens when *dukkha, anicca,* and *anatta* concepts are brought to the history of Israel's covenant life. The context is basically unfamiliar and even threatening. It is not a smooth transition.

The fish which lived in the salt water (the thought-world of "detachment") is now laved in the fresh water (the thought-world of "attachment"). When the principle of detachment is embraced by the principle of attachment, the former will inevitably be "altered." But this special "alteration" is a theologically valuable "alteration." *Dukkha, anicca,* and *anatta,* by themselves, contain high spiritual values. The "altered" *dukkha, anicca,* and *anatta* yield tremendous theological value for the people of Thailand. Insights of the Enlightened One and the theology of the covenant God are mutually related in a paradoxical way. The former contradicts the latter, but simultaneously, the former participates in the latter by supplying the valuable raw material without which theological values cannot be established for the people of the thought-world of detachment. In a similar way, theological covenant-awareness rejects the Buddhist doctrines, but at the same time, it theologizes them and thus accepts them.

Dear Elder Malunkyaputta,

I am afraid that I have involved you in a discussion very unfamiliar to you! Pardon me. It has been more a discussion with myself, a monologue. I do not hesitate at all in showing my sincere respect to the Buddha. He was one of the greatest sages that humankind ever produced. I listen to him. I want, then, to see how I can theologically historicize him. Yes. You are right. This business of what I call "theological historicization" (what a monstrous expression!) is *my* concern and not yours. For me, what the Buddha said will be tremendously significant if I place it, yes, all of it, in the context of the life of that strange (and insignificant) people called Israel. I am not speaking of the Israel of today. The biblical Israel is the Israel that attracts so much of my attention. I do not want to ignore the words of wisdom of your Master. I try, instead, to place it in my theological existential context of thinking — the covenant-relationship between God and Israel (and the church).

My sincere thanks to you for opening up my discussion by that wonderful parable. My God is (to say this is pretty hot already! isn't it!?) a "hot" God! This hot God cannot be approached by way of "whethers . . ." God will burn all the "whethers. . ." God burns them, not by the principle of detachment, but by that of attachment! It is a creative and life-giving attachment! (How strange this must sound to you!) I have an interesting and special story to tell you on this point. That is the story of someone who came, chronologically speaking, after you — Jesus of Nazareth. But that has to wait for the moment.

"Let the poison be pulled out immediately. The situation is that of emergency! Speculations must go out the window!" This great *spirit* of the parable must be deeply appreciated by all of us. In my case this sense of urgency has a special message since I historicize this spirit of urgency *and* the contents of urgency by placing them in the context of specific historical urgency. The basis which enables me to do this placing is that God "warms" the cool person not by rejecting, but by accepting human *dukkha, anicca,* and *anatta.*

Sincerely yours,

CHAPTER 13

Apostle James in Thailand

- Apostle James! You have a special appeal to the people of Thailand.
- Your religion is *cool* yet *hot*! Hot yet cool! This is tremendously accommodating!

Welcome! Welcome Apostle James to this wonderful country of Thailand! How wonderful to see you here! You look very well. Tell me, how was your trip from Jerusalem? We are very happy to receive you here in the "City of Angels" (*Krungthep* — Bangkok).

Yes, Apostle, these are Buddhist monks. This is the country of Buddhism. Bangkok, the capital of Thailand since 1782, has dozens of great Buddhist temples, such as Wat Benjamabopit (Marble temple) and Wat Peca Keo where the Emerda Buddha is. Right. You have flown into the heart of *Buddha-dom*. The headquarters of the World Buddhist Fellowship is here in Bangkok. The King? Yes. The King of the Kingdom of Thailand is constitutionally defined to be a Buddhist. Theravada Buddhism has given so much to the people of Thailand during the last 700 years. I am quite impressed how deeply the doctrine of the Buddha is venerated among the ordinary people here.

Well, since you ask me — who am I to tell you about Buddhism? — let me say a few words about Buddhism in Thailand. Buddhism is a "cool" religion. One of the basic beliefs of Thai Buddhism is that "to be *cool* is better than to be *hot*." Perhaps I may go further and say that "to be cool" is salvation, and "to be hot" is damnation. "Cool" and "hot" here, of course, are not said in terms of a thermometer. It is about the "cool heart" and "hot heart." Is your heart cool!? Don't get it heated up!

How does a person prepare his or her heart to be cooled? By detachment! When one is "attached," then one's heart warms up and becomes hot. The important point is that when the Buddha spoke of detachment, he was not speaking of the ordinary kind of detachment, but a very radical one. For instance, detachment from oneself! Now I am a person called Koyama. Koyama must not attach himself to the idea of the person called Koyama. The idea of the personality is an illusion. Free yourself from this incorrigible and deep-rooted illusion of personality. Yes, indeed, it is a very thorough-going doctrine! I am sure that this must be indeed the way to achieve the "cool heart" if one is to be successful.

Yes, Apostle, you ask me what we (I am speaking for the people of Thailand) think of your letter? We find it very interesting. We feel in a certain way quite at home with the spirit of your letter. Your letter is short and precise. It is practical and picturesque. You are very good in the use of picture-language . . . "the one who doubts is like a wave of the sea . . .;" "the one who does not practice what he hears is like one who observes his natural face in a mirror . . .;" "the tongue boasts of great things. It is like a very small rudder that controls the big ship" . . .; "a person's life is like a mist that appears for a little time and then vanishes;" and so on. These images remain with us. Actually, we forget some important parts of your discussions in the letter, but these mental pictures are very much with us. We like your picture-language!

You are wondering why I say that "we feel, in a certain way, quite at home with the spirit of your letter." Well, let me tell you that — I hope that this will not surprise you — the letter sounds to us like a "cool" letter. You speak of the value of the "cool heart," which is quite readily understandable to us. This is, briefly, why we find your letter specially helpful and meaningful to us in Thailand. I notice you are surprised! Yes, I know when you were writing the letter, you were not thinking of us in the Kingdom of Thailand. But the letter is, so far as we are concerned, a big hit!

You ask what is it in your letter that made us think you are a "cool" Apostle. Let me try to tell you about the *cool elements* in your letter. "The rich will pass away like the bloom of a wild plant. The sun rises with its blazing heat and burns the plant; its bloom falls off, and its beauty is destroyed. In the same way the rich man will be destroyed while busy conducting his affairs" (1:10-11).

> Now, you rich people, listen to me! Weep and wail over the miseries that are coming upon you! Your riches have rotted away, and your clothes have been eaten by moths. Your gold and silver are covered with rust, and this rust will be a witness against you, and eat up your flesh like fire (5:1-3).

This, Apostle, is the basic sentiment in Thai religious life. All decays! All is transient! When one realizes the philosophy of "all decays," then one will learn the high value of detachment and begin to walk in the path leading to tranquility, coolness itself. Since this comes almost at the beginning and at the end of your letter, we feel close to you and interested to study further your letter. Then, you say, "A person is tempted when he is drawn away and trapped by his own evil desire" (1:14). Right! Indeed! This is exactly what we understand. One's *own* evil desire! In our religious life, we do not meddle with someone else's concern. We look at ourselves, particularly our own evil *desire* which is the cause of producing within us a most undesirable "hot heart." The "hot heart" comes from "evil desire!" Agreed! This is the message of our own "cool Buddhism." But what makes us more at home with you is what comes immediately after this "evil desire." You continue that "his evil desire conceives and gives birth to sin; and sin, when it is full-grown, gives birth to death" (1:15). This "chain reaction!" This "cool" chain reaction! This is what we like so much. There is, deep in our Thai hearts, a firm faith in the operation of this chain reaction from evil desire to death. It is a cool objectivity that works here and produces death. The chain reaction is not "hot," it is "cool." It does not need a radiator to cool off. The engine of its mechanism does not produce heat at all! It is an inevitable automatic arrangement. There is no supernatural or subnatural somebody to interfere in the process. "When it is full-grown" — You said it! This inevitable process of A producing B, B producing C, C producing D . . . is our Thai "process theology" of cool religion. The logic here is the same as *tham di dai di, tham chua dai chua* (if you do good, you will reap good, if you do wrong, you will reap wrong). Then we find you to say that God "does not change, nor does he cause darkness by turning" (1:17). Whoever the God is, "he does not change" strikes the right tune to us. All decays. All changes. All passes away. That there is someone who is *detached* from that which decays, changes, and passes away is good news! It is the good news of detachment. He or she does not change when he or she is detached from the changeables. We feel at home with this doctrine! This God, then, must be a cool God. God who "does not change" means God who "does not heat up." Isn't this true? Apostle, one after another, we feel you are speaking to our deep religious sentiment. You are a marvelous preacher! Please let me go ahead with this study of "cool elements" in your letter.

"Everyone must be quick to listen, but slow to speak, and slow to become angry" (1:19), you write. We like this word "slow." Everything around us is becoming rapid and fast. We are getting more and more impatient. Impatience breeds anger, of course. And anger is a state of hot heart. Be slow. Take time. There is no rush. That is the way to keep your heart "cool." This simple one word "slow" reminds us of a well-known Buddhist tradition, a very interesting one:

> Suppose, O Monks, there was a huge rock of one solid mass, one mile long, one mile wide, one mile high, without split or flaw. And at the end of every hundred years a man should come and rub against it once with a silken cloth. Then that huge rock would wear off and disappear quicker than a world-period, i.e. *kappa*.

What a long time a *kappa* is! We don't bother to know what it is which is measured by the unit of *kappa*. All we know is that it has something to do with life in the *Deva* planes. But this image of "every hundred years one rubs with a silken cloth" is consciously or unconsciously with us. We appreciate this "slow" movement and thus unhurried "long time." When, Apostle, you say "slow to anger," the image of *kappa* comes to us. We do have, may we say, a "metaphysical basis" to be "slow" and "unhurried."

Then, Apostle, you say, "Man's anger does not help to achieve God's righteous purposes." Here is the reason why "hot mind" (anger) is something terribly undesirable in that it does not contribute to what God intends to do for humankind in a concrete situation. Human "hot temper" will frustrate the work of God in history! I see the point. Indeed, Apostle, often one's "hot mind" does not achieve the righteous purpose of God, but, at the same time, Apostle, may I ask if his or her "cool mind" will achieve the righteous purpose of God? Pardon me, Apostle, I wonder if you are *too* "cool" here. As I understand the Old Testament, the prophets are all "hot," the first being Moses who came down from the Holy Mountain of God with "anger burning hot" (Exod. 32:19)! Jeremiah was an "angry man" who made his people angry toward him. Amos was a man of super-anger. He blasted against nations! So, Apostle, I have difficulty in understanding fully what you mean. But, of course, I would understand if you would say that a certain *kind* of "anger does not help to achieve God's righteous purposes." That is quite true. In general, Apostle, we feel that you are, at this specific point, very close to the Thai concept of coolness: "Whatever the situation is, *be cool*, don't get excited and heated up!"

"Bridle your tongue" (1:26), your letter says to us. Right indeed! The tongue "heats up" so easily. The man or woman with a "hot tongue" does not know the way to peace, *nirvana*. Think of a ship: big as it is, and driven by such strong winds, it can be steered by a very small rudder, and goes wherever the pilot wants it to go. "This is how it is with the tongue: small as it is, it can boast about great things" (3:4,5). The wise person knows how to bridle the tongue. If person has a "cool tongue," one is saved! The Buddha, the Enlightened One, said the same thing:

> Monks, if while the monk is attending to the thought-function and form of those thoughts, there still arise evil unskilled thoughts associated with desire and associated with aversion and associated with confusion, monks, that monk, his teeth clenched, his tongue pressed against his palate, should by his mind subdue, restrain and dominate the mind.[1]

"His tongue pressed against his palate" is not a "cool" situation. "Pressed" conveys a sense of emergency and a "hot" situation. But by pressing his tongue against his palate, the monk must *subdue* "heat," "restrain and dominate the mind." This is the way to reach the "kingdom of coolness." Then

---

1. I. B. Horner (ed.), *The Middle-Length Sayings*, Vol.1, Luzac, 1967, p.155.

you continue and say something which strikes us with a special force: the tongue sets "on fire the cycle of life" (*watta heeng chivit* in Thai, precisely, "the wheel of birth," 3:6)! This is our basic principle by which we understand our life. Life circles. Our previous life, present life, and future life are in the same wheel circling and circling. Apostle, where did you get this idea (*ton trochon tes geneseos*)? Did you get it from the Buddhist canon? Apostle, are you here borrowing the Stoic ideas concerning different aeons of the world? They spoke about the destruction of the universe in fire. The tongue, a tiny member of our body, can become an instrument to bring doom to the universe. But the point we are interested in is, of course, your *courage* (?) to use this characteristic phraseology, "the wheel of birth." Are you agreeing with the concept of "the wheel of birth?" Or are you just using this idea in order to communicate the seriousness of a poisoned tongue? I think you are just using it because it is very understandable to your audience which is influenced by the Stoic cosmology. Am I right? It is very interesting that the Stoic "wheel" happens to be similar to the Buddhistic "wheel." So when you are courageous enough to use the phraseology, you, without realizing it, communicate directly to us Thai! The "hot tongue" heats up even the cool universe to conflagration! We understand this, Apostle!

"Where do all the fights and quarrels among you come from? They come from your passions, which are constantly fighting within your bodies" (4:1). Passion, "hot" passion (*tanha*), is the source of all "fights and quarrels." Passion is the zeal for attachment. It is the opposite of detachment. "I want more . . . I want more . . ." — this is passion. Detachment and coolness eliminate "fights and quarrels." Then you put your "detachment theology" in a nutshell: "Don't you know that to be the world's friend means to be God's enemy?" What a strong statement! This is as *radical* as "free yourself from the illusion of I." But we feel we can understand your extreme position because actually it will lead us to the possession of a cool heart.

> If you regard this world as (fleeting as) a bubble or a mirage, then the King of Death cannot seize you (any more). Come! Look at this world as a beautiful royal chariot wherein foolish men are fascinated. But the mind of wise men is not bound to it. . . . More excellent than the glory of an emperor, more excellent than the glory of a universal ruler is the fruit of "Entering the Stream" (which leads to complete extinguishment).[2]

Understand the world through wisdom! But do not attach yourself to the world. Do not cultivate friendship with "a bubble, a mirage, a beautiful royal chariot!" By making yourself attached to the world you will lose sight of the glory more excellent than all glories put together, the glory of "extinguishment" ("perfect coolness")!

---

2. *The Dhammapada*, #170, 171, 178.

Apostle, perhaps I can go still further. But I would like to stop here for the moment. I wonder if you now have some idea why your letter occupies a special place for the people of Thailand. Your message is "cool!"

You ask me if this is the *whole* story of your letter? Well, Apostle, you are right. This is not the whole message of the letter. Indeed, your letter has a very strange quality. It is, as I have told you, cool. Yes, it is cool. But it is a "cool" *coexisting* with "hot." The story gets cooler and cooler *in order* to get hot! Apostle, this is the reason why your letter is not only very understandable but also *fascinating*. What is more fascinating than a story "cool" and "hot," yet not lukewarm? A story in which "detachment" is attached to "attachment?" This is the way we find your letter. Well, Apostle, let me try to elaborate a little on this. We are specially grateful for this unique quality of your letter.

When we read your introduction, "James, a servant of God and of the Lord Jesus Christ" (1:1), we feel, of course, that this letter is heading for the "hot" religion. Servant of God! — this implies, basically, that you are servant to someone other than yourself. Our uneasiness about this is that if this someone to whom you are a "servant" happens to be "hot," how can you be "cool?" Is the combination of "hot" master and "cool" servant possible? Furthermore, we notice that you do not say "someone," you say "God" and "Lord Jesus Christ," don't you? God is not just someone. God is a person. We know that "person" is a "hot" concept. *Dharma* is a "cool" concept. *Dharma* exists and works with "cool objectivity" and makes all things "cool." But a "person" is unpredictable and changeable. A "person" lives in "hot subjectivity." A "person" emanates all kinds of undesirable heat!

We are persons. We know that. But we are careful about our "personhood" since it may generate heat. Since God is a person, a human related to this person is in danger of heating up or becoming "defrosted."

"But if any of you lacks wisdom, he should pray to God, who will give it to him; for God gives generously and graciously to all" (1:5). We humbly realize that we lack "wisdom" (*panna*). This realization is a decisive step toward the "cool heart." So far you are cool. But you bring in *God* here. This, we feel, is a step toward the "hot heart." We understand that wisdom is something self-generated and self-enlightened. You say that we must ask God for it. Can we be sure that we will get the *right kind* of wisdom from God, the kind we want? The wisdom to make a cool heart within us? We do not feel at ease at this point. Self-generated wisdom is "understandable" wisdom to us. It comes from us. But your suggestion involves a risk. Risk is a "hot" situation. Will you be kind enough to say that the kind of wisdom that comes from God is similar to the wisdom that is self-generated? Then we would be on "cool" ground. But I notice that you do not say this in your letter. So here, just as we have rejoiced in your message on *panna* and are made to feel at home, we are thrown out into the world of "hot risk!"

"My brothers! In your life as believers in our Lord Jesus Christ, the Lord of glory, you must never treat people in different ways because of their outward appearance" (2:1). Show no partiality! We respond immediately that *dharma* is impartial! If *dharma* is partial, then *dharma* becomes a problem for us. But your basis of impartiality is not *dharma*, but faith in "our Lord Jesus Christ, the Lord of glory." In other words, our impartiality, according to your view, must be based on personal commitment to Person. What a difficult assignment! But, certainly, this gives us a new insight into our idea of community life.

> Does anyone think he is a religious man? If he does not control his tongue, his religion is worthless and he deceives himself. This is what God the Father considers to be pure and genuine religion: to take care of orphans and widows in their suffering, and to keep oneself from being corrupted by the world (1:26,27).

If a man has a "hot" tongue, his "God-fearing" (religion) is useless. The genuine religion is to take care of one's neighbors who are in need. It is practice, *doing*, that is the life of religion. Religion is not just a matter of controlling the tongue, it has to do with "orphans," "widows," and some definite attitude toward the world. Religion is then *involvement* in the matters relating to the marginal people, "orphans" and "widows," but in the very involvement one must be not corrupted by the world. One may avoid corruption by the world by living at a distance from the world. But this is not, I understand, Apostle, what you are talking about. You are saying that one should get involved in the world, primarily with orphans and widows. Then, one is free from "being corrupted by the world." The reason is that in this case the involvement with the world is the very point of God-fearing. Thus, perhaps, one can speak of the primacy of attachment — provided it is the God-fearing attachment — which contains within itself a special kind of detachment, a detachment not from the world, but from the corrupting influence of the world. Thank you!

PART IV

Interpreting the Christian Life

CHAPTER 14

In Search of a "Personality"
of Theology in Asia

- Abraham's going-out is a great symbol, for the greatest going-out took place for us in Jesus Christ.
- Why is the word "cross" the center of the good news of God? The cosmic rule emanates from the "prince of glory (who) died on the cross!"
- Apostolic life is the life of "the scum of the earth, the dregs of humanity" and the cast-out life!
- In our Asian "kidneys" (the most secret stirrings of the soul were thought of as resident within the kidneys in the Old Testament), we must learn to appreciate the theology of the cross.

Jesus heard that they had cast him out, and having found him he said, "Do you believe in the Son of man?" He answered, "And who is he, sir, that I may believe in him?" Jesus said to him, "You have seen him, and it is he who speaks to you." He said, "Lord, I believe;" and he worshipped him. Jesus said, "For judgment I came into this world, that those who do not see may see, and that those who see may become blind." Some of the Pharisees near him heard this, and they said to him, "Are we also blind?" Jesus said to them, "If you were blind, you would have no guilt; but now that you say, 'We see,' your guilt remains" (Jn. 9:35-41).

A man was blind from his birth. What a darkness! Jesus, the "True Light" (Jn. 1:9; 8:12; 12:46), saw him. "He spat on the ground and made clay of the spittle and anointed the man's eyes with the clay" (v.6). With this simple sacrament, he said to the blind man, "Go, wash in the pool of Siloam (which means sent)" (v.7). The blind man followed Jesus' instruction and received — experienced — his sight. The light instantly flooded his body and soul. He was emancipated from the imprisonment of hopeless darkness by the touch of Jesus (Matt. 11:4-6). The messianic good news prophesied by Isaiah has been realized! His experience of the new light and new life is, however, immediately challenged by another group, one which is against the coming reality of the gospel. The man who had just been made "free" by the one whose fingers are the fingers of God (Lk. 11:20) was now *cast out* (*exebalon* — violently pushed out, thrown out!) of the very community in which he was reared and to which he belonged. "Theologians" cast him out! They threw out the man with whom Jesus became neighbor (Lk. 10:36, 37). The man's chief offense was that he bore witness that he was given new life by "someone" other than Moses, whom, the religious authority and theologians say, "we know" (v.29). But "this man" is "a sinner" (v.24) and "we do not know where he comes from" (v.29)! Besides, "he does not keep the sabbath" (v.16)!

Thus Jesus, God's good news itself, was judged to be a "sinner" and a nobody. When *Christ the Incognito* comes to "theologians," he becomes a stumbling block! The one who was thrown out, however, found the one who had been cast out. The two *incognitos*, as it were, met in order to reveal the coming of good news and the effect of the good news to all the world. At this moment of encounter between the healer and the healed, the emancipator and the emancipated, good news himself and the recipient of good news, the former pronounced judgment and hope on the world. Remember, it took place *outside* the great stream of religious practice and theological tradition of the people. Its theological background was "being cast out!" This "outside" is not an ordinary "outside." Its quality can only be *christologically* defined.

There is a profoundly disturbing dimension in the biblical proclamation that God, in God's saving rule of history, let "being thrown out," "being pushed out," "being edged out," and "being rejected" of some (election!) take place for the many (Matt. 20:28; Mk. 10:45; I Tim. 2:6). The amazing thing is that this "arrangement" belongs to the heart of God's salvation history (reconciliation history), and it is in this way that God will "unite all things in him, things in heaven and things on earth" (Eph. 1:10).

I wish to speak on two critical events in the life of the biblical Israel in order to prepare us to meet *Jesus Christ, the one cast out* for our sake.

First, the biblical narrative on primeval history and the call of Abraham: in this we see the salvation-significance *for many* ("nations" — *goyyim*) of the *man* who "went *out*, not knowing where he was to go" (Heb. 11:8). Gerhard von Rad, the eminent Old Testament scholar, traces the narrative of the progression of human sin in primeval history: the Fall, Cain, the son of Lamech, the marriages of the angels and the Tower.[1]

Each progression of sin is visited by the increasingly severe judgment of God. Yet that is not the whole story. At each step of the increase of sin, the grace and mercy of God also visit humankind. The first pair were banished from the garden, but God clothed them. Cain, who did not keep his own brother, was given divine protection (Gen. 4:15). When God was contemplating the universal destruction of "*man* and beast and creeping things and birds of the air" (Gen. 6:7), "Noah found favour in the eyes of the

---

1. Gerhard von Rad, *Old Testament Theology*, I, pp. 163f.

Lord" (v.8). Out of the destruction of the Flood came a new beginning. "Where sin increased, grace abounded all the more" (Rom. 5:20). But, how about the story of the Tower of Babel? It ends without grace (Gen. 11:1-9)! "Therefore its name was called Babel, because there the LORD confused the language of all the earth and from there the LORD scattered them abroad over the face of all earth" (v.9). What of the further relationship between God and the scattered peoples (nations)? "Is God's grace finally exhausted?"[2] *No!* The answer to this crucial question comes from God's call of Abraham, through whom God purposed that "all the families of the earth shall bless themselves" (Gen. 12:3).

Quite abruptly, in the midst of the "unsolved problems of Yahweh's relationship to the nation,"[3] appears the man called Abraham. He comes at this critical juncture between primeval history and salvation history as the man who leaves "his country, kindred, and his father's house" (Gen. 12:1). He leaves Ur of the Chaldeans (Gen. 11:31), and this "leaving" was the beginning of the story of God's renewed peace directed to all people of all nations. He left in order to come back. He left without a saving message in order to come back with the saving message. In his leaving, he is coming back! In his abandoning Ur, he is rescuing Ur.[4] What a paradox! His election was to the service of the nations. The Abrahamic life is bound to be a *hard* life (Heb. 11:32-38; Lk. 24:26). It is a life *called* to serve in the design of the "reconciling God" for humankind.

Second, the activity of Deutero-Isaiah came between the destruction of Jerusalem in 587 B.C.E. and the downfall of the Babylonian empire in 539 B.C.E. Counting from 612 B.C.E., the year of the fall of the Assyrian Nineveh to the newly emerging power of the Medes and the Babylonians, the lifespan of the great Babylonian empire of Nebuchadnezzar was only a matter of seven decades until the troops of the Persian Cyrus entered the city of Babylon in 539. The mighty world-empire had fallen. Deutero-Isaiah's ministry was concentrated sometime after 550, when the rise of Cyrus was beginning to appear on the horizon of the Fertile Crescent power-struggle. At this critical juncture of world history, Deutero-Isaiah spoke of Israel in the great "trial" dispute in which Yahweh opposed his own people Israel (43:22-28; 50:1-3).

> Yet you did not call upon me, O Jacob; but you have been weary of me, O Israel! You have not brought me your sheep for burnt offer-

---

2. Ibid., p. 163.

3. Ibid., p. 164.

4. "The Old Testament does not state that the election of Israel means the rejection of the nations. The fact that the Old Testament knows nothing of the passive definition (that Israel is the chosen people), but the active announcement that Yahweh chooses, makes it impossible to speak of the nations as 'rejected.' And this never occurs in the Old Testament" (Johannes Blauw, *The Missionary Nature of the Church*, Lutterworth Press, 1962, p. 25).

ings, or honored me with your sacrifices. I have not burdened you with offerings, or wearied you with frankincense. You have not bought me sweet cane with money, or satisfied me with the fat of your sacrifices. But you have burdened me with your sins, you have wearied me with your iniquities (43:22-24).

First, Deutero-Isaiah passes an outright critical judgment upon the nation's sacrificial worship as Amos, Hosea, Isaiah, Micah, and Jeremiah did. Israel keeps saying, "We serve you with our sacrifice!" Yahweh answers: "You did not really serve me. In actual fact you made me into a servant!"[5] Let me quote Westermann at some length, because this trial controversy permits a glimpse into the heart of the reconciling God.

> This, however, is no more than a clumsy rendering of the Hebrew, which turns on the two forms of the same verb *'ābad* (to serve or to work) in v.23b and v.24b: *lo' he 'ebadtī ka* and *ak he'ebadtānī*: I did not make you work (serve) and you made me work (serve). This key-passage for Deutero-Isaiah's proclamation contains an echo of the catchword of the servant songs (*'ebed*, from *'ābad*). In order to understand this connection, we must realize that the words — and it is God who speaks them — "you have made me serve (made me into a *'ebed*) with your sins" are offensive to, if not indeed impossible for, the Old Testament concept of God. God is lord; in all semitic religions what constitutes the nature of divinity is lordship. If God is made into a *'ebed*, if he is made to serve, he has his divinity taken from him.
>
> Here in 43:24, this reversal of the natural relationship between God and man, in which God is lord and man God's servant, flashes out for just a moment. It fades again immediately, for in v.25 God again acts precisely and decidedly as a master who can as such simply blot out Israel's guilt. However, what here is the momentary sounding of a note, is to be taken up again in the poems about the *'ebed*, the servant of God: there is to be a servant who, at God's behest, is to take the sins of the others upon himself.[6]

What a message! What we are allowed to see in this one glimpse can be *stammered* in "fear and trembling" as something like this: the reconciling God is ready to become *'ebed*-God! And it happened in Jesus Christ! Is there anything, any situation greater, more amazing, more life-giving, than this, God's "going out?" Could such a thing be?

The Abrahamic "going out" is a "going out" with intense expectation. It is a response to a sending God who sends God's Word. "The Word became flesh and dwelt among us" (Jn. 1:14). "Behold, the Lamb of God!" (v.29). All

---

5. Claus Westermann, *Isaiah 40-66*, SCM Press, 1969, p. 131.
6. Ibid., pp. 131f.

Abrahamic "goings out" point to the one who "came in the name of the Lord" (Jn. 12:3) and who was "spat upon, mocked, and stripped and crucified" (Matt. 27:28-31; Mk. 15:16-20). The ultimate meaning of all "goings out" in God's election is found in Jesus Christ, the one cast out. The Abrahamic expectation of the blessing to "all the families of the earth" is fulfilled in the one who "is before Abraham was" (Jn. 8:58), and in whom the ultimate "going out" *for all* took place. This is a story of the '*ebed Yahweh* which "no eye has seen, no ear heard, nor the heart of man conceived" (I Cor. 2:9). Indeed, "many prophets and righteous men longed to see what you see, and did not see it, and to hear what you hear, and did not hear it" (Matt. 13:17; Jn. 8:56).

At this point I should go back to the story of the man born blind. But I am still not ready to do so. I must speak on Jesus Christ, the '*ebed Yahweh*, in whom — in his being thrown out! — judgment and hope became, in their finality, the contents of good news!

The New Testament tells us precisely and unequivocally that Jesus Christ was "forsaken" by God himself. "My God, my God, why hast thou forsaken me?" (Mk. 15:34). "No one was ever so forsaken!"[7] The psalmist says, "He who keeps you will not slumber" (Ps. 121:2). But God refuses to be the keeper to the Son on the cross. "If I make my bed in Sheol, thou art there!" (Ps. 139:8). On the cross, Jesus agonized because "thou are not there!" God "did not spare his own Son but gave him up for us all" (Rom. 8:32; Jn. 3:16). God made "him to be sin who knew no sin" (II Cor. 5:21). Christ "became a curse for us" (Gal. 3:13). Jesus Christ lived in an inviolable communion with God (Jn. 14-17). It is this Jesus Christ who was made a "curse" for our sake.

If the cross of Christ is such a terrible event — and it is! — why does it occupy the *center of good news*? Why does Paul write to the troubled church in Corinth triumphantly: "I decided to know nothing among you except Jesus Christ and him crucified" (I Cor. 2:2)? Why is the gospel *essentially* "the word of the cross?" (I Cor. 1:18). Why must theology speak about the one who is so *absolutely* rejected and thrown out? Why is it that all theologies must be theology of the cross? Why can't we, constantly and forcefully, keep saying that our theology is an unconditional assertion that "the LORD is your keeper; the LORD is your shade, on your right hand. The sun shall not smite you by day, nor the moon by night" (Ps. 121:5-6)? And thus, wouldn't we develop a pleasing and attractive personality, as it were, to our theology — to our theology in Asia? Why emphasize the story of "being pushed out," "being rejected," and "being edged out?" Let me speak about the place of the cross of Christ in the divine career of the Son. What I wish to say is summarized in II Corinthians 8:9:

> For you know the grace of our Lord Jesus Christ, that though he was rich, yet for your sake he became poor, so that by his poverty you might become rich.

---

7. Luther, Weimar Edition, V, pp. 614-36.

In this context the simple words "rich" and "poor" are loaded with tremendous theological meaning. Paul is, of course, thinking neither in terms of economic capacity nor even in the sense of the rich young Francis of Assisi giving all and becoming poor. The Lord Jesus Christ was "in the form of God" (Phil. 2:6). "He is the image of the invisible God, the first-born of all creation" (Col. 1:15; I Cor. 8:6). He was the Word in the beginning with God (Jn. 1:1f.). This is the richness of "our Lord Jesus Christ." Yet *for your sake*, says the apostle Paul, the Lord became poor. "And the word became flesh and dwelt (*skeneo* — "to live in a tent") among us" (Jn. 1:14). Flesh (*sarx*) in John "represents human nature as distinct from God."[8] "He came to his own home, and his own people received him not" (1:10). Only "we" (the apostolic church) "beheld his glory" (1:14). The life of the Lord is heading toward the crucifixion "outside the gate" (Heb. 13:12). "None of the rulers of this age understood this" (the story of the "rich Lord" becoming the "poor Lord"), "for if they had, they would not have crucified the Lord of glory" (I Cor. 2:8). His "poverty" assumes incomparable depth at the death on the cross, as we have seen. The resurrection validates that "God shows his love for us in that while we were yet sinners Christ died for us" (Rom. 5:8). The crucifixion and resurrection thus stand in a vital relationship; Christ "was put to death for our trespasses and raised for our justification" (Rom. 4:25).

With the resurrection, the new age has come! The cross is the moment of God's supreme love (*agape*) revelation. The resurrection is the confirmation of God given to the reality of *agape* that "Christ loved us and gave himself up for us" (Eph. 5:1). The ascension does not mean a temporary absence of Christ from the history and world. On the contrary, it decisively means the participation of the Risen Christ in the kingly rule of God over the totality of history (Acts 2:33; 5:31; 7:55; Rom. 8:34; Eph. 1:20; Col. 3:1). But this exalted Lord is, according to the hymn of Philippians 2:5-11, the one who "emptied" himself to the point of "being spat upon and mocked and crucified." "*Therefore* God has highly exalted him" (v.9). John makes a tremendous assertion, quoting Jesus: "'I, when I am lifted up from the earth, will draw all men to myself.' He said this to show by what death he was to die" (12:32-33; cf. 3:14; 8:28). Here crucifixion is already seen as exaltation! Christ goes up on the tree with his crown of thorns as if the cross is the royal throne! Hung on the cross, he says, "I will draw all men to myself!" The cosmic rule emanates from the "Prince of glory (who) died on the cross!" "Worthy is the Lamb who was slain, to receive power and wealth and wisdom and might and honor and glory and blessing" (Rev. 5:12).

In this brief survey of the career of the Son, what I am trying to say is that the word of the cross is the word that summarizes the mission of Jesus Christ, the '*ebed Yahweh*. It is clear that Paul's theology and his life revolve around the good news-reality of the cross-resurrection ("mission accomplished").

---

8. C. K. Barrett, *The Gospel according to St. John*, SPCK, 1955, p. 138.

In what ways does the cross become *the* ground for reconciliation? Paul here uses a variety of images trying to say something about the "inexpressible gift" of God in Christ (II Cor. 9:15). It is expiation, atoning sacrifice, paying the price, service, vicarious suffering, representative penalty. And Luther says: "*Selige Tausch*" (blessed exchange)! It is all these, yet even all these combined are powerless to explain the "inexpressible gift" of the reconciliation-event of Jesus Christ (Rom. 11:33-36). While Paul the apostle is professing his believing reaction to "Jesus Christ and him crucified," he is himself participating in *that* kind of life, the life of "being thrown out." He *experiences* the word of the cross. He writes of his amazing apostolic style of life:

> For it seems to me God has made us apostles the most abject of mankind. We are like men condemned to death in the arena, a spectacle to the whole universe — angels as well as men. We are fools for Christ's sake, while you are such sensible Christians. We are weak; you are so powerful. We are in disgrace; you are honored. To this day we go hungry and thirsty and in rags; we are roughly handled; we wander from place to place; we wear ourselves out working with our own hands. They curse us, and we bless; they persecute us, and we submit to it; they slander us, and we humbly make our appeal. We are treated as the scum of the earth, the dregs of humanity, to this very day (I Cor. 4:9-13).

This is a straight narrative of life-experience from the apostle of the "word of the cross." Does this not reflect the life of the Lord Jesus Christ? Is not this life of "the most abject of mankind," "condemned man," "disgraced man," . . . to "the scum of the earth, the dregs of humanity," a life of an outcast? Are not "scum" and "dregs" something one *must* throw out? Is not this life a life-size experience and expression of the powerful word of the cross (I Cor. 1:18; 2:4-5)? Let me quote from another context:

> Are they Hebrews? So am I. Are they Israelites? So am I. Are they descendants of Abraham? So am I. Are they servants of Christ? I am a better one — I am talking like a madman — with far greater labors, far more imprisonment, with countless beatings, and often near death. Five times I have received at the hands of the Jews the forty lashes less one. Three times I have been beaten with rods; once I was stoned. Three times I have been shipwrecked — a night and a day I have been adrift at sea; on frequent journeys, in danger from rivers, danger from robbers, danger from my own people, danger from Gentiles, danger in the city, danger in the wilderness, danger at sea, danger from false brethren; in toil and hardship, through many a sleepless night, in hunger and thirst, often without food, in cold and exposure. And, apart from other things, there is the daily pressure upon me of my anxiety for all the churches (II Cor. 11:22-28).

What a life! Yes! But this life *is* the *apostolic* life! This total life is the life experiencing and communicating the life of Jesus Christ who was "made a curse for our sake." The theology of the word of the cross must be expressed and communicated "bodily." "I wear on my body the marks of Jesus" (Gal. 6:17). How can one be an '*ebed* to the '*ebed* of God unless one expresses servanthood in one's pattern of life? "Not reading books or speculating, but living, dying and being damned make a theologian!"[9]

Some years ago I gave a series of lectures on the book of Exodus to a group of Christian farmers in northern Thailand. They were delivered on hot afternoons and the lectures had to be extraordinarily interesting in order to keep the students and lecturer awake. One such afternoon, an elderly farmer stood up and asked me, "Acharn, (i.e., teacher) what is the . . . o . . . l . . . ogy?" Instead of answering, I picked up a piece of chalk and drew a picture of a chicken. (The farmer saw it and said: "That duck has a small beak!") I proceeded:

> This is a chicken. You know how a chicken lives, what it eats, how it lays its eggs, how it gets exercise, how it gets sick. . . . Such understanding of the chicken is called "chicken-ology" since "logy" means "understand." So, theology means the "theo" (God) and "logy" (understanding), the "understanding of God." Do you follow this far? Fine! There is, however, a great difference between "chicken-ology" and "theo-logy." We can study and understand a chicken much more easily than God. We can observe the chicken. We can catch it. We can even open it up and study its inside! But with God can we do this? No! We cannot put God on the table to observe. We cannot cut God open and see inside! Never! The "logy" of theo-logy is a special kind of "logy." Is is not a "logy" that comes from "observing" God. It is a "logy" that develops within our heart, soul, and mind (Matt. 22:37) when we obey, repent, hope, love, believe, worship God. It is a "logy" of obedience, repentance, creation, hope, judgment, love, faith, worship and eternal life. It is an unusual "logy" indeed!

So far what have I said? I have said two things: (1) "Election for service to the many" belongs to the heart of the proclamation. "Going out," "being cast out," "being rejected," is the structure of the "word of the cross" which is folly to "those who are perishing" (I Cor. 1:18,21,23,25). The good news of reconciliation reaches its final realization in Jesus Christ crucified. (2) Theology can only stammer about the person and work of Jesus Christ. It is because the Lord of *agape* crucified is the subject of theology. The one who engages in theology does so to "understand" (*epignosis*, Eph. 1:17), "touch" (*pselaphao*, I Jn. 1:1-4) and "do the truth" (*poiōn tēn alētheian*, Jn. 3:21). He is to reflect in either a hidden or an open way, on the direction

9. Luther, Weimar Edition, V, p. 163.

and quality of "becoming the scum" of humanity, since this "becoming" is not a peripheral issue but a matter of essential importance in the history of salvation. Theology must be engaged not only in the heart (heart is "not only the seat of the whole of the emotions, but also of the reason and the will") but in the *kidneys* ("the most secret stirrings of the soul were thought of as resident within the kidneys:" Ps. 73:21; Jer. 17:10).[10] The church universal is watching us today to see how our "Asian kidneys" respond specifically to the message of the word of the cross.

At this point I wish to go back to the story of the man born blind. He *experienced* the saving touch of the emancipator. He inevitably caused an identification-dispute within his own community (v.8). He said: "I am the man" (v.9). So far, he was not so much of a problem. He was, however, then taken to the theological examination conducted by the Pharisees. He insisted on one thing: "One thing I know, that though I was blind, now I see. . . . Never since the world began has it been heard that anyone opened the eyes of a man born blind. If this man were not from God, he could do nothing" (vv. 25,32,33). His witness to the unknown emancipator (v.12) was expressed "bodily" and "empirically." It was simple and forceful. Then he was expelled. At this moment, he was called to walk in his own manner in the same path of the Abrahamic "going out." Without understanding the theology of the cross, he began to participate empirically in the great apostolic tradition. The Lord of the word of the cross (remember, "nobody has ever been so forsaken!") approached him and the divine word of invitation came to him. "Do you believe in the Son of *man?*" (v.35). His "heart" (and his "kidneys") responded to the man who gave him full peace. He (from the depth of his "kidneys") worshipped him. This incident took place *outside* the "regular" and "approved" theological investigation to which he had been subjected. But when the moment of divine self-introduction confronted him (v.37), he *understood precisely* what it meant. It was he, the emancipator, speaking to him! In this meeting of two outcasts (Matt. 11:28), the Lord pronounced the judgment (*krima*) of separation (*krisis*) upon the world. The separation is that "those who do not see may see, and that those who see may become blind" (v.39). This judgment comes from the one "who was rich, but for your sake became poor." It is pronounced within the living context of the divine *agape*. "Man's life lived within the context of finitude and mortality is also lived within the context of God's blessing."[11] In the context of God's blessing? Yes. It is so in the good news of Jesus Christ who has gone to the uttermost "outside" on the cross.

At this point, theology becomes missiology, and missiology becomes theology. Is not theology a stammering description of the sending God culminating in the word of the cross? Is not missiology an understanding of God who *is* and *acts* in unsearchable and immeasurable strength of love cul-

---

10. Gerhard von Rad, op. cit., p. 153.
11. D. T. Niles, *A Testament of Faith*, Epworth Press, 1972, p. 7.

minating in the person and work of Jesus Christ? Where else can these two accomplish this unity outside of that particular christological and apostolic "outside?" And isn't it obvious that all cheap grace, cheap judgment, and cheap hope are denied entrance to that special "outside?" Isn't it true that that "outside" is a costly outside because there the great price is paid (I Cor. 6:20; 7:23)? Confronted by this theology-missiology, the totality of God's reconciling history, who can say "We see," as though we had become counsellors to God (Rom. 11:34)? And if we say "we see," we will hear from Jesus Christ crucified, "Your guilt remains," because we refuse to *participate* in the saving history of the costly grace of God.

Theology in Asia must assume her own personality. It must bear "the marks of Jesus" (Gal. 6:17) at the depth of our Asian "hearts" and Asian "kidneys." What is appropriated in our "hearts" and "kidneys" must be expressed in *our* obedience to the word of the cross, the foundation of theology-missiology.

> In heaven, where all see the glory of God, they want no one to show it forth and declare it. But, on earth, where the glory of God is by no means received, seeing that, it works in a manner contrary to all human ideas, so that God seems more to forget his people than to be mindful of them, there is need that his glory should be set forth by the word, and understood by faith (Luther).

This is happening and this will happen whenever Asians are captivated by the word of the cross (II Cor. 10:5). Let us call our total missiology-theology or theology-missiology theology of the cross. Is there any other center for our theological existence than this theology of the cross? Theology of the cross must be rooted in this time in our Asian souls thus able to bring forth a living, dynamic, and *free* "personality" of theology in Asia (Jn. 8:32).

CHAPTER 15

Tokyo and Jerusalem

- Jerusalem of 587 B.C.E. and Tokyo of C.E. 1945.
- Both Christian institutions and charismatic people are under the judgment of the Word of God.
- The constant awareness that we are under the judgment of the Word of God is the first and fundamental gift from God through which God may or may not make a person a Jeremiah. "God is able from these stones to raise up children to Abraham!" (Matt. 3:9)
- "Too many Jeremiahs" is a sign of danger rather than of salvation!

The word that came to Jeremiah from the Lord: "Stand in the gate of the LORD's *house, and proclaim there this word, and say, Hear the word of the* LORD, *all you men of Judah who enter these gates to worship the* LORD. *Thus says the* LORD *of hosts, the God of Israel. Amend your ways and your doings, and I will let you dwell in this place. Do not trust in these deceptive words: 'This is the temple of the* LORD, *the temple of the* LORD, *the temple of the* LORD'" (*Jer. 7:1-4*).

Strangely, there is a similarity between Jerusalem of 587 B.C.E. and Tokyo of 1945. Jerusalem was destroyed by the Babylonian Nebuchadnezzar, and Tokyo was demolished by the American President Truman. It was a shocking experience for both Jerusalem and Tokyo. The Japanese people believed that no matter what might happen, Tokyo would not fall *because* it was the seat of the divine emperor. He is the successor to the sun goddess. He is God incarnate. His divine protection is with the city and the land. "This is the palace of the emperor, the palace of the emperor, the palace of the emperor!" Ultimately, the victory will be with us! The Japanese theology of the imperial system did not permit the Japanese people to conceive of any other possible outcome. But "the sacred land of the sun goddess" was demolished!

The land God promised to the people of the covenant was not a peaceful island like Hawaii or Tahiti under sunny skies, surrounded by blue sea

137

and with a refreshing breeze blowing through the tall coconut palms. On the contrary, it was situated between two imperial powers. To use a Thai image, the promised land was situated "between a crocodile and a tiger." The crocodile of the North (Assyria and Babylonia) and the tiger of the South (Egypt) were constant threats to the people of the covenant living in the tiny land corridor. What a "promised land" that was! The Assyrian Sargon II destroyed Samaria in 721 B.C.E. Then Judah was immediately exposed to the threat from the North. She was thrown into the international power struggle, a game of treacherous military alliances and turncoat politics. In the complicated international situation, Pharaoh Necho came to help Assyria (Egypt's traditional enemy!) against the rising Babylonian power. The king Josiah, gambling his lot with the Babylonians, tried to stop the army of Necho at Megiddo and lost his life! The horizon was getting darker and darker for Judah. It was exactly at this point of Judah's life that the voice of the Lord of history came through a man called Jeremiah. Judah will be demolished! This was his message. What a message! Jeremiah was bitterly opposed by ruler and people. "Whatever happens, Jerusalem will be safe and protected. It is the city of God. God's temple is there. It is God's *seat*. How can God allow heathens to come and demolish God's own city? In this city is the temple of the Lord, the temple of the Lord, the temple of the Lord! This is our *theological* conviction," the people said. Jeremiah said, "This catchword of yours is a lie!" (NEB) The sacred city of God, Jersualem, was demolished by the Babylonians in 587. It became like Shiloh (v.12).

Jeremiah's attack was not directed at the temple of the Lord itself. It was primarily directed at the deceptive theology hanging around the sacred institution. He did not pick on some "mini" institutions in order to make his protest heard. He spoke of "the temple of the Lord," the greatest institution in the life of the covenant people! Little wonder that he was almost lynched by the people (see ch. 26).

Our Christian life is surrounded by institutions and establishments. And their number is legion. Some institutions are sacred and others are less sacred. Some institutions are more useful to the good of the community than others. Institutions have their respective histories. They tend to become rigid and inflexible. They die hard. Their self-denial occurs only very rarely. The real danger of institutions must be located not in the institutions themselves, but in the "theology" that surrounds them. The penetrating analysis of the deceptive theology is summarized by Jeremiah as "This is the temple of the Lord! — *therefore* we are safe!"

The deceptive theology characterized by "this is the temple of the Lord" can be at work in diversified forms: "This is what the Pope says," "This is what the Church Council decides," "This is what the theological faculty thinks," "This is what the House of Bishops decrees," "This is what the mission board says," "This is what the denominational headquarters agreed on," and so on — *therefore* we are safe! "No," protests Jeremiah, the *protes-*

tant. "Beware of these deceptive words! Institutions can become deceptive — even including the temple of God! — *unless* you mend your ways and your doings. Live the life of the covenant people! Emancipate yourself from the illusion of institutional salvation secured by institutional religious life!" What a protest! Christian institutions must be, then, placed under the judgment of vv. 5-7:

> For if you truly amend your ways and your doings, if you do not oppress the alien, the fatherless or the widow, or shed innocent blood in this place, and if you do not want to go after other gods to your own hurt, then I will let you dwell in this place, in the land that I gave of old to your fathers for ever.

On this basis, Christians *can* and *must* be critical about institutions related to the church. We are not called to serve institutions as our end. That would be idolatry. Institutions are only *humble means* by which we may participate in God's work in history. We are called to serve God and humanity, sometimes upholding and sometimes demolishing institutions, sometimes within and sometimes outside of them. It belongs to the very life of "freedom of a Christian" to discern the positive Christian value in any given institution, and to protest, as Jeremiah did, whenever he finds the deceptive theology of institutional "therefore-we-are-safe." But *know* that God places a Jeremiah in the institutions, too. God may reject the protester who claims to be a Jeremiah. Not all protesters are Jeremiahs. Only God can place a Jeremiah — in or out of the institution.

CHAPTER 16

Is Christ Divided?

- There were four groups: the Paul group, the Cephas group, the Apollos group, and the Christ group in Corinth! What the apostle Paul could not accept at all, we today accept without difficulty.
- What are the positive values in denominational traditions? They represent *humble* theological attempts to stammer out some fragments of the fullness of God's glory in Christ (Isa. 6:1-8). Denominations must be appreciated in their *theologies* and *histories* (not in their organizational or financial capacities!).
- Is "contribution-drive" basically Christian drive? In what way can we make our contribution edify the name of Christ?
- Asia has waited long to witness denominationalism being "mocked, spat upon, scourged, killed and cast out!"

What I mean is that each one of you says, "I belong to Paul," or "I belong to Apollos," or "I belong to Cephas," or "I belong to Christ." Is Christ divided? Was Paul crucified for you? Or were you baptized in the name of Paul? (I Cor. 1:12,13).

I Corinthians was written in 53 or 54 C.E. Very early in the life of the Christian church there were already divisions! There were four groups; the Paul group, the Cephas group, the Apollos group, and the Christ group. It is very difficult to determine what each of these groups stood for. Most likely these groups (including the fourth one!) arose because of their different understanding of the gospel. If so, it was theological issues that divided the church in Corinth, and perhaps a little bit of "personality-cult." Paul could not accept this. Never! He wanted to heal the divisions. So he asked three fundamental questions of the divided church.

(1) Is Christ divided? Theology that gives any suggestion of a structure that supports Christ divided is fundamentally wrong. He is the One in whom "all things hold together" (Col. 1:17). This must be the theme of theology. "In him all things scatter asunder" cannot be the subject of theology. Is there any division in this? At this fundamental level?

(2) Was Paul crucified for you? Theology that gives the impression that someone other than Jesus Christ was *crucified for you* is fundamentally wrong. He was crucified for all people. In him, the Crucified One, all things are held together. Is there any division in this? At this fundamental level?

(3) Were you baptized in the name of Paul? Incorporation into the body of Christ, the church, is through people's identification with the death and resurrection of Jesus Christ symbolized in baptism (Rom. 6:3,4). How did you become Christian? In whose name? In the name of the One who holds all things together in his death and in his resurrection! Is there any division in this? At this fundamental level?

Why, then, divide into four groups when all have the same doctrine? (*a*) Jesus Christ is not divided; (*b*) Jesus Christ is crucified for us; and (*c*) it is into Jesus Christ that we are baptized.

Paul is not asking difficult theological questions. He is focused on Jesus Christ. "I decided to know nothing among you except Jesus Christ and him crucified" (I Cor. 2:2). Concentration on the One who holds all things together in his suffering and in his victorious resurrection is *the* way to overcome divisions. "Disunity is fundamentally a matter of *mind* and *opinion*, that is, of doctrine, and it is here that restoration and reconciliation must take place; neither at this point nor later does Paul suggest that the church can be mended by ecclesiastical politics."[1]

After all, there were "only" four groups with four different theological positions. It was not so serious, was it? Paul called the situation a "tearing apart" and a "rending." He could not accept it. For him, it was a matter of life and death for the Christian church. "Is Christ divided?" he shouted! What Paul could never accept, we today accept without much trouble. David O. Moberg informs us that there are two hundred fifty-four denominations in the United States. Within the Methodist family there are twenty-one kinds, in the Lutheran seventeen, the Baptist twenty-seven kinds.[2] The divisions multiplied for varieties of reasons: historical, political, racial, cultural, linguistic, and theological. Some reasons for division were weighty while others were clearly petty issues. The fact remains that the Christian church — the church of the One who holds all things together — is perhaps the most divided religious institution existing. "For he is our peace, who has made us both one, and has broken down the dividing wall of hostility . . ." (Eph. 2:14). But the tragic historical fact is that the church itself set up the "dividing wall" which Christ the Lord of the church had broken down.

I like to maintain that there is a difference between denomination and denominationalism. In brief, denominations — I am thinking mainly of the major denominations — are valuable products of the history of the Christian church. For the most part they came into being from *theological* debates. They had serious *theological* beginnings. Theological insights given

---

1. C. K. Barrett, *The First Epistle to the Corinthians*, A. and C. Black, 1968, p. 42.
2. David O. Moberg, *The Church as a Social Institution*, Prentice-Hall, 1962, p. 31.

through them are valuable even outside the confines of the West. But it is of great importance for us to remember that these theological insights are *humble* theological insights. They are *servants*, not masters, to the "inexpressible gift" of God in Christ (II Cor. 9:15). They cannot exhaust and prove the depth of God's purpose in Christ (Rom. 11:33-35). The theology of Luther is an expression of his deep personal appreciation of "Christ and him crucified." And so it is with the Wesleys' theology. Because they concentrated on Jesus Christ, their theologies are edifying and helpful to us Asians. But let us remember that their theologies are *humble* theological attempts to express some fragment of the fullness of God's glory in Christ (Isa. 6:1-8). Luther does not hold all things together. If he did, there would be a theological justification in calling a church a Lutheran church. Once he said that if someone started a "Lutheran church" after his death, he would jump up in his grave with red hot anger! Luther was right. There may be historical and sociological conveniences in calling a church Lutheran, but there is no biblical or theological justification for doing so. The church must be called only by the name of the one who promised, "Upon this rock *I* will build *my* church" (Matt. 16:18), who was crucified for us, and in whose name we are baptized. For this reason, the church must be called always and universally the "church of Christ" with the designation of locality: "church of Christ in Thailand," "church of Christ in Cambodia," "church of Christ in Hong Kong," "church of Christ in Ephesus," "church of Christ in Corinth," "church of Christ in Galatia." This is the only theologically defensible way to speak of the church.

"Methodist Headquarters" is a sociological concept. It is like "Sony Headquarters" or "Cathay Organization Headquarters." But "Methodist church" is an impossible concept. Church is always "church of Christ." "Methodist church," "church of Methodism," or "church of Wesley" — such concepts will directly militate against the biblical image of the church. God is a jealous God (Deut. 4:24). "I am the LORD, that is my name; my glory I give to no other" (Isa. 42:8). Was Wesley crucified for you? Were you baptized in the name of Wesley? Instead of calling the church a Methodist church, we should say, "Church of Christ in Singapore," appreciating the *humble theological insights* given by the tradition of Methodism in our understanding of the "inexpressible gift" of God in Christ.

Humble theological insights! Why do we give the mystery of the body of Christ, the church, the name of a humble theological insight? I personally prefer "Jeremiah-ist church" or "Deutero-Isaiah-ist church" to "Methodist church" or "Baptist church." The former helps me far more than the latter in my understanding of God's purpose in Christ for us. But Jeremiah-ist church is as dangerous an idea as Methodist church! The church belongs solely to the one who "died for us."

I realize that I have made myself a fool in my theological exposition of "Methodist church" or "Lutheran church!" No one who is Methodist or Lutheran would say that Luther or Wesley was crucified for us. Furthermore, this way of naming the church has been in use for a long time. It is accepted! Only a neurotic theological mosquito would hum around accepted expressions such as Methodist church and Lutheran church. Yet, for my part, I insist that the current system contains the possibility of "humble theological insights" becoming "dominating theological insights," as though those insights were large and strong enough to package the whole life and energy of the gospel of Christ. When Wesley or Luther become more central than Jesus Christ — can we say outright that this has never happened and will never happen? — then humble theological insights (denominational traditions) become something else. There emerges the theological structure for *denominationalism.*

This theological structure is sick. Here theology is "puffed up" (I Cor. 4:6) and takes precedence over the "inexpressible gift" of God. Theological contributions made by historical groups of Christians deserve positive evaluation only as long as they are not unduly elevated. That is to say, as long as they all point to the "Christ and him crucified" as *humble* theological insights. This same thing must be said to the Paul group, the Apollos group, the Cephas group, and the Christ group. When "humble theological insights" become puffed up, then, together with many other non-theological factors — such as the powerful sociological and financial factors — denominationalism is in the process of development.

Denominationalism is deadly. It is demonic. It is the source and the force for "tearing apart" and "rending." Denominationalism monopolizes Christ theologically. This is an extremely arrogant undertaking! It has the backing of financially powerful organizations.

It is of considerable importance for Christians to *belong* to one of these denominational organizations because of the sociological and financial implications. Inside, they seem to enjoy a seemingly enviable "sacred" security. The theological understanding of denomination is often pushed aside. Instead, an organizational, institutional denomination steps forward. Indeed, often Lutherans do not study the theology of Luther, and Methodists do not investigate the theology of Wesley. They are accidentally Lutherans and automatically Methodists.

The anthropology of denominationalism is devastatingly simple. Denominational affiliation determines the quality of our image of God! People "shall not live by bread alone, but by the words that proceed out of the denomination authority!" A president of the Southern Baptists, in relation to the subject of expected exodus of "liberals" from the Southern Baptist ranks, remarked, "There are some things that make a Baptist a Baptist, and if you don't believe them you ought to leave."[3] "Something that makes a Baptist a Baptist" — is this "something" something other than "Christ and him crucified?" If so, what is it? Can one be a Baptist but not a Christian? If not, why does that "something" command such importance? Isn't this an

---

3. Reported in the *National Catholic Reporter,* 17 April 1970.

elevation of a tradition over the foundation of the Christian faith itself, "Christ and him crucified?" If "Christ and him crucified" becomes the center of our theological thinking, then "something that makes a Baptist a Baptist" will become an issue of second, third, or fourth importance. The anthropology of "something that makes a Baptist a Baptist" is dangerous and harmful to the Christian life!

Inevitably the question arises. Who is a Lutheran? Who is a Methodist? A Lutheran is, it seems to me, one who appreciates the theology of Luther — the way Martin Luther expounded the explosive truth of God in "Jesus Christ and him crucified" — and who is helped to see the depth of "what no eye has seen, nor ear heard, nor the heart of man conceived" (I Cor. 2:9) through Luther's *humble* theological attempt. Therefore, the basic identification is that one is a Christian. One never becomes a Lutheran unless one holds that "Luther was crucified for me." But people may call themselves a Lutheran when they know that the sole reason for calling themselves Lutheran is a "theological" reason. Such people find "theological help" in the tradition of Luther. The "help" must not usurp the place of the Crucified One. When one says, "I am a Lutheran," "I am a Methodist," or "I am a Baptist," it involves a theological discussion. "What theological insights of Luther are a help to you personally when you look up to the 'Prince of Peace who dies on the cross'?" If one can answer this, one may *humbly* (and preferably *privately*) call oneself a Lutheran. (All the same, what an unfortunate and dangerous way to call oneself!)

Then it is not just going to a Lutheran church which makes a Christian a Lutheran. Going through the Lutheran catechism does not make a Christian a Lutheran. The relationship with the Lutheran Mission Board does not make a Christian a Lutheran. To be the Executive Director of the World Lutheran Federation does not make a person a Lutheran. To draw a salary from a Lutheran institution does not make one a Lutheran. To be a Lutheran is not an automatic process. It has nothing to do with institutional or organizational affiliation. It is a conscious theological process that makes a Christian a Lutheran. It involves the awareness that Luther's theology was a stammering (humble) attempt to appreciate the wealth of Christ.

Frequently I have heard that the Lutheran church has its special contribution to make to the churches in Asia; the Methodist church has its special contribution to make to the churches in Asia; the Anglican church has . . .; the Baptist church . . .; the Presbyterian . . .; and so on. The "contributors" decide that the Asians need these specific contributions in order to have a full life in Christ. Without exception these contributions are positive, good, and helpful. Certainly, they will enrich the life of the church here in Asia.

Suppose, however, one evening three women, an American, a Thai, and a Japanese, were to try to prepare a dinner together for guests. The American lady would say, "Steak, steak! This is my contribution." The Japanese lady would say, "Raw fish, raw fish! This is my contribution." The Thai lady would say, "Sticky rice with coconut sauce! This is my contribution." What a confusion that would be! Can their guests eat steak, raw fish, and sticky rice with coconut sauce? Will they not get stomachaches? Or, perhaps one guest could eat steak, another raw fish, and the third sticky rice with coconut sauce! But then where is the spirit of eating *together*? In either case, don't we need some coordination in the kitchen? If it is a matter not of general contributions, but of special contributions, is not intensive coordination required all the more?

It is, in fact, not simply a matter of coordination. If it were simply a matter of coordination, it would not be so difficult. But the question goes deeper than that. It is the relationship between the special contribution of denominations and the apostolic contribution in the image of "refuse." Are all these *special* contributions participating in the apostolic "becoming refuse?" Otherwise, isn't there a possibility that Jesus Christ in Asia will be "contributioned-out?" Has not this happened already? One tradition emphasizes a certain form of liturgy, another the concept of the transcendence of God; one, the idea of justification, another the idea of sanctification, and so on. Every denomination is so concerned about its *own* contribution that it has hardly any time to consider the merits of other contributions. An American lady is a dedicated "steak lady;" a Japanese lady is an equally dedicated "raw fish lady;" a Thai lady is a confirmed "sticky-rice-with-coconut-sauce lady." They have no time to appreciate each other's dishes. Then enthusiasm for one's own contribution can become a polite religious imperialism. When special denominational contributions are directed toward the apostolic contribution of "becoming refuse" (I Cor. 4:9-13), they will throw much light on to the ultimate fullness of Jesus Christ. When they are not, they will blur the glory of Jesus Christ, the crucified.

What is your contribution? Does it carry that apostolic quality of "becoming refuse?" Is your contribution "refuse"-related contributions? Or is it only distantly so related or not related at all?

The "refuse-related contribution" is a strange concept. It belongs to the nature of "refuse" to be "cast out" (*peripsama* — offscouring — comes from *peripsao* — "to wipe off all round;" "that which is wiped off"). To be treated like "refuse" means to be mocked, spat upon, cursed, killed, and cast out! Thus, some years ago, when a Methodist theologian told me with great zeal and passion: "We Methodists must make this particular contribution! It is the God-given task of Methodism to do so," I felt some strange sensation within me. Is not this self-assertion? Isn't this the opposite of renunciation? Isn't this a refusal to be mocked, spat upon, cursed, killed, and cast out? On what basis must Methodists make this or that contribution? Is there any other basis than that One who is treated like "refuse" and whose life the apostle Paul imitated? That same Methodist theologian would perhaps share my discomfort were he to hear from a Lutheran theologian: "We Lutherans *must* make *this* contribution!" He is not interested in the

Lutheran contribution. His value judgment does not reach beyond *the* Methodist contribution. Isn't there a serious danger in this? Doesn't it increase divisions in the life of the church in Asia? Isn't it high time that each denominational tradition understood all *other* contributions? Only *after* it understood others, then, and only then, it may make its contribution as the "refuse-related contribution."

Of course, we must go further. Isn't it a basic rule of life that one cannot make a contribution unless one is ready to accept another's contribution in return? Otherwise, "making a contribution" may become only a convenient expression for an egoistic "keeping our contributions to ourselves." There is a difference between "keeping" and "giving." When Methodists say, "We Methodists wish to make this distinctive Methodist contribution," are they sure that they are not saying, in fact, "We Methodists wish to *keep* and perpetuate this special Methodist tradition to ourselves?" "To make a contribution" is to "give away" the "pearl of great price" of one's own tradition. In the process of "giving away," not in the process of "keeping" and perpetuating, some changes, yes, even some radical changes, may take place in that very distinctive contribution the tradition wishes to make. The whole situation is not so static, since one having something is now going to give that something to someone else. "Giving" is a dynamic *theological* process which influences *both* the giver and the given. A tradition cannot "give" something without "receiving" something from others. It belongs to the wonder and mystery of the Body of Christ, the church, that the Methodist contribution cannot survive without the Lutheran contribution, as the Presbyterian contribution, also, cannot survive without the Methodist contribution, and so on. All are interrelated by the principle of the One who denied himself (Phil. 2:6-7). Why don't we understand our contributions in the theological context of Mark 8:34f.: "If any man would come after me, let him deny himself and take up his cross and follow me. For whoever would save his life will lose it; and whoever loses his life for my sake and the gospel's will save it."

Placing denominational contributions under the judgment of the above passage entails a serious consequence. It may threaten the very existence of the denominational theological contribution! Or, at least, it challenges the "distinctive" quality of any given tradition. We may wish to say, "We are Lutherans. No matter what, we cannot allow our *distinctive* theological quality and contribution to be challenged and crucified! We may take anything else, but not *this*! Never!" Here we come to the nerve center of theological discussion. Namely, what is the theological value of this being "distinctively Lutheran?" Does the value come from something other than "Jesus Christ and him crucified" (I Cor. 2:2)? Or is it so unique and superior a theological interpretation of "Jesus Christ and him crucified" that one cannot find it in any other tradition? If so, what exactly is that valuable theological interpretation? What is the relationship between this particular interpretation and other theological insights given by the other traditions? Exclusive?

Inclusive? Supplementary? And finally, perhaps the most difficult question arises: What is the *relationship* between the particular Lutheran interpretation and "Jesus Christ and him crucified?" And how should a certain theological interpretation live and behave if it reflects the apostolic quality of "becoming refuse?"

In the wider context, the "contribution drive" is present in the heart of all the great world confessional families. In 1956 John A. Mackay, the President of the World Alliance of Reformed Churches, said that each confessional family seeks to make "its specific contribution to the 'ecumenical treasure house of Christian faith and life.'"[4] One item on the executive agenda of the 1957 World Alliance of Reformed Churches is about "the contribution which a resurgent confessionalism can make to the enrichment of that (ecumenical) movement."[5] This is said, of course, in the spirit that "the tendency to absolutize confessional structure or loyalties is a thing of the past."[6] But this line of assessment of confessionalism does not ring a realistic note, particularly when it is heard in Asia. Perhaps we find in Visser't Hooft an articulate expression of our Asian feeling in this issue.

> Do we always remember that denominations by their nature are provisional in character, or do we sometimes think and speak about them as if they were final embodiments of Christian truth? Now Martin Luther and John Calvin and John Wesley have all made it abundantly clear that they did not think of the church formation which they saw growing up in their lifetime as the last word. On the contrary, they all thought in terms of the Church Catholic and prayed for the restoration of the full catholicity and unity of the church. And should we be more confessional than our confessional leaders? More confessional than Luther or Calvin, or more than Wesley? Surely not![7]

The Asian impression of the world confessional families is often that the present-day leaders of the confession are more "confessional than Luther, Calvin and Wesley!" To say that "the tendency to absolutize confessional structure or loyalties is a thing of the past" is a vastly optimistic and dangerously misleading estimation. In the view of the East Asia Christian Conference Bangalore Working Committee in 1961, "The very vitality of these confessional loyalties often creates serious obstacles in the life of the younger churches." The Bangkok Assembly (1964) posed a challenge to the world confessional families. The three questions asked in Bangkok are of extreme importance for the life of the churches in Asia:

---

4. Harold E. Fey (ed.), *The Ecumenical Advance*, SPCK, 1970, p. 121.
5. Ibid., p. 122.
6. Ibid. (Dr. Mackay).
7. Ibid., pp. 123f.

(1) Do the world confessional organizations rest on theological principle or do they simply gather together churches because of a common history and tradition?

(2) Even where world confessional organizations are seeking to preserve for the universal church some fundamental insight into an aspect of Christian truth, is this best done by an organization built around that truth?

(3) Are the confessions and doctrines which are the historical basis of these world confessional organizations living realities among the people in these confessional families?[8]

Bangkok 1964 has expressed the concern of all Asian church leaders about the world confessional families.

These three questions the EACC asked are hard questions to answer! But they point to the crucial theological issues hidden in the influence of the world confessional families upon the Asian churches. EACC is appreciative of the confessional theological insights. The three questions are challenging the *relationship* between their *theological heritages* and *organizations*. "Is this (the preservation of the confessional theological insights) best done by an organization built around that truth?" This is a theologically significant question. Aren't they too possessive of their theological insights? Can't they release them? Aren't they ready to be "cast out?" Would not precious theological insights contribute to the church ecumenical if they were freed from "organizations built around that truth?" If churches of the same confession are getting together simply "because of a common history and tradition," then will not that organization hinder the possibility of exciting the theological formation we need in Asia today? Could not confessional families take the self-denial of the "grain of wheat" more seriously? (Is it the best arrangement that "raw fish" is always "possessed" by the Japanese lady, steak by the American, simply because they are respectively Japanese and American?)

Then comes the third question: are these theological insights "realities among the people in these confessional families" including the Asian family members? Are they realities? Are they not "boxing as one beating the air" (I Cor. 9:26)? What do the theological traditions of Luther, Calvin, and Wesley mean, *in reality*, particularly to the Asian churches? This will put the first two questions into the context of radical historic evaluation. "Do the world confessional organizations rest on *theological principle?* Is this theological principle something which can be immediately air-mailed from the Western headquarters of the confessional family to Thailand, Indonesia, and Hong Kong? If not, what would happen if confessional organizations were to come into Asia carrying their own respective theological "principles?" "Organizations" may be able to come more easily than "theological principles" because the latter must go through the process of showing forth

---

8. Ibid., p. 125.

the power of God in Christ by assuming the quality of "refuse." It takes time to achieve this. It may take thirty years or fifty years, and perhaps more. In the meantime the confessional organizations are actively at work *as though* theological principles are well accepted or adjusted or indigenized. In fact, *they are not!* Here is the critical *discrepancy* between the theological dimension and the organizational dimension. This is, in the perspective of theology in Asia, a very critical issue.

This discrepancy, naturally, complicates the implications of the contribution each confessional family desires to make. But when organization makes itself felt in the form of money-power, its influence upon theological insights is clearly negative.

The Bangkok meeting has really asked far-reaching, important theological questions. The extensive theological implications of these three questions must be dealt with soon by Asian theologians. In this brief chapter I have only opened the subject. My basic position is that "theological insights" of the world confessional families will make ecumenical contributions *if* it is understood that their contributions and the contents of their theology reflect the *glory* of the one who was mocked, spat upon, scourged, killed, and cast out! Theologically speaking, Asia has waited long to witness denominational theological contributions "mocked, spat upon, scourged, killed and cast out!" — in order that they may *contribute* to the newness of Christian life in Asia

CHAPTER 17

Toward a Crucified Mind

- It is more rewarding to know a Buddhist than to know Buddhism.
- Appreciation of the complexity of history can control "theological inflation."
- God is the initiator of the salvation event, "dead-alive — lost-found" (Lk. 15:24).
- The communicator communicates.
- The mind of the communicator is a crucified mind. The crucified mind is neither neurotic nor unbalanced. It is a mind of self-denial based on the self-denial of Christ.

The seminaries did not teach me. I had to discover it by myself. They did not teach me that it is more interesting to know a Hindu than to know Hinduism; it is more rewarding to know a Buddhist than Buddhism, a Marxist than Marxism, a revolutionary than revolution, a missionary than missiology, wife than the "marriage and the family" course, Jesus Christ than christology.

My life is being lived basically within the constant interaction of the five living persons that make up my family. If I were living in the interaction of five "logies," my life would be much easier, but also much less interesting and colorful. I speak, I shout, I spank, I laugh, I think, I eat. In all these doings I am forced to feel the difference between "I" and "I-logy" and between children and "children-logy." Personal encounter (human community) is pregnant with unpredictable possibilities. The living person who confronts me defies the best possible definition of him. He is far more mysterious and complicated than I can possibly delineate, even with the help of Freud, Marx, Dostoevsky, and Heidegger. I look at missionaries. I am one of them. I find that "missionary" is indeed more complicated than "missiology." Missiology I can tame, but missionary I cannot. That "a person is made in the image of God" may sound simple. But the living person who stands in front of me is a staggering anthropological, sociological, and historical complexity. Permit me to make some clumsy remarks. Missiology does not sweat, thirst, complain, cry, laugh, or practice family planning. But missionary does! She is a *full* person whether she likes it or not.

I am sorry that I did not realize this simple distinction much earlier. I should say, to be more precise, that I am sorry that I have not personally appropriated and experienced in my whole existence this simple distinction and what it means. If I had, it would have contributed greatly to my manner of appreciating other persons when I came to meet them. Is it perhaps possible — what a dreadful thought! — that the study of theology blinded me in this respect? Has not theology inflated my language and thought? Has this inflation kept me from real contact with people? Truly, theology is more manageable than God. "Wife-logy" is more tranquil than any wife. While I was in Thailand, I studied Buddhism. What a wonderful time I had in the quiet library of the seminary as I went undisturbed through the pages of the Buddhist Canons. Thanks to some knowledge of library-Buddhism, I began to say a few sensible words about Buddhism. But when I realized the difference between library-Buddhism and street-Buddhists, my library-Buddhism was paralyzed. Library-Buddhism and street-Buddhists are, of course, related. In fact, I felt quite often that the street-Buddhists should study more about library-Buddhism. Yet it is the street-Buddhists who are the brothers and sisters whom I see, with whom I speak, and with whom I live. To love them *as they are* in all their complexity and not just to love anthropological, sociological, theological "formulations" of brothers and sisters is the command of God whom we have not seen (I Jn. 4:20). Only through such love can my theological "inflation" be brought down. I began to examine as carefully as I could the relationship between "the idea of a person walking in the idea of history" and "the living person in the concrete historical situation." Here, for example, is an unemployed man. He has to live with the devastating awareness that his community does not need him! He has no income. He is a Thai. He is walking the streets of Bangkok with an empty stomach. The sun beats mercilessly down upon him. He is bitter about his lot. In his tired head he searches for a way to get a scanty meal. He has had only three years of formal education. I observe him. I may even produce a book about him as voluminous as Gunnar Myrdal's *Asian Drama*, yet I am afraid that he may elude my best definition of him. He is a living person. A person is an unfathomable complexity. He exercises freedom.

Let me insert an illustration. I realized one day that an almost insignificant thing about me has a complicated historical background. Why do I have a miserable English pronunciation? It is because my father, my grandfather, and my great-grandfather spoke the Japanese language. My difficulty in distinguishing the short *a* from the short *u* sound ("please flash the toilet") does not derive from my private shortcomings but from the historical chain of Japanese ears and tongues. I could make the same point about my preference for eating raw tuna, trout and squid, though I do not enjoy raw oyster. It is because the community from which I derive my sense of taste did not appreciate raw oyster. Why do I have this or that particular type of emotion, psychological reaction, or sense of value? What is it that attracts me to the idea of nothingness or absolute detachment? Why am I always suspicious of activism? Where did I get my appreciative understanding of *hara-kiri*? Why is there pantheistic emotion within me, even though I reject it theologically? What brings me to appropriate the gospel in a particular way? Why do I see three Koyamas or perhaps five Koyamas within one Koyama? Which Koyama is the Koyama who is now writing? There must be some complicated personal and historical answer to all these questions.

The realization of the complexity of human existence has concurred with the realization of the complexity of history. A person is as complicated as history. History is as complicated as a person. Appreciation of this correlation became a point of new departure for my missionary thinking. As I began to appreciate the complexity of history, I began to see the hidden values of history. History became, as it were, personal, and my personal life became, as it were, historical. I realized a strange thing; the appreciation of the complexity of a person and history had opened my eyes to a more meaningful appreciation of the love of God in history. One aspect after another of my life came under scrutiny until emotionally, at one point — and this may sound irrational and perhaps ridiculous — I felt the love of God in the fact that my tongue fails to say "flush toilet" and my stomach accepts rice naturally and accepts hamburger unnaturally!

The theological statement "God in history" is a stupendous assertion when we stop to think about what it means. In all the immense complexities of the histories of Egypt, Assyria, Babylon, Persia, Rome . . . "God experiences history."

> "Are you not like the Ethiopians to me, O people of Israel?" says the LORD. "Did I not bring up Israel from the land of Egypt and the Philistines from Caphtor and the Syrians from Kir?" (Amos 9:7)

Isaiah speaks of God's might over the complexities of history.

> In that day the LORD will whistle for the fly which is at the sources of the streams of Egypt, and for the bee which is in the land of Assyria. And they will all come and settle in the steep ravines, and in the clefts of the rocks, and on all the thornbushes, and on all the pastures. In that day the LORD will shave with a razor which is hired beyond the River — with the king of Assyria — the head and the hair of the feet, and it will sweep away the beard also (7:18-20).

Look at the man called Zacchaeus. He was a tax collector. He must have heard about the famed rabbi from Nazareth, so he wanted to take a good look at him. We know why he went up the tree. His calculation was right. He had a trained sense of estimation! Jesus came along. He stopped under Zacchaeus's tree. He looked up at him and called, "Hurry down, Zacchaeus, for I must stay in your house today" (Lk. 19:5). Zacchaeus nearly dropped from the tree in surprise. Now, that was *all* Jesus said, but see what that word of "hotel arrangement" did to that man! It was a declaration of acceptance. What happened was like the breath of God "breathed into his nostrils" (Gen. 2:7). He changed! The old Zacchaeus was discontinued. Listen to his confession of faith in the language of a tax collector: "Listen, sir! I will give half my belongings to the poor; and if I have cheated anyone, I will pay him back four times as much" (v.8). This is the only language he knew to express the change which took place in the depths of his spiritual life. What had happened? Jesus explained it: "Salvation has come to this house today" (v.9). What happened was salvation. He was emancipated into a new relationship with his neighbors. What a fascinating and unpredictable story! Is it a simple story? Jesus accepted Zacchaeus and Zacchaeus changed. As simple as that? Perhaps, but why this simple acceptance of Jesus (hotel arrangement) produced a spiritual revolution within Zacchaeus has a complicated history.

One day some years ago I met a missionary couple from the West at the Bangkok Airport. They had just arrived. They expressed the view that Thai Buddhism is a manifestation of demons. How simple! Thirty million people in the Buddhist tradition of 700 years were brushed aside in one second. The remark betrayed super-arrogance and super-ignorance. I was further told that the Peoples' Republic of China, with her 800 million who are all atheists and therefore unsaved, is positively the enemy of the gospel! This unfortunate display of arrogance and ignorance derives from an inability to appreciate the complexity of people in history. Here is a case of extreme "inflation." Inability to meet people produces a superficial grasp and appreciation of history. "Human failure," as it were, results in "historical failure." That which is human is historical, and that which is historical is human. God comes to us becoming as human being and therefore historically. "The Word became a human being and lived among us" (Jn. 1:14 TEV). "We write to you about the Word of life, which has existed from the beginning of the world: we have heard it, and we have seen it with our eyes; yes, we have seen it, and our hands have touched it" (I Jn. 1:1 TEV) expresses the ultimate coming of God to us who live in historical and human complexities.

My aim so far has been to bring out the meaning of the distinction between a living, real person and a "logy" about that person. I have also emphasized the danger of "inflation" when we fail to appreciate the complexities of a person and of history. Now, the historical and human coming of God — this is an awkward expression — is the coming of Jesus Christ. In the coming of God in Jesus Christ we see God's good intention to save us.

"God was in Christ reconciling the world to himself" (II Cor. 5:19). God's saving will is most movingly described in one of the parables of Jesus. When the younger son returns, the father in the parable says, "Let us eat and make merry; for this my son was dead, and is alive again; he was lost, and is found" (Lk. 15:24). Here God's experience of history is summarized. He is deeply involved in the history of "dead-alive — lost-found." God's presence in the historical process of "dead-alive — lost-found" must be our primary concern. In our confession of faith the order "dead-alive — lost-found" and not "alive-dead — found-lost" is essential. Note the Deuteronomic "Apostles' Creed" which summarizes the whole theology of the Pentateuch:

> My father was a homeless Aramaean who went down to Egypt with a small company and lived there until they became a great, powerful, and numerous nation. But the Egyptians ill-treated us, humiliated us and imposed cruel slavery upon us. Then we cried to the LORD the God of our fathers for help, and he listened to us and saw our humiliation, our hardship and distress, and so the LORD brought us out of Egypt with a strong hand and outstretched arm, with terrifying deeds, and with signs and portents. He brought us to this place and gave us this land, a land flowing with milk and honey. And now I have brought the first-fruits of the soil which thou, O LORD, has given me (26:5-10).

This experience of emancipation from imprisonment (dead-alive — lost-found) has decided the character of the biblical faith. In the historical experience of dead-alive — lost-found, Israel and the church saw "a strong hand and outstretched arm." It is the content of the apostolic witness. "A strong hand and outstretched arm" reaches its ultimate form in the incarnation of the Son. "We have beheld his glory!" (Jn. 1:14). God is the God who involves Godself in the historical and human drama of dead-alive — lost-found. And what does "dead" mean in Asia today? What does "alive" mean? What does "lost" and what does "found" mean? We must ask these questions in the midst of historical and human complexities. *There* God becomes real to us. There? Yes. There only! God's presence is not what one may call "general presence." God visits us in our "specific" time and place of complexity. Love is the mind that tries to understand specific needs of this man and that woman, this community and that community. That "God is love" is not a general statement applicable to the general overall situation. God is "specifically" love.

> And the LORD God made for Adam and for his wife garments of skins, and clothed them (Gen. 3:21).

This is the way the theologians of the Pentateuch expressed God's "specific" act of love.

But how do we *communicate* this saving truth of God which I have summarized — "God in history of dead-alive — lost-found" to our neighbors? Communicate? Yes, the communication of that novel idea of "God in history of dead-alive — lost-found" is now our problem. Well, if it is just an "idea" we are asked to communicate, it must not be too difficult. One can, perhaps, communicate it just as one would communicate the state of the Hong Kong housing situation to Japanese visitors. What is to be communicated, however, is something more than an idea. It is life, history, hope, and love. Here the simple word "communication" suddenly assumes a profound and mysterious dimension. Communication becomes difficult and costly in that it demands tremendous spiritual energy and commitment. The God who involves Godself in the history of the salvation process of dead-alive — lost-found is the God who says "Your problem is my problem." God commits Godself. "Behold, he who keeps Israel will neither slumber nor sleep" (Ps. 121:4). God does not sleep, not because God is neurotic, but because God is the "keeper." God gives Godself. Now how to communicate such a reality of God to our neighbors? Neighbors who are not "neighborology" but real living neighbors who are in the midst of human and historical complexities?

This communication is only possible through the medium of a living person, the communicator himself or herself. The God who says "Your problem is my problem" cannot be made real through "communicationlogy," but only through the life of the communicator. The message and the messenger must become one. If the message is incarnated in the messenger and produces a messageful person, the message will be communicated. It is then no longer an "idea" but an "event." Incarnational communication is the way in which God's event is communicated. "Communicator" is more fundamental than "communication." In the life and person of Abraham, God sends a message to the nations. God's message is personalized in Abraham. I am not saying that "one who has seen Abraham has seen the Father." The ultimate and complete unity of the message (the Word) and person took place only in the person of Jesus Christ. What I am saying is that Abraham became a communicator by the initiative of God. Since God decided to make him God's communicator, Abraham, in his acts of obedience and disobedience, in his scheme of tricking others and in being tricked, in his believing and doubting, becomes the "walking message" for the nations. As soon as Abraham steps into the promised land, he is beset by famine. What a disappointing promised land! He goes down to Egypt. Upon entering Egypt, he plans a certain strategy because his wife is "very beautiful." He accepts Sarah's advice to have an heir . . . in all these events he remains a communicator. It is not a matter of how well (skillfully) he communicates the mind of God. It is a matter of simply remaining a communicator. Abraham is not assigned to the task of communication. He is called to be a communicator.

Jeremiah's trouble begins with God's decision to make him his communicator.

Before I formed you in the womb I knew you, and before you were born I consecrated you; I appointed you a prophet to the nations (1:5).

Jeremiah tries to refuse this appointment, but in his refusal he is already acting and living as a communicator. He was appointed before he was formed in the womb!

> My anguish, my anguish! I writhe in pain! Oh, the walls of my heart!
> My heart is beating wildly; I cannot keep silent; for I hear the sound
> of the trumpet, the alarm of war (4:19).

The impending danger from the north is internalized in Jeremiah. History's crisis is incarnated to "the walls of my heart." His heart beats wildly since history's heart beats wildly. His total personality cried out under the pressure of "being a communicator."

> O LORD, thou hast deceived me, and I was deceived; thou art stronger
> than I, and thou hast prevailed. I have become a laughing stock all
> the day; everyone mocks me. . . . If I say, "I will not mention him, or
> speak any more in his name," there is in my heart as it were a burn-
> ing fire shut up in my bones, and I am weary with holding it in, and I
> cannot (20:7,9).

This is no ordinary lament. These are words that indicate the destiny of the communicator. In this interior struggle and conflict of the person of communicator, God speaks to the nations. The whole person of Jeremiah carries the message.

There are songs which are called Servant Songs in Isaiah (42:1-4; 49:1-6; 50:4-11; 52:13 — 53:12). The writer of the Servant Songs portrays the image of the Servant who goes through the destiny of humiliation and exaltation. Scholars hold differing views on the identity of the Servant. He may be the nation of Israel, or an individual, or both. The point I wish to make is that the Servant, whether Israel as a nation or an individual, is the communicator of God's purpose in history.

> I gave back to the smiters, and my cheeks to those who pulled out the
> beard; I hid not my face from shame and spitting (50:6).

The Servant accepts unbearable humiliation (see Jer. 11:19-21; 15:17; 18:18; 20:10). To be a communicator of God is not at all an "armchair-affair." It is a "calamitous" assignment. It is not a "part-time job." It requires *all* of a person's life. In the conviction that "the LORD God helps me" (50:7), he must accept rejection and humiliation. He becomes the rejected, the humiliated, and the misunderstood (53:4). This rejected, humiliated, and misunderstood person is the communicator of the saving acts of God in history. He gives his "cheeks to those who pull out the beard." What an image of the communicator!

Paul's apostolic preaching is done with his "body." "I bear on my body the marks of Jesus" (Gal. 6:17). The marks may be the scars of lashes. Paul speaks about himself in the tradition of the other great communicators of God:

> For I think that God has exhibited us apostles as last of all, like men sentenced to death; because we have become a spectacle to the world, to angels and to men. We are fools for Christ's sake, but you are wise in Christ. We are weak, but you are strong. You are held in honor, but we in disrepute. To the present hour we hunger and thirst, we are ill clad and buffeted and homeless, and we labor, working with our own hands. When reviled, we bless; when persecuted, we endure; when slandered, we try to conciliate; we have become, and are now, as refuse of the world, the offscouring of all things (I Cor. 4.9-13).

Called to be a communicator of God's saving event, Paul's whole manner of life has changed. The scars symbolize his historical and human participation in God's concrete drama of dead-alive — lost-found. His whole existence and theology demonstrate his personal experience of the power of God that stages the saving event of dead-alive — lost-found. Does not "reviled-bless — persecuted-endure — slandered-conciliate" have an amazingly similar note to that "dead-alive — lost-found?" He identifies himself as "refuse of the world, the offscouring of all things." Does this not, again, sound similar to the self-denial of the Servant who let others pull out his beard?

A few letters attributed to Paul were written in prison. A great deal of Paul's message of the emancipating Christ comes from the wall of imprisonment. From the prison he writes to the Philippians. Outside some are preaching Christ in envy and rivalry and others from good will. He cannot walk out of prison and speak to the people involved in this tragic division. He, the communicator of the gospel, seems to be rendered helpless. But even in prison he senses the advance of the gospel of Christ. In his imprisonment — in the situation of, as it were, having his beard plucked out — he witnesses the advance of the reality of Christ's emancipation among people. "If I must boast, I will boast of the things that show my weakness" (II Cor. 11:30).

In reviewing, even though briefly, some of the communicators of the saving act of God in history, I have tried to point out how deeply biblical communication is communicator-communication. God uses people in all their complexity. God lets a person participate in God's purpose in history. God does this in the midst of historical and human complexity. God's love (*agape*) expresses itself not as a general philosophical principle of the world, but concretely and historically in the confusion of complexity.

God calls people and lets them participate in God's purpose. God calls people *freely*. God calls people without regard to degrees, whether Bachelor of Theology or others. God calls one who happens to be a Thai Buddhist for God's purpose. Theology one can tame, but the living God no one can tame. No one can tell God what God should do. In the broad sense, a missionary is anyone who increases by participation the concretization of the love of God in history. Some years ago, I visited a remote village in north Thailand. A group of government health officers were spraying a chemical at that time. Eradication of the malaria mosquito is one concretization of the love of God. In this sense those officers are missionaries. Is "missionary" an inclusive or exclusive concept? Is it a broad or narrow concept? It is a *theological* concept. "Theological" here means that the definition of being a missionary comes ultimately from God who missions people. God who missions knows the missionary.

A missionary is never a finished product. "Missionary" is a continuous participation-concept. A missionary lives with the consciousness of participating in the saving drama of dead-alive — lost-found. He or she grows. Her missionary quality is enhanced as she lives a life of participation in the Pauline sense.

Then the question "What makes a missionary?" brings us to the question of the nurture or growth of the missionary. As she grows, she remains a missionary.

First, the missionary must live *in* the complexity of history. This call comes from God who loves people. Love is the mind that appreciates complexity. The appreciation of complexity of history nurtures the missionary's life.

Second, the missionary's missionary-quality will be nurtured in his or her life-participation in the apostolic existence of reviled-bless — persecuted-endure — slandered-conciliate. God calls people. In the call is included the call to go through the experience of "letting someone pull your beard out!" There are some historical connections and projects which form a portion of the proud beard of the mission boards. But the implication is that they may have to come out. It will hurt. But if that is the way to enable our richer participation in that apostolic life, then it has to happen.

Third, the missionary's missionary-quality will be nurtured as he or she travels in the direction of the "unity of message and messenger." No missionaries will ever reach this unity. But that does not mean that one should not walk *toward* that goal. A missionary must have "spiritual exercise." What direction should he or she go in spiritual growth? The direction of the unity of message and messenger!

This chapter is called "Toward a Crucified Mind," not "The Crusading Mind." When I meet missionaries from the West in the varieties of localities in Southeast Asia, what I call the Johannine principle, "He must increase, but I must decrease" (Jn. 3:30), comes to my mind. John the Baptist introduced Jesus in these moving terms. Jesus must increase! Missionaries must decrease *if* their decrease points to the increase of Jesus Christ. Increase of Jesus Christ? Yes! Increase of Jesus Christ in the given Southeast Asian locality. How is Jesus Christ to be increased in Hong Kong? Jesus is increased when the local people are increased in the knowlege of Jesus Christ in whom the dead-alive — lost-found history came to its final substance and expression. Missionaries must decrease, then, in order to make the local people increase. However, as soon as the given local people are increased, they must decrease for the sake of the increase of other local people. The chain reaction of increase and decrease must continue. This continuity of increase and decrease is the wave of salvation-history, the beginning and end of which is Jesus Christ.

The Johannine principle of increase and decrease goes through a tremendous upheaval when Jesus decreases in order to make "us" increase.

> For you know the grace of our Lord Jesus Christ, that though he was rich, yet for your sake he became poor, so that by his poverty you might become rich (II Cor. 8:9).

He is the author of reconciliation. In decreasing himself to an incomprehensible degree, he becomes the foundation of reconciliation (Phil. 2:1-11). At this point the Johannine principle is, as it were, swallowed up by the Christ principle. If missionaries decrease themselves, they are doing so not only in the light of the Johannine principle, but also in the revolutionary principle of Christ. Here lies the secret of the dynamic identity of the Christian missionary.

If missionaries decrease themselves, they are doing so not only in the light of the Johannine principle, but also in the revolutionary principle of Christ. What is this principle of Christ? It is expressed in the life-style of the apostolic discipleship; "when reviled, we bless; when persecuted, we endure; when slandered, we speak kindly."

> Have this mind among yourselves, which you have in Christ Jesus, who . . . (Phil. 2:5-11).

The mind that speaks kindly when slandered is based on the mind of Christ that spoke kindly when slandered. " "Love does not insist on its way" (I Cor. 13:5). The crucified mind is not a pathological or neurotic mind. It is *love* seeking the benefit of others. This mind sees a person "as he is seen" (I Jn. 4:20). This mind creates the communicator's mind. This mind appreciates the complexity of people and history. It participates in the dead-alive — lost-found history in the way Christ participated. This must be the mind of the missionary. This mind is radically different from the crusading mind which bulldozes people and history without appreciation of their complexities. The crusading mind is not the mind of the biblical communicators. It must not be the mind of the missionary.

The crucified mind, not the crusading mind, must be the mind of all missionaries, indeed of all Christians. Does not the Crucified One create the crucified mind within us and nurture it? Is it not true that only the crucified mind can respond joyously to the call of the Father reclaiming his lost son to "dance, music and feast" in the event of dead-alive — lost-found?

CHAPTER 18

Three Modes of Christian Presence

- The Christian faith is a "noisy" faith of God's attachment to people.
- Christ in whom all things hold together is the Christ of whom only the "word of the cross" can adequately bear witness.
- Who are we? We are the crucified-Christ-with us. This is our new identification.
- This new personal identification will express itself in three modes of Christian presence in the world:
  - stumbling presence. Can a house unshaken bear witness to the earthquake?
  - "discomforted" presence. Can Christians who do not involve themselves in the great "discomfort" of the nailed Christ point to the source of all comfort?
  - "unfree" presence. Christians are called to participate in all situations of life as the Incarnate Lord fully did. Yet this participation must not lead them to "drink the cup of the demons."
- All scattered things are held together in the *glory* of the *crucified* Lord!

In the steaming afternoon stillness of a Buddhist temple in northern Thailand I was engaged in a conversation with a Buddhist monk. We were discussing the first chapter of the gospel of John.

In the beginning was the Word, and the Word was with God, and the Word was God.

Responded the monk:

My friend, this is quite a *noisy* religion. I am afraid that we are getting further and further away from the bliss of tranquility and detachment. At least in the beginning there must have been Nirvanic silence, deep tranquility and *non-attachment*.

160

I said to myself: "This quick intuitive observation of the monk is on the right track indeed! The Christian faith is a noisy faith. Because it lives in believing in God's decisive and irreversible *attachment* to people in Christ."

In the Bible, there is a striking progression of God's "noisy attachment." In "the time of expectation" (Karl Barth) — which was the time of God's covenantal attachment with the people Israel — God sent the prophets, "the agitated persons."[1] The progression of attachment gained a new intensity when the Eternal Word which was in the beginning "became a human being and lived among us" (Jn. 1:14). He is the One who said "I am the Truth," which meant for the primitive church the extraordinary redemptive truth of God who was "in Christ personally reconciling the world to himself" (II Cor. 5:19). This reconciliation has been accomplished "by virtue of the sacrifice of the cross" of Jesus Christ (Col. 1:20; Eph. 2:13). The Word which was in the beginning became, in Jesus of Nazareth, the crucified Word. The Lord of creation (Col. 1:16) is *now* the head of the church (Col. 1:15-17 progresses into 18-20). None of us can halt this divine progression! Christ in whom all things hold together is the Christ of whom only the "Word of the cross" can adequately bear witness. The Christian faith is agitated "adhesion to God" (Luther). The apostle Paul spoke for the whole *oikoumene* throughout the centuries when he wrote to the Corinthians:

> I resolved that while I was with you I would think of nothing but Jesus Christ — Christ nailed to the cross (I Cor. 2:2).

In Dr. B. D. Napier's *Commentary on Exodus* we find an exciting piece of exegesis:

> Who am I? asks Moses. Child of Israel-Egypt? Fugitive? Priest's son-in-law and Midianite shepherd? No, responds the Word. Your identity now is to be understood only in relation to Me. You are God-with-you.[2]

The Word says to us today: "Your identity now is to be understood only in relation to the crucified Lord. You are the crucified Lord-with-you." Paul declares this new identity in Galatians 2:20:

> I have been crucified with Christ: the life I now live is not my life, but the life which Christ lives in me; and my present bodily life is lived by faith in the Son of God, who loved me and sacrificed himself for me.

We are thus invited to see that "in him all things hold together," in the light of the crucified Lord. There is no possibility of holding all together without him or outside his time. Verse 17 has nothing to do with the gnostic

---

1. Abraham J. Heschel, *The Prophets*, Harper & Row, 1962, p. xiii.
2. B. D. Napier, *Exodus*, Layman's Bible Commentaries, SCM Press, 1963, p. 30.

holding together (emanation) and the *karmic* (action-reaction) holding together (apathetic operation of causality). On the contrary, it points to the crucified Lord who in his suffering accomplished the holding of all things together in him and carried this holding together to the ultimate point of consummation in the history of God's salvation.

The crucified Lord holds all things together as the king, the priest, and the prophet.

(1) Crucified, yet Christ is sovereign over *all* (the king).

(2) Crucified, yet Christ comforts *all* (the priest).

(3) Crucified, yet Christ frees *all* (the prophet).

This is how our theme presents itself when it is seen from the theology of the cross.

These critical ingredients of the theology of the cross are pressing themselves upon our minds with overwhelming force of immediacy. Mr. Ashol Mehta, India's Minister of Planning, spoke of the world's final proletariat, some 900 million people who are among the very poorest in the world today:

> . . . this is perhaps one of the most important tasks with which we must identify ourselves . . . reclaiming . . . 900 million people of the world who are today in a state of abject depression. This *human reclamation*, requiring its peculiar type of social engineering, is to my mind the big challenge that all men of religion, all men of God, have to face.

The world is scattered asunder! We are pressed between two realities. On the one hand, the reality that "in him all things hold together," and, on the other, the reality that all things are confounded, scattered, and sick. The former is a theological, eschatological reality (a hidden reality). The latter is a brutally obvious reality to all. The Christian church confesses that the language which can bind these two realities is the language of the cross, and the ointment which can effect the healing of the breach between these two realities is the ointment of love poured by the woman over the head of the Anointed of God (Lk. 7:36-50). The lordship which can relate these two truths is the crucified lordship! Here is the global significance of theology of the cross. Theology of the cross is not a monopoly of the sixteenth-century Reformers or of present day neo-orthodoxy, or of any particular segment of the Christian church. If human suffering is "ecumenical" (throughout the inhabited world), then naturally the study of the message of the healing ointment must assume ecumenical horizons and quality. Theology of the cross will give us a perspective in which we can look at, and participate in, the suffering of humankind. The suffering of the world is costly, and equally costly is the way Christ holds all things in his suffering. Apart from theology of the cross we will be held guilty of advocating, more or less, Christ in the inspiration of Mary Poppins who can hold things together easily by a snap of her fingers!

THREE MODES OF CHRISTIAN PRESENCE

"Crucified, yet . . ." is the summit of the paradox of God's glory in the act of holding all things together in Jesus Christ. Christian presence, which is rooted in and participates in the crucified Christ, must demonstrate the quality of Christ's glory in suffering, his exaltation in rejection.

Our Stumbling Presence

It is difficult to stake one's life on a man who was crucified between two thieves outside the gate of Jerusalem, trusting him to be the Lord in whom alone God's final restoration of all things was effected (Eph. 1:10). It seems "sheer nonsense" (I Cor. 1:23, J. B. Phillips) to insist that the time of crucifixion was the time of exaltation and glorification of Christ (Jn. 12:23; 13:31f.) and thus the time of demonstrating the lordship of Christ. In short, the rejected and crucified lordship is the scandal of the cross of Christ. With sheer good sense the very people from whom Christ came stumbled at him (Rom. 9:32,33; Matt. 13:57). With sheer good sense, the people who lived at a distance from Abraham stumbled at him (Acts 17:32). With sheer good sense the people who live in proximity to the Buddha stumble at Christ as well. The lordship of Christ in the theology of the cross — the crucified lordship! — is universally "sheer nonsense" to humans (Gal. 5:11).

Christians are, we often say, those who have safely overcome, by the grace of God, the stumbling block of the crucified Christ and who have entered into the new life nourished by "Christ the power of God and the wisdom of God."

Precisely here, however, the theology of the cross presses a critical question: can unstumbling Christians point to the shaking of the foundations caused by the crucified Lord? Can Christians bear witness to Christ's crucified lordship unless they themselves are stumbled at it? Can a house unshaken bear witness to the earthquake which is going on?

As we live in the turbulent history of humankind today, we confess that Christ, the crucified and hidden Lord, stands at the center of history. When we try to live history seriously and try to interpret our life in Asia today "in the light" (Ps. 36:9), we begin to stumble. It is neither in the light of the Buddha nor of science, but in the light of the God of Israel, who has accomplished the design of holding all things together in Jesus Christ, that we begin to stumble! The block of stumbling is called "eschatological already-not-yet" — the scandal of history. Why does God intend *today* that both "wheat and tare" should grow together until the appointed Last Time (Matt. 13:24-30)? This decision of God is not peripheral but fundamental to the New Testament. It is the deep mystery of God.[3] Is not this mystery of

---

3. Julius Schniewind, *Das Evangelium nach Matthäus*, Vandenhoeck and Ruprecht, 1937, pp. 165, 171.

the suspended salvation and judgment within our historical time, the great ground-swell that causes all kinds of havoc and shakings in our life and in our history? And does not this "not-yet" contain the answer as to why the theme "In him all things *hold together*" has a sub-division called "A *divided* church in a *broken* world?" Our Hong Kong Consultation on "Faith and Order" (1966) frequently bears witness to the earthquake. Here is one found in the chapter "Confessing the Faith in Politics:"

> Confessing the faith in Asia today means bearing witness to Jesus Christ as Lord and Saviour of all political concern and activity. In His life, death, resurrection and the coming of His Spirit. He *has overcome* all principalities and powers. . . . His presence there is still hidden but faith confesses the hope that He *shall establish* His kingdom *in the end* and all things will be renewed and fulfilled in Him (italics added).[4]

This eschatology in Christ involves all the history of all humankind. *All* are, therefore, disturbed and shaken by the ultimate mystery of God.

> We confess that Christ is the Lord, the Judge and Fulfilment of all history. Therefore, we affirm that He is at work even now in the Asian revolution which is under His judgment and mercy and which *in the fullness of time He will redeem.*[5]

Isn't it true that our only responsive stance toward this "scandal of history" is to sell all we have in order to buy the precious "pearl" of the Messianic Reign (Matt. 13:44-46)? Is not this great challenge hidden from the world? Can our existence remain unshaken when we are challenged by the hidden reality of the reign of God right in the confusion of history? Are we not stumbling here because of our little faith? But in our very stumbling we wish to confess Jesus Christ is the Lord in history. How? Can it be? Christ sustains us!

> Simon, Simon, behold, Satan demanded to have you, that he might sift you like wheat, but I have prayed for you that your faith may not fail; and when you have turned again, strengthen your brethren (Lk. 22:31-32).

Is not this the hidden quality — theological quality — of our stumbling?

Here lies a peculiar quality and position of the Christian presence. Our Christian presence is a presence firmly established upon the glory of the

---

4. *Confessing the Faith in Asia Today*, EACC, 1966, p. 73.
5. Ibid.

crucified Christ, yet at the same time this very glory shakes our presence and makes it a stumbling one! The supreme example of the nature of this Christian presence is given in Christ himself who was nailed to the cross. "My God, my God, why hast thou forsaken me?" (Mark 15:34) reveals Christ who is stumbling at the forsaking of the hidden God, yet who is firmly trusting and triumphing in God. Christ believed in God *against* God. Faith is "to flee to God against God" (*ad deum contra deum confugere*) says Luther.[6] Christian presence, which is the presence of faith, must live this crucial tension. No one is permitted to escape from the tension between stumbling and triumphing trust.

There is such a thing as a stumbling quality in the Christian presence. We do not make our presence a stumbling one. God makes us so in the Son. It is not artificial but given. Our stumbling presence guards us from falling into superficial triumphalism of faith, which misunderstands the depth and width of faith's eschatological assertion that "in him all things hold together." The danger of the triumphalism of faith lies in its insidious charm which clouds our eyes fastened to the nailed Lord.

Triumphalism encourages us, as it has done with stubborn tenacity at many critical times in church history, to make a quick jump from "stumbling" to "unstumbling," from Good Friday to Easter. This jump must be carefully avoided. Barth writes:

> Human experience and human thought might as such, in accord with their own dead weight, proceed in a straight line from despair to deeper despair, from seriousness to still greater seriousness (there is also a negative *theologia gloriae*), or from triumph to higher triumph, from joy to still greater joy; *to faith this straight line movement is forbidden by the Word of God, which calls us from despair to triumph, from seriousness to joy, but also from triumph to despair and from joy to seriousness. This is the meaning of theologia crucis* (italics added).[7]

Luther fought against the scholastic unstumblingness ("from triumph to higher triumph, from joy to still greater joy") of his day. Perhaps the fundamental contribution of the theology in Asia to the church universal is to describe, in her own language, theology that stumbles.

In remaining stumbling, we are in a better position to communicate *why* we are stumbling — which is no less than evangelism itself — to our neighbors. The grace that makes our presence stumbling prefers to be channeled to others through the stumbling agents. To assert Christ's lordship of holding all things together through our stumbling presence is indeed a singular way of self-assertion of the church of Christ in the stumbling world today!

---

6. Weimar edition, V, pp. 204-8.
7. Karl Barth, *Church Dogmatics* I,1, T.&T. Clark, 1936, p. 204.

Our "Discomforted" Presence

The first question of *The Heidelberg Catechism* is this: "What is your only comfort, in life and in death?" The answer is given: "The only comfort is in that I belong to Jesus Christ."

> If we live, we live for the Lord: and if we die, we die for the Lord. Whether therefore we live or die, we belong to the Lord (Rom. 14:8).

> Then what can separate us from the love of Christ? Can affliction or hardship? Can persecution, hunger, nakedness, peril or the sword (Rom. 8:35)?

Christians are comforted people in virtue of belonging to Jesus Christ.

Precisely here, however, the theology of the cross presses a critical question: Can comforted Christians bear witness to the Lord who comforts all *from the cross?*

> As Christ's cup of suffering overflows, and we suffer with him, so also through Christ our consolation overflows (II Cor. 1:5).

> He was rich, yet for your sake he became poor, so that through his poverty you might become rich (II Cor. 8:9).

Can Christians, who do not involve themselves in the great "discomfort" of the nailed Christ, point to the source of all comfort? Isn't it true that precisely because they are comforted by the crucified Lord, they are inescapably involved in "discomfort" of the crucified Lord? We belong to Jesus Christ. Exactly because of this specific belonging, we are christologically comforted and christologically discomforted. We are to live sharing the painful *pathos* of God's saving will expressed in the striking images at the crucial moments of salvation-history.

> Now I will cry out like a woman in travail. I will gasp and pant (Isa. 42:14).

> Now my soul is in turmoil . . . (Jn. 12:27)

This is the nature of "discomfort" which we are called to share. Our comforted life displays its explosive energy in our "discomforted" life. To live in this peculiar paradoxical framework is our special mission to the world. It is a prophetic style of life.

What does this "christologically discomforted" mean in the Asian context today?

In the first place, let me repeat that the source of our discomfort is neither in the Enlightened Buddha nor in a certain kind of noble religious and ethical idea, but in the crucified Lord. We do not make ourselves dis-comforted. It is the work of God in Christ. We are deeply comforted and deeply discomforted by the same Christ. Our "discomfort" is to reflect the nature of Christ's "discomfort," *suffering.* The Apostle Paul was confident of his call to the glorious apostleship because his life really participated in Christ's suffering (II Cor. 4:7ff.; 6:4ff.; 11:23ff.; Col. 7:24; Rom. 8:17; Phil. 3:10).

Christ suffered because he was involved with others. He died for others (Rom. 8:32; 14:15; Gal. 2:20; I Pet. 2:21; I Thess. 5:9; Heb. 2:9; Jn. 10:11; 15:13). In this act of dying for others Christ has completed his image of the New Human. Christological discomfort is not a monologue in any sense of the term. It is a dialogue, an active participating reality. The "christologi-cal" implies immediately "the neighborological." They are inseparable. How do we participate in the *newness* of Christ, the New Human? By living a paradoxical life deeply comforted and deeply discomforted by Christ in the midst of our neighbors — this is the way to participate in the newness of Christ's presence in Asia.

In the second place, when we are christologically discomforted, we share christological comfort. In particular, we will be bypassing Christ's discomfort if we approach our people with doctrinal statements. The realism of Christ's comfort and the comfort of our human doctrinal statements, no matter how accurate and profound they may be, cannot be treated on an equal footing. Doctrinal persuasion is a falsely comfortable way to come to the hearts of our neighbors. To quest after the right doctrinal formulation is important, but to share the comfort which is in Christ is far more imperative and crucial. The famous Athanasian Creed *Quicunque vult salvus esse* (whoever wishes to be saved) has rendered, no doubt, a great service to the church by clarifying the awesome mystery of God's essential mode of existence and God's saving acts for humankind in history. The *spirit*, however, dictating this great con-fession of faith, is partially paralyzed when it imprisons the *comfort* of Christ into propositional paragraphs with almost "divine" certitude. I wonder if this spirit, the activity of which we can detect at various points of church history, has hindered the communication and sharing of the comfort of Christ. Isn't it true that not doctrinal formulation, but comfort can reach all, uneducated farmers, a Toynbee, and a Ramakrishnan alike? The reality of being com-forted by Christ must leave some impact upon the peoples who are com-forted by the Buddha, or Marxism, or technocracy.

We are called to reject the position of false comfort, and imitate Christ's discomfort in the very sharing of Christ's comfort.

I feel the pangs of child-birth all over again till Christ be formed within you . . . (Gal. 4:19f.).

Participating in Christ's work of holding all things together by being deeply discomforted — what a singular form of mission in the discom-forted world today!

Our "Unfree" Presence

Christ frees us from the power of darkness. The healing of the man born blind (Jn. 9:2-5) is one of the most inspiring illustrations of the power of emancipation which is in Jesus Christ. The story goes, in effect:

> Disciples, your approach to this man's tragedy is wrong! Your minds are still busily occupied to find its cause in the man himself. Indeed, good reasons for his blindness may be found in him or in his parents. But, *now*, you must not pursue that possibility. Discontinue it! You must look at me and see how I, in my own painful way, hold all things together. Now, because I am here, you are in the new age, in the new world illumined by my involvement. The question of "whose sin this is, his own or his parents" has lost its significance since I am here. *Discontinue* your old theology and old style of living. See this tragedy in relation to me, through and in my presence!

When Christ touches *one*, and *one* is led to touch him in faith — even "the fringe of his cloak" (Matt. 9:20-22) — that person is restored to wholeness, to the abundant life in the covenant relationship with God. The touch of the New Human—even through the humble instrument of "spittle and clay" — makes a person new (Jn. 9:6f.). This special newness in Christ is the source of the freedom in Christ. In the light of this amazing appropriation of the newness of life in Christ, "the new creation" (II Cor. 5:17), Paul was able to call even the best portion of his own spiritual possession "garbage" (Phil. 3:4-9). Christ's word reached Zacchaeus in the tree and his darkened life was restored to the full light of the covenantal relationship with people and with God (Lk. 19:4-10). The life restored is the life complete. Wherever Christ walked, people were summoned to listen to him and when the people responded with "the ears that can hear" (Matt. 13:9), "christological discontinuity" took place.

Indeed we are brought into the wholeness of life in Christ. Precisely at this juncture the theology of the cross asks a critical question. Should not this freedom be crucified, following the Son of God who crucified his freedom for others in the form of a servant (Phil. 2:7; Lk. 22:27; Isa. 53)? In the light of the crucified Christ, can our freedom express itself in any other way than in the life of "unfreedom of the servant?"

On the basis of I Corinthians 9:19, Romans 13:8, Galatians 4:4, and Philippians 2:6f., Luther, the great exponent of the theology of the cross, has given us two great sentences of truth about Christian life:

> A Christian is a perfectly free lord of all, subject to none. A Christian is a perfectly dutiful servant of all, subject to all.[8]

---

8. Martin Luther, *The Freedom of a Christian Man.*

The first proposition (lordship) must be put into action through the second proposition (servantship). Then it portrays the structure of the crucified lordship of Christ. Christian presence in the world moves between the two points, between christological discontinuity — freedom from "the elemental principles of this world" (Gal. 4:3) — and christological continuity — "unfreedom" in the form of servant to serve all. In this remarkable perspective of freedom, christological discontinuity participates in God's holding together all things in Christ.

Here we are confronted by the problem of the Lord's table and the other tables. We are not free to forget Christ's table which reminds us of his baptism of suffering (Lk. 12:50; 22:14-16) "until he comes" (I Cor. 11:26). Our *attachment* to the Lord's table makes us "distinguishable" from the world[9] and frees us from the "saving messages" of the "other tables," such as those of secularism, technocracy, communism, and the great ancient religions. Here, however, is a paradox. We are made free from the other tables because of our remembering the Lord's table. But this emancipation will make us concerned about the messages of those other tables.

"They are not of the world, even as I am not of the world. . . . As thou didst send me into the world, so I have sent them into the world." The gospel not only makes the church distinguishable within the human community: the gospel also creates a new identifiability with the human community.[10]

This new identifiability given to us in our attachment to the Lord keeps us from falling into the act of idolatry. St. Paul warns us of the incompatibility between the Lord's table and the table of demons (I Cor. 10:21). There is a demonic sacramental depth in all these great other tables which invite us to the feast of worshiping them. This "fearful reality" must be discerned by the light of the table of the Lord.[11]

We join others in the expression of their joys and sorrows, but refrain from actions and activities which deny or compromise our faith. Occasions of social intercourse, celebration and ritual activities such as births, birthdays, betrothals, marriage, illness, funerals, remembrance of death, often present Christians with opportunities for expressing their fellowship and sensitivity as well as their discernment.[12]

---

9. *Confessing the Faith in Asia Today*, p. 75.
10. Ibid.
11. Dietrich Wendland, *Die Briefe an die Korinther*, Vandenhoeck and Ruprecht, 1954, p. 74.
12. *Confessing the Faith in Asia Today*, p. 54.

We are called to participate in all the situations of life as the Incarnate Lord fully did. Yet this participation must not lead us to "drink the cup of the demons."

CONCLUSION

We do not make ourselves stumbling, discomforted, and unfree. God makes us so through the Son, in spite of our desire to be free from this strange mode of life.

In him *all* things hold together — this *all* is stumbling, discomforted, and unfree. But if this *all* is thus profoundly stumbling, discomforted, and unfree, so are we *in* and *because* of Jesus Christ. To face the all which is stumbling, discomforted, and unfree as the one (individual and community) who is stumbling, discomforted, and unfree is to participate in the ministry of the "holding together" of the hidden Lord. This is the basic form of our Christian calling and presence.

> Called "impostors" we must be true, called "nobodies" we must be in the public eye. Never far from death, yet here we are alive, always "going through it" yet never "going under." We know sorrow, yet our joy is inextinguishable. We have "nothing to bless ourselves with" yet we bless many others with true riches. We are penniless, and yet in reality we have everything worth having (II Cor. 6:9-10, J. B. Phillips).

In this eschatological hour, we are called to share the pathos of God,[13] God's *pathos* toward all scattered things which are held together in the *glory* of the *crucified* Lord.

---

13. A. Heschel, op. cit., p. 126.

Epilogue

My Pilgrimage in Mission

Born in 1929 in Tokyo, Japan, I was about ten years old when I was introduced to John Bunyan's *Pilgrim's Progress*. I still remember the excitement with which I held the book in my hands and examined the picture of the weary traveler, kneeling before the cross. It was the first theological book I read in my life. Though my understanding of it was limited, its symbolism beyond my comprehension, I was drawn by the devotion of Christian, the main character of the book. His determination to reach the goal, overcoming all obstacles and temptations on the way, left a deep impression on my soul. Finally, he arrives at the cross, and the burden he has been carrying falls from his shoulders. The strange impression of this travelogue has stayed with me as though it were my personal secret. Today I can see that the book introduced me to the Christian understanding of history. Our lives, and even the great panorama of human history, have beginnings and ends that contain the movement (i.e., the pilgrim's progress) toward God. This understanding of life and of history gives a fundamental orientation for the Christian understanding of mission.

PILGRIM'S PROGRESS VERSUS DEMON PROGRESS

About the time I encountered *Pilgrim's Progress*, the Japanese military was already active against Manchuria and China. The war thus begun eventually became the Fifteen-Year War. At the time of Japanese surrender in 1945, Japan was at enmity with fifty-two nations. Between 1941 and 1945 I experienced utter confusion, violence, and destruction. Night after night the bombs rained down upon us. Yet, somehow, the idea that our life, personally and collectively, must be a movement toward God survived in my soul. I sensed, though vaguely, a great contrast between pilgrim progress and the "demon progress," as it were, of the cult of emperor worship. I concluded that Japan became a heap of ruins because it engaged in the cult of a false god — in idolatry. Perceiving that this would sound extremely strange to my friends, I kept it to myself. My thought was simple. The emperor is human. It is not right to say that he is divine. Idolatry, a theme foreign to Japanese culture, became a part of my mental vocabulary. It came together with the experience of the terrifying violence of war. I was

171

baptized during the war years not so much from an awareness of my personal sinfulness as from the immediate experience of the destruction of my country by war. The minister who baptized me told me that the God of the Bible is concerned about the well-being of all nations, even including Japan and America. To hear this at the same time that we were being bombed by America was quite startling. This was my first ecumenical lesson.

My life, spanning the bulk of this century, has been continuously invaded by the violence of wars. The twentieth century has been a century of genocide and wars. When I pray, "Lead us not into temptation," I am, in fact, saying, "Lead us to the eradication of violence." It is violence, not temptation, that has defined my life in this century.

The Christian faith came into the Koyama clan when my paternal grandfather became a Christian some 130 years ago. With his grandfatherly authority, he encouraged us to read the Bible and to freely discuss our thoughts about it. Strange names — Adam, Eve, Moses, Elijah, Jeremiah, Paul, Peter — gradually became familiar to us. Because of my grandfather's wisdom, the Bible has always been for me a companion book that initiates fascinating and serious discussion about our life in the world. I hold today that the Bible is the Word of God not because it is so defined by the church, but because it speaks to us urgently and deeply. Many years later my mother told me that my grandfather had been praying for one of his grandchildren to become an evangelist. Without knowing this, I entered the preparatory course of Tokyo Union Theological Seminary in 1946. Tokyo was desolate, and I was tormented by hunger.

I remember that one morning at chapel Dr. Kuwada, president of the seminary, read from 2 Kings 25:6-7. The American president, Mr. Truman, he said, treated the Japanese emperor Hirohito far more mercifully than Nebuchadnezzar, the king of Babylon, had treated Zedekiah, the king of Judah. I felt thankful for that. On the day when the top Japanese war criminals were hanged, Dr. Kuwada spoke of international justice. But, I thought, had Japan won the war, they would surely not have been hanged. Through these "international" events, I learned to pronounce the names of Nebuchadnezzar and Zedekiah, turning them over on my tongue in my Japanese accent with great delight. They sounded impressive!

I graduated from Tokyo Union Theological Seminary in 1952 with a thesis on St. Francis of Assisi. In my mind St. Francis's ability to converse with a wild wolf was united with his mystical reception of the holy stigmata of Christ. I concluded that the lifestyle of the stigmata overcame all barriers to communication, even between the animal and human worlds. I seemed to detect an Oriental (India, China) element of saintliness in Francis.

A TIME OF CULTURAL AND THEOLOGICAL "FLOATING"

From 1952 to 1959 I studied "Western theology" in theological schools in Madison and Princeton in New Jersey. During those years I was convinced that whatever my professors taught me was universally valid, since, after all, Christian theology had been developed in the West. Almost intentionally, I ignored my own culture and language, deciding that they were worthless. It was a time of cultural and theological floating that continued for seven years. I was able to obtain the doctoral degree in theology from Princeton Theological Seminary without bringing what I learned in New Jersey to dialogue with my own spiritual and cultural roots. Vaguely, however, I was aware of the need for integration.

One steamy night in August 1960, I flew with my young family into Bangkok, Thailand. We were missionaries sent by the United Church of Christ in Japan (Kyodan) to the Church of Christ in Thailand. Through the desk of Ecumenical Relations of the Kyodan, the financial support for this project came mostly from Presbyterian, Disciples, and Baptist churches in America. Though we were called "missionaries from Japan," the Kyodan was not able, at that time, to support us fully. This dependence arrangement continued for fifteen years, supporting me and my immediate Japanese successor in Thailand. I learned that any ecumenical project involves complicated financial arrangements.

In Bangkok we immediately plunged into language study. For one full year our life was totally circumscribed and consumed by language study. Being unable to produce certain sounds, my tongue was twisted, my lungs pained, and my intelligence humiliated. Learning the Thai language was my second spiritual baptism, a baptism into the unfamiliar sounds and symbols of a different culture and religion. Today I am tempted to say that anyone who wants to understand multiculturalism or religious pluralism would first have to endure this linguistic baptism. It was the language study that grounded me from that rootless floating. For all the tongue twisting and mental humiliation, after a year of language study I ventured to lecture in Thai at Thailand Theological Seminary in Chiengmai. My students heard the countless mistakes, both hilarious and dangerous, that I made in the classroom.

Coming to Thailand, I entered the young yet venerable heritage of Asian ecumenism, which began in 1949 with the Bangkok conference entitled "The Christian Prospect in Eastern Asia." Under the leadership of D. T. Niles, U Kyaw Than, and Alan Brash, the East Asia Christian Conference (EACC) was formed in 1957. The theme of its inaugural conference at Prapat, Indonesia — "The Common Evangelistic Task of the Churches in East Asia" — was still echoing when I arrived in Chiengmai. I experienced firsthand the reality of the community of faith spread throughout Asia. My theological ministry found a new strong context in the "Common Evangelistic Task."

LUTHER'S THEOLOGY IN CHIENGMAI

With the kind help of John Hamlin, the principal of the seminary, and of faculty colleagues, my appreciation of the Thai Theravada Buddhist–

animist culture gradually deepened. This new development shook my confidence in the New Jersey theology. When one day in the classroom I realized that my lecture on Luther's theology was a complete flop, I panicked. The waves of the panic reached back all the way to my wartime experience. The realization that many of my EACC friends also knew the war, but as the victims of Japanese imperialism, was important for my new theological orientation.

What, I asked myself, is the connection between Chiengmai and Wittenberg? I could not justify myself by saying that for my New Jersey professors, Wittenberg was important. There was a serious question of relevance here, as the EACC was pointing out. Between northern Thailand and New Jersey there are such vast differences in religion, culture, and language. If I speak about Luther's theology in Chiengmai, I must know what my Chiengmai students need to know and understand about such theology. If I did not face these questions, how could I participate in "the Christian prospect in Asia?"

This simple question of relevance was for me Elijah's hand-sized cloud that became, in a short time, a storm. I found the question far more difficult to answer than I at first anticipated. I saw that I must first understand the history of the Thai people and their religion and culture. This would take, I said to myself, more than my lifetime. To begin with, why did I, a man from Tokyo, think Luther's theology was meaningful to me? This question revealed to me how long I had been floating from my own roots. Even this personal question I was not sure how to answer! Suddenly I was confronted by the question of my own personal and theological identity. I realized that the last time I was really I was during the daily bombings of the war. Under the bomb I was totally vulnerable and naked. *Kyrie eleison* (Lord, have mercy!) was the only word left for me then. And that was a strong identity!

Yet I could not allow what I learned in New Jersey to simply disappear like a mist. I needed to reconstruct my theological knowledge in terms of my experience in Thailand. I was involved in a triple accommodation process with Tokyo, New Jersey, and Chiengmai. Should I look at New Jersey and Chiengmai from Tokyo? Or Tokyo and New Jersey from Chiengmai? Or Tokyo and Chiengmai from New Jersey? How could I come to some kind of meaningful integration of my theological thought that would express itself in Japanese, English, and Thai? Gradually, the intense wartime experience of *Kyrie eleison* reclaimed the center of my theological thinking.

The experience of vulnerability under the bomb began to cast its light upon the confusing triple accommodation process. I became Tokyo-centered, but this Tokyo has, in my theological map, remained ever desolate. Tokyo, in being reduced to a ruin, participated in the ancient story associated with Nebuchadnezzar and Zedekiah. From that memorable day when I lectured on Luther in Chiengmai up to the present, I have been continuously challenged by the question of "one Gospel and many cultures." Often this challenge comes to my mind with the image of King Zedekiah, his eyes torn out and taken into exile. The theme of "Christ and culture" and my firsthand experience of the destruction of Japan were welded together in my soul. Ecumenism is a serious subject because it affects the destiny of nations. Japan, behaving like Nebuchadnezzar, "put out the eyes" of countless Asians. How do we affirm the ecumenical gospel in the face of global violence?

SINGAPORE: THE DECOLONIZATION OF THEOLOGY

In 1968 I moved to Singapore to take up the position of dean of the South East Asia Graduate School of Theology (SEAGST), which was formed in 1966. This school was an outcome of a historic theological education consultation held in Bangkok in 1956. In the record of the consultation we read, "The teaching of systematic theology must be relevant to the environment. It must, on the one hand, be grounded in the Bible; and on the other, related to the actual situation . . . . The Christian faith should be presented in relation to the totality of questions raised by the local situation, and *it should not be assumed that certain questions are relevant to all times and situations*" (italics added). Repeating in my mind the last line of the above quotation, I succeeded John Fleming from Scotland. With the 1956 Bangkok conference, we consciously began the process of the decolonization of theology. The selfhood of the Asian church became a subject of serious discussion.

Though my office was located at Trinity Theological College in Singapore, I was kept busy most of the time flying around in the countries of Southeast Asia. From the beginning, the SEAGST faculty knew that there are not one but many religious and cultural contexts in Asia. In fact, the variety in Asia is both staggering and impressive. The SEAGST focused its attention on the academic and historic strength of schools in various cultural contexts. Thailand offered Buddhist studies, while Indonesia and Malaysia were responsible for the study of Islam. Hong Kong and Taiwan presented Confucian studies. The Philippine seminaries were the locus for the study of church history. In 1975, after three years of study and discussion, the Senate of SEAGST came to a consensus to adopt a "Critical Asian Principle" in theological education. It urged the schools to be contextual to regional situations and called the faculty's attention to at least four principles: situational, hermeneutical, missiological, and educational. The Senate approved the presentation of graduating theses in the students' own Asian languages if they preferred. Studying Christianity under these principles, my students of a Buddhist land and students of other Asian cultures could see afresh their own religious heritage, and in doing so, they saw Christianity afresh. By providing theological students with the opportunity to study in other Southeast Asian countries, SEAGST made it possible for them to get out of their own cultural turf for a while in order to become more communicative in theology and language. This is what makes ecumenical education exciting.

While I was the dean, some eighty Ph.D.s constituted the federated faculty of professors who taught in the theological schools in several countries of Southeast Asia. The degrees of all of these professors, including my own, were earned from theological schools in the West. All of the professors were people of two cultures ("fork and chopsticks"), committed to the direction of theological education expressed at the Bangkok conference of 1956. In our Senate discussions we explored together the nature and limits of cultural accommodation of the Gospel not from the North Atlantic theological perspective but from the contexts of diverse local cultures in Asia. A marked absence of paternalism and imperialism among these multicultured faculty members nurtured the healthy growth of the school.

The SEAGST viewed Asia as one part of the global web of cultures and languages. It affirmed an ecological image of interrelatedness instead of viewing Asia as an independent, isolated entity. In my mind the ecological opposes violence, and the image of interrelatedness replaces that of "superiority." I decided not to use the language of superiority within the context of theology. Superiority is a cultural, not theological, concept. To say that Christianity is superior to Buddhism, or vice versa, is empty talk. The Gospel is not to be called superior. It calls us to bear "good fruits" (Matt. 7:17). The "no other name" theology (Acts 4:12) signifies an exclusiveness whose character is "full of grace and truth" (Jn. 1:14). Unlike the ordinary cultural concept of exclusiveness, this Christological exclusiveness, drawing its life from love of unfathomable depth (1 Cor. 13:13), goes far beyond any comparative discussion of superiority or inferiority of religions.

The SEAGST, from its inception, has been a busy center of ecumenical theological discussion. John Fleming, Shoki Coe, Erick Nielson, D. T. Niles, U Kyaw Than, Ivy Chou, Alan Brash, M. M. Thomas, Alan Thomson, Henry P. Van Dusen, John Bennett, and Charles West, just to mention a few, were dear friends, always ready to become most serious discussion partners with SEAGST.

AN UNEXPECTED "BOMBING" IN NEW YORK

In 1974 I left Singapore for New Zealand, where I was senior lecturer in religious studies at the University of Otago. Six years later, in 1980, I received a long-distance call from Donald Shriver, president of Union Theological Seminary in New York, inviting me to become professor of ecumenics and world Christianity. In this exciting environment I experienced a "bombing" quite different from that I had known during the wartime of my youth. There, for the first time, I encountered the Jewish and black peoples. New York abruptly forced me to respond theologically to the fact of enormous violence suffered by these two peoples. My concept of theology, which is ecumenical by nature, did not allow me the excuse that I come from a land in which these two peoples had no historical connections. I sensed that my identity would be directly threatened if I did not come to terms with the twofold encounter. My happy confidence that I was bringing the excitement of Asia to Union was thus shaken soon after I came.

In Asia I had learned that culture is an extremely ambiguous concept. The male-dominated culture of China, in its ten centuries of foot binding, had crippled one billion women. For centuries Hindu caste culture has delegated millions to lives of hopeless poverty and despair. In my thinking, I had come to a *theologia crucis* (theology of the cross) in which love, becoming completely vulnerable to violence, conquers violence. In my Asian *theologia crucis* "Christ and culture" and "Christ and liberation" were united. New York approved the essential relatedness of the two, but it questioned my *theologia crucis*.

The experience of blacks and Jews challenged the heart of the Christian faith as I understood it at that time. I came to see that their critical appraisal of Christian faith derives from their historical experience of violence. It is sad to know that Christian theology and the church have participated in the violence they suffered. These two peoples are a symbol representing millions of other people who have suffered violence and perished in the course of human history. Their very presence in our midst raises the ultimate question of violence in human civilization. This was the same question I had whispered to myself in the war years; why is it that someone throws bombs upon us from the sky?

Previously, I had read books by Martin Buber, Abraham Heschel, and Louis Finkelstein. But the living presence of a vibrant Jewish community, with their erudite and influential rabbis, their lively theological education, and the ongoing ancient tradition of the synagogue worship in which I participated from time to time in the city, impressed upon me the truth of the continuity of the Abrahamic covenant. One must not speak easily, I said to myself, of the superseding of the Old Covenant by the New Covenant. With this monologue, my Jewish-Christian dialogue in New York began. I noticed that the theology of superseding has given to Christians a specious sense of superiority, not only over Jews, but over peoples of other faiths as well, an attitude that has contributed to the increase of violence in the world. A sense of superiority too quickly becomes a self-righteous complex that generates violence.

Theologically, I began to notice a difference between the Jesus I had known in Tokyo and the Jesus I found in New York. My Tokyo Jesus was the divine redeemer of the Gentiles. His Gospel could be proclaimed without making one reference to the Jewish people of today. There is Christology in Tokyo.

In New York, however, Jesus is, first of all, a Jewish person of great spiritual stature. And equally important as Jesus of Nazareth is the name of Rabbi Akiba. There is no Christology here. One has to come to New York to experience Jesus the Jew without a trace of Christology. This absence of

Christology shakes the foundation of the Christian faith. The *theologia crucis* may speak of the theology of the Suffering Servant of God (Isa. 53) but nothing more. What the name Jesus stands for is no more than a part of the historical experience of the people of Israel. In the same way that the message of Jeremiah is universal, Jesus is universal. Jesus in Jewish New York is "down-sized." Here, he is no longer *vere Deus vere homo.*

A critical moment came to me when I finally came to feel the enormity of evil of the holocaust of European Jewry. In Asia I had been able to engage in theology at a safe distance from Auschwitz. In New York that distance once for all disappeared. All civilizations are violent, I saw. But why should Christian civilization be so especially violent?

Again, in Asia I had engaged in theological work at a safe distance from the history and the effects of black slavery in the United States. Even in my student days in New Jersey, only rarely had my professors mentioned the violence of the Crusades, of the Inquisition, of the colonization and settling of the Americas, of slavery, and of the Holocaust. Asians are color-conscious racists. Yet it took New York to confront me with the violence of racism. For the first time in my life I asked what had seemed a strange question. Was Jesus white? Was Augustine black? The New Testament and the creeds of the church never mention the color of Jesus. The enormity of the suffering of black people in the time of slavery and the continuing reality of vicious racism today has made me speak carefully about *theologia crucis.*

"I DESIRE MERCY AND NOT SACRIFICE"

Theologia crucis must not approve or encourage "sacrifice-making." To say that as Jesus sacrificed himself, we too should sacrifice is dangerous because it could suggest that sacrifice-making itself has Christian value. Sacrifice (*sacer,* holy; *facere,* to make) makes human life holy only when it is an expression of love. Sacrifice itself is tragedy. Over the years in New York I have came to see a connection between sacrifice and violence. Sacrifice is often another name for self-protection and even for self-righteousness. In view of the tremendous gap between the affluent and destitute sections of humanity, we find it difficult not to accept the equation that sacrifice *is* violence. We need to remember that *theologia crucis* is a doctrine of love, not of sacrifice. The predicament of black people has compelled me to meditate upon the words of the prophet Hosea: "I desire mercy and not sacrifice" (6:6).

The primary duty of *theologia crucis* is to confront violence and destroy it. Grace is global. Violence also is global. My New York *theologia crucis* began to have the two themes simultaneously: grace and violence. I came to understand that grace is the grace of God, but it must become our inner power to resist and eradicate violence as personally demonstrated by Martin Luther King, Jr. In this empowerment the grace of God becomes real.

The power of bombs is naked violence. The Hindus say that those who bomb others will eventually bomb themselves. This is the law of "action and reaction," or *karman*. Impressive as the *karman* philosophy is, the *theologia crucis* is not identical with it. If I were to say that they are identical, all of Asia could be easily evangelized. "Action and reaction," though profoundly understandable, cannot be the final words to bring about the elimination of violence. In fact, somehow the chain of "action and reaction" must be cut. It is the power of grace that can cut this chain. At this cutting, the Semitic faiths (Judaism, Christianity, and Islam) encounter the Hindu spiritual world.

What if the *karman* doctrine were to bring forth a less violent world than the Semitic doctrine does? The final test for the truthfulness of the *theologia crucis* is whether this Christian teaching truly contributes toward the removal of violence in the world. Our commitment to the removal of violence must express itself in a number of important areas. That is the content of ecumenism and mission. In interreligious dialogue we must study how each tradition struggles against violence. Inquisition is violence. Inquisition is the death of evangelization. I believe we can speak forcefully and intelligently about Christian faith only when we are engaged in the common battle against violence. Christian speech on the uniqueness of Christianity would speak to the world if the world had been impressed by Christian work toward the elimination of violence.

The *oikumene* Christ loves is full of violence. Bombing is going on everywhere. Every bomb strikes the God of Jesus Christ. Every bomb is a denial of the "breath of God" that came into our nostrils (Gen. 2:7). Does not this one word — *bombing* — characterize the mode of human life upon this planet in the twentieth century? Perhaps, in different ways, previous centuries were as violent as ours. But we are living in the twentieth century and are responsible to this century and its future. Why is the human being so violent? Why are all civilizations — but in particular, why is the Western civilization, informed by Christianity — so violent? The source of human violence is a mystery. It takes the mystery of the Eucharist to counter it. Someday, with the help of the Jewish people, black people, and many others, I may be able to stammer a few words about the mystery of the Eucharist that can expose the mystery of violence and thus move toward its elimination more courageously and intelligently.

My pilgrimage in mission began with my uncomprehending reading of *Pilgrim's Progress*. I have lived all my life from one war to another. My experience of bombing has caused me to be less interested in individual salvation or a blessed eternity after death, and more passionate about salvation now, in this life. Christian "eschatology" is focused on the present. For me the Christian mission is to bring forth the wholesomeness of abundant life to all upon the earth. In this way, perhaps *only* in this way, can we proclaim confidently and joyously the name of Christ.

Acknowledgments

Parts of this book originally appeared as follows; much of the material now appears in a revised form. Permission to reproduce it here is gratefully acknowledged.

"From Waterbuffaloes to Theology in Thailand," *International Review of Mission*, October 1964

"Theological Situations in Asia and the Mission of the Church," *Journal of the Protestant Episcopal Theological Seminary, Virginia*, Summer 1974

"Gun and Ointment" appeared under the title "The Future of the Christian World Mission in Asia," in William Danker (ed.), *The Future of the Christian World Mission: Studies in Honor of R. Pierce Beaver*, Eerdmans, Grand Rapids, 1971

"Bangkok and Wittenberg" appeared as the editorial, "Bangkok, Wittenberg and Jerusalem," *The South East Asia Journal of Theology*, Vol.5, no.1

"Aristotelian Pepper and Buddhist Salt," *Practical Theology*, Vol.14, no.3

"Neighborology" first appeared as "Confessing the Faith in Thailand — Prelude to Neighbourology," *The South East Asia Journal of Theology*, Vol.8, nos. 1 and 2

"The Wrath of God in a Culture of Tranquility" appeared as "Wrath of God vs. Thai *Theologia Gloriae*," *The South East Asia Journal of Theology*, Vol.5, no.1

"Ten Key Theological Issues Facing Theologians in Asia," *The South East Asia Journal of Theology*, Vol.15, no.1

"Theological Re-Rooting in the Theology of the Pain of God" appeared as a book review in *Sinugo* 2, April 1970

"Buddhist, not Buddhism," *Asia Focus*, April 1969

"Three Modes of Christian Presence" first appeared as "Christian Presence in the Light of Our Theme: 'In him all things hold together,'" *The South East Asia Journal of Theology*, Vol.10, no.1

Index

Abraham, 128-131
accommodation, 78, 82, 86, 89; prophetic, 15-19
agape, 55, 68, 99, 132
"agent" concept, 86-87
aging, 104
ahimsa ointment, 38-41
akkodhana, 105, 108
Albuquerque, Alfonso de, 33-35, 37, 41
analogia doloris, 88-89
anger, 121
animistic world, 81
anus-sada, 105
apatheia, 104, 107, 108; the ideal of, 68, 69, 106
apatheia-person, the ideal of the, 99-103, 105, 107
apetabheravo, 105
Apollos group, 140, 143
apostolic life, 132-133
arhat, 103, 105, 110-112
arhat-ship, 102, 107
Aristotelian philosophy: Buddhism and, 56-63
Asian spirituality and religion, 19
Asokanization, 61
assault, theology of, 54, 55
attachment vs. detachment, 118-120, 122-124; Christianity and, 60-61; to existence, 102-103; to history, 114

Baillie, John, 65, 99
Bainton, R. H., 53
Bangkok, 53-55
Bangkok Assembly (1964), 147-149
Bangkok conferences, 173, 175
baptism, 141
Barth, Karl, 165
Bhikkhu, Venerable Buddhadasa, 105
Bible, authority of the, 78

birth, 104-105; wheel of, 122
Black, C. E., 35, 44
black people, 176-178
Blauw, Johannes, 129 n4
blind man, 135; sight restored by Jesus, 110-111, 127-128, 168
blood, 59
Brunner, Emil, 66
Buddha, 6, 21, 97; Four Noble Truths of, 48, 100-101, 105
Buddhism: Aristotelian philosophy and, 56-63; compared with Judaeo-Christianity, 94, 112; distinguished from Buddhist, 93-95, 150, 151; and illusion of "I," 103-105, 110; influence on Thai no-pathos, 70-71; vs. Stoicism, 70-71; Ten Virtues in, 5; Theravada, 5, 16, 59, 69, 112, 118
Bunyan, John, 170
Burma, 11-12

Cephas group, 140, 143
change, 44-45
Chiang Kai-shek, 13-14
Chiengmai, 58, 173-174
China, 40; history of, 6-8, 37-38, 80
Christ, 42, 45, 63, 65-67; Aristotelian, 62-63; Asokanized, 61, 62; discomfort of, 167; as divided vs. undivided, 140-141; shape and form of, 19
Christian denominations, 140-143; theological vs. organizational dimension of, 148-149
Christian institutions, 138-139
Christian mission: future of, 32-33; participation in history and, 36-42
Christian presence, modes of, 163; "discomforted" presence, 166-167, 170; stumbling presence, 163-165, 170; "unfree" presence, 168-170

Christianity Not Mysterious (Toland), 73-75
communication and communicators, 154-157
Communist Party of China, 6-7
confession, 147-148
contextualization, 15-16, 18; authentic *vs.* false, 15
"contribution-drive," 144-147
cooperation, mutual, 10-11
cosmic regularity, 22, 25, 28
cosmic rule, 132
cosmos, 41
covenant: biblical concept of, 108-110; between Israel (church) and God, 114-116
Creator, 25, 29, 30
cross, theology of the, 131-133, 135-136, 162
crucified mind, 158-159; missiology of the, 18
Crucified One, 41-42; in world of technological efficiency, 44-49
cyclical patterns, 28, 122; in history, 72; in nature, 22-24, 31, 71-72

Dahlberg, B., 74-94
David, Son of, 55
"dead-alive—lost-found," 153-155, 157-159
death, 104, 105, 120
deism, 72 n7
denominationalism, 141, 143-144, 146-147
dependent origination, Buddhist doctrine of, 56, 61
Deutero-Isaiah, 129-130
Dhammapada, 105
dharma, 59, 61, 123, 124
dialogue: proclamation and, 79
doctrinal clarity, 81
dukkha, ideal of, 112-117; ideal of *apatheia*-person and, 99-102

East Asia Christian Conference (EACC), 173, 174
efficiency, 44-49
Eightfold Path, 100
Ekasila, 10

ekklesia (church), 41
Eliade, Mircea, 98
embracing, 84-86
eros, 55
eschatology, 164
evangelism, 18
evil, 24, 119-120
existence, 102-103

faith, 54-55, 165
faiths, followers of other, 78-79
frogs, seasonal croaking of, 20-22
Frois, Luis, 81

Gandhi, Mahatma, 38
Geertz, Clifford, 10
God: attachment of, 60, 161; biblical, 25, 37; "hot," 108-112; judgment of the Word of, 138; love of, 46-47, 60, 69; participation in history, 27-28, 41, 109, 112; by the promise of, 25; purpose of, 30; reconciling, 130, 153-154; as ruler of nature, 25-26, 30-31; strange work of, 73; warms the cool person, 117
God-fearing, 124
God's wrath: obscured by ideal of no-pathos, 68-69; *vs.* theology that "neglects history," 72-75
"goings out," 128-131, 134, 135
gospels, 6
gotong-royong, 10-11
"gun and ointment" perspective of the West, 32-36, 79; and participation in Christian mission, 36-39

healing, 35, 110-111. *See also* "gun and ointment" perspective of the West
Hebraization, 115
himsa gun, 40
Hinduism, 17
history, 28, 109; biblical linear view of, 31; in the light of the Word of God, 76-77; neglect of, 70-74; "once-for-all" *vs.* "many-times" qualities of, 22-24; primary truth of, 17
"holy life," the, 106
Holy Spirit, 11, 76, 77
"homelessness," principle of, 106-108

Hong Kong, 7-8
Hooft, Visser, 77
human beings, as the "image of God,"
  94-95
humanization of the gospel, 78

"I": illusion of, 103-105, 110; Jesus as
  restoring and strengthening, 110-
  112
ideals: of *apatheia*, 68, 69, 106; of the
  apatheia-person, 99-103, 105, 107; of
  dukkha, 99-102, 112-117; of no-
  pathos, 68-75; of poverty, 16-17; of
  tranquility, 68, 69, 74, 75
idolatry, 13-14, 171
incarnation, 94
indigenization, 15, 17, 82
Indonesia, 9-11
inevitability, 60, 61
Israel, 113-116, 129; history of, 26-29,
  115

Jahweh, 27 n7
James, Apostle, 118-123
Japan, 12-13, 137; industrialization in,
  12-13
Japanization, 115-116
Jehovah-Jesus, 57-59
Jeremiah, 136-139, 155-156
Jeremiah's message, 8
Jerusalem: and Tokyo, 137
Jesus Christ, 6, 41, 61, 123-124; crucifixion of, 131-134, 136, 141, 161,
  163; power of emancipation, 168;
  rejection of mother's plea for help,
  53-54; restoring sight to blind man,
  110-111, 127-128, 168; and salvation, 17-19, 79; story of, 53, 58, 152-
  153; use of Buddhism and Aristotelian philosophy, 56-63
Jewish people, 176-178
Johannine principle, 158, 159
judgment, 138, 139

kammic, 102
kappa, 120-121
karman, 179
karmic, 162
khwamrak, 60, 63

kidneys, 135, 136
Kierkegaard, Søren Aabye, 62
Kingshill, Konrad, 21, 22
Kitamori, Kazo, 69; case study of work
  of, 83-89
"kitchen theology," 60-63
Koyama, Kosuke. *See* mission, Koyama's
  pilgrimage in
Kyodan, 173

Lactantius, 68
Latourette, Kenneth S., 72 n7
legalism, 67
logos, 71
Lord, the, 47, 108-109, 113, 131; crucified, 162; "who sits enthroned over
  the flood," 24-31
love, 63, 68, 99, 132; Christian concept
  of, 60; human/natural vs. divine
  self-giving, 55
Luther, Martin, 54, 69; theology of,
  173-175
Lutheranism, 142-144

Malacca, 34
Malunkyaputta, 97-99, 107, 116
Mao Tse-tung, 6-7, 37-39, 80; "theological language" of, 37-38
Marxist-Leninism, 6-7, 37-38
Matthew, 18
maya, 16, 64, 65
McGilvary, Daniel, 56-59
meedtaa-karunaa, 4-6
mercy, 4-6, 78-79; *vs.* sacrifice, 178-179
Methodism, 142-143, 146
mind, 62; warm-blooded, 61, 62
Ministry in Context, 15-16
missiology, 18-19, 136, 150
mission, Koyama's pilgrimage in, 171;
  decolonization in Singapore and,
  175-176; desire for mercy *vs.* sacrifice in, 178-179; Luther's theology
  in Chiengmai and, 171-175; *Pilgrim's Progress vs.* demon progress in,
  171; unexpected bombing in New
  York and, 176-178
missionaries, 19, 150, 158
missionary ointment, 41-42
modernization, 35-36, 40-42, 44

monastic order, 106
monks, 106-107, 118, 121
morphe, 41
Mount Sinai, 14
Myanmar, 11-12

na paritassati, 105
Napier, B. D., 161
nature, 24-31; "beyond-nature," 25-26;
    as cyclical, 22-24, 31, 71-72; influ-
    ence on Thai no-pathos, 71-72
"neighborology," 64-67
Newbigin, Lesslie, 71
Nibbana, 70, 102
nirvana, 5, 16, 59, 61, 102, 109
"no-self," 70-71
non-violence, 38-39

oikoumene, 14
once-for-all style of life, 23
opus alienum dei, 73
opus proprium, 73
orderliness vs. disorderliness, 61-62

Panikkar, K. M., 34
panna, 123
Pantja Sila, 10, 11
patheia, 104
paticca samuppada, 61
Paul, 140, 141, 157
perturbation, 70-72, 74, 75
Phaja-Madcura-d, 21-24
Philippines, 8-9
Pilgrim's Progress (Bunyan), 171
Pope Nicholas V, 37 n14
poverty, religious ideal of, 16-17
prawàdtisaad, 28 n8
proclamation, 78, 79
"proletariat ointment," 37-41

rahu, 106
reason, 71-73
religion, 124
re-routing. *See* theological re-routing;
    suffering
resurrection, 112, 132
revelation, 72-73

salvation, 18-19, 110, 154; Jesus and, 17-
    19, 79; technology and, 46
samyojaniyehi vippamutto, 105
sangha, 106
santo, 105
santusito, 105
satyagraha, 38, 40
self-identity, 9, 103-104, 110; shared, 9
sexuality, 106
sin, 128-129, 131
Sinai, 14
Singapore: decolonization of theology
    in, 175-176; theological issues in, 3-
    4
sotapanna, 102
sotas, 102, 106
soul: body and, 97
South East Asia Graduate School in
    Theology (SEAGST), 175-176
spirit(s), many *vs.* One, 9-10
"spiritual poverty," 16, 48
spirituality, 81
Stoicism, 68, 70
Stream, 102, 106
suffering, 17, 100, 104, 166-167; anal-
    ogy of, as rerouting principle, 88-89;
    felt for the sake of others, 84-86
Sukarno, Achmad, 10-11
sukhin, 105
swaraj, 38
syncretism, 78

Taiwan, 13-14
technology and technological effi-
    ciency, 44-49
Thai no-pathos, leitmotifs of, 70-72
Thai people, basic continuity in lives
    of, 4-6
Thailand, 12, 68-69, 74; Buddhism and
    Aristotelian philosophy in, 56-63;
    theological issues in, 4-6; view of
    nature, 24
theologia crucis, 177
theologians in Asia, theological issues
    facing, 76-81
Theological Education Fund (TEF),
    15, 16, 45
theological inflation, 153

theological questions needing doctrinal clarity, 81

theological re-routing: analogy of suffering as principle of, 88-89; of "God is fighting with God," 84-86; of the gospel of Jesus for the Japanese mind, 86-87

theology, 76, 134-135; as history in the light of the Word of God, 76-77

theology-missiology, 136

Theology of the Pain of God, 82-84

third world, mission of the, 18

thong samhang, 21

time, 71-72

Tokyo: and Jerusalem, 137

tranquility, ideal of, 68, 69, 74, 75

truth, 29

tsurasa, 85-86

tsutsumu, 84-86

Udana, 70-71

uung-aang, 23-25, 28

U Thant, 38-39

Vietnam, 12, 80

Visser 't Hooft, W. A., 77

water buffalo, 22-23

West, the: "gun and ointment" perspective of, 32-36, 79; influence on Asia, 79; as threat and salvation for the East, 33-39, 79

will, 110

Wittenberg, 53-55

World Council of Churches, 45

worship, 18

Yangon, 11-12

Zacchaeus, 152-153